birthright

Stephen R. Kellert

birthright

People and Nature in the Modern World

Yale UNIVERSITY PRESS/NEW HAVEN & LONDON

Yale University Press books may be purchased in quantity for educational, business,
or promotional use. For information, please e-mail sales.press@yale.edu (U.S. office) or
sales@yaleup.co.uk (U.K. office).

Designed by Mary Valencia.
Set in Stone Serif type by Newgen North America.
Printed in the United States of America.

Library of Congress Cataloging-in-Publication Data

Kellert, Stephen R.
   Birthright : people and nature in the modern world / Stephen R. Kellert.
      p.   cm.
   Includes bibliographical references and index.
   ISBN 978-0-300-17654-4 (cloth : alk. paper)   1. Human ecology—Philosophy.
2. Human beings—Effect of environment on.   3. Philosophy of nature.   I. Title.
   GF21.K46 2013
   304.2—dc23

                                                                          2012019768

A catalogue record for this book is available from the British Library.

This paper meets the requirements of ANSI/NISO Z39.48-1992 (Permanence of Paper).

10 9 8 7 6 5 4 3 2 1

For the love of
Symplocarpus foetidus, G. Dicentra cucullaria,
Oncorhynchus mykiss, Cervus canadensis

CONTENTS

INTRODUCTION: BIOPHILIA

Humanity is the product of its evolved relationship to nature, countless yesterdays of ongoing interaction and experience of the natural world. Our senses, our emotions, our intellect, and even our culture developed in close association with, and in adaptive response to, the nonhuman world. Moreover, our physical and mental health, productivity, and well-being continue to rely on our connections to nature, even as our world becomes increasingly fabricated and constructed.

This contention defies what many have come to believe is the foundation of human progress and the hallmark of contemporary civilization: the conquest and transformation of nature and our seeming triumph over our biology as just another animal species. Many people today view society, far from depending on nature, as having overcome reliance on the natural world through the wonders of science, engineering, and mass production. They marvel at our ability to communicate in seconds, gather vast amounts of information, defeat diseases that once ravaged millions, and obtain goods and services that even the most privileged could not have imagined a few centuries ago. They wonder, do we really need nature for anything but raw materials that can be adapted to better uses, and perhaps for an occasional outdoor experience, which might be nice but certainly is not necessary?

Contemporary society is justifiably proud of its standard of living, physical health, and all the material comforts it has achieved. Still, to be successful and sustainable, not just materially but also psychologically and spiritually, these achievements must rest on a bedrock of positive and nurturing relationship to the natural world. This dependence is not just a matter of raw materials, clean water, productive soils, and an array of ecosystem services. More fundamentally, it is related to our capacity to feel, to think, to communicate, to create, to solve problems, to mature, to form a secure and meaningful identity, and to find meaning and purpose in our lives. As in the past and for the conceivable future, the core of our humanity will reflect the quality of our connections to the natural world. We will never be truly healthy, satisfied, or fulfilled if we live apart and alienated from the environment from which we evolved. Much of what we value and cherish as distinctively human—our capacity to care, reason, love, create, find beauty, and know happiness—continues to be contingent on our diverse ties to nature.

This reliance on nature reflects our biological origins as a species. We evolved in a natural world, not an artificial or human-created one. For more than ninety-nine percent of our history, our fitness and survival depended on adaptively responding to the ongoing demands of the natural environment, which drove the development of our senses, emotions, intellect, and spirit. For a tiny fraction of our history as a species, we have lived seemingly apart from nature, assuming these relatively recent practices to be normal: the domestication of plants and animals, which goes back just ten thousand years; the harnessing of energy beyond the human body, beginning five thousand years in the past; the invention of the city, some four thousand years old; the mass production of goods and services during the past five hundred years; the defeat of major diseases, only a few centuries old; or the currently evolving products of modern electronics and engineering.[1]

Rather than being vestigial or irrelevant, our inherent inclination to affiliate with nature remains crucial to our physical and mental health and well-being. This dependence on nature has shaped and continues to shape our capacities to feel, reason, think, master complexity, discover, create, heal, and be healthy. Whether we choose to be farmers or financiers, foresters or professors, to labor with our minds or toil with our bodies, our safety, security, and survival remain contingent on the quality of our connections to the natural world.

Contact with nature is not, however, some magical elixir, which readily bestows success and fulfillment. Life is always a struggle with uncertain outcomes. Yet the natural world remains the substrate on which we must build our existence. Lacking beneficial contact with nature, our physical, psychological, and spiritual well-being inevitably suffers. In a society estranged from the natural world, our sanity becomes imperiled, no matter the material comforts and conveniences we enjoy. By contrast, a life of affirmative relation to nature carries the potential to be rich and rewarding. As the writer and biologist Rachel Carson eloquently remarked:

What is the value of preserving and strengthening the sense of awe and wonder, the recognition of something beyond the boundaries of human experience? Is the exploration of the natural world just a pleasant way to pass the golden hours . . . or is there something deeper? I am sure there is something deeper. . . . Those who dwell . . . among the beauties and mysteries of the earth are never alone or weary of life. . . . There is something infinitely healing in the repeated refrains of nature.[2]

I do not intend to belittle the accomplishments of modern life. A return to some idyllic existence removed from modern technology and an increasingly urban and created world is not my intention. Still, I will argue that our fitness and fulfillment as individuals and as a society require ongoing physical and psychological connection to the nonhuman world. If we deny or subvert our inherent need to affiliate with nature, we invite our decline every bit as surely as we do with the more obvious threats of war and disease.

Unfortunately, modern society has become adversarial in its relationship to nature. This antagonism has engendered an array of profound environmental and social challenges: large-scale loss of biological diversity, widespread resource depletion, extensive chemical pollution, degradation of the atmosphere and the specter of catastrophic climate change, and a host of related health and quality of life problems—even a crisis of the human spirit. These challenges have been spawned by a contemporary society that has lost its bearings in relation to the world beyond itself.

Despite these challenges, this book is not about impending disaster. I am confident that humanity can restore a positive and nurturing relationship to nature born of a profound realization of human self-interest. This recognition will require, however, a much deeper and fuller understanding of the many ways we are inherently inclined to affiliate with nature, and of its role in our health, fitness, and capacity to flourish as individuals and as a society.

Humanity stands at a crossroads, having greatly undervalued the natural world beyond its narrow material utility. We have deluded ourselves into associating human progress and civilization with the dominance, transformation, and transcendence of nature. What we require now is a new realization of how much our health and well-being continue to rely on being a part of rather than apart from nature. The writer Henry Beston emphasized the necessity of this understanding as the basis for achieving a true humanity, arguing:

Nature is a part of our humanity, and without some awareness and experience of that divine mystery man ceases to be man. When the Pleiades and the wind in the grass are no longer a part of the human spirit, a part of very flesh and bone, man becomes, as it were, a cosmic outlaw, having neither the completeness and integrity of the animal nor the birthright of a true humanity.[3]

The foundation for this book's exploration of the human physical and mental dependence on nature is the notion of "biophilia," defined as the inherent inclination to affiliate with the natural world instrumental to people's physical and mental health, productivity, and well-being. The concept of biophilia was first advanced by the biologist Edward O. Wilson in a book of that title, and by Wilson and me in a subsequent volume, *The Biophilia Hypothesis*.[4] Previously, the term had been used by the psychologist Erich Fromm to argue that a love of life is essential for human mental health.[5] The literal translation of the Latin word *biophilia* is love of life. Love is certainly an important aspect of people's inborn affinity for the natural world. But biophilia as Wilson and I have shaped the term is a complex process encompassing an array of values and qualities that constitute a broader affiliation with nature. Biophilia reflects fundamental ways we attach meaning to and derive benefit from the natural world. These include:

- *Attraction*: appreciation of the aesthetic appeal of nature, from a superficial sense of the pretty to a profound realization of beauty.
- *Reason*: the desire to know and intellectually comprehend the world, from basic facts to more complex understanding.
- *Aversion*: antipathy toward and sometimes fearful avoidance of nature.
- *Exploitation*: the desire to utilize and materially exploit the natural world.
- *Affection*: emotional attachment, including a love of nature.
- *Dominion*: the urge to master and control the natural environment.
- *Spirituality*: the pursuit of meaning and purpose through connection to the world beyond our selves.
- *Symbolism*: the symbolic representation of nature through image, language, and design.

In the chapters to come, I explore the development and occurrence of each biophilic value as well as their bearing on our health and well-being. Like much of what it means to be human, biophilia is a biological urge that must be learned and developed to become fully functional. We may be born with an inclination to affiliate with nature, but its adaptive occurrence depends on experience and the support of others. This reliance on learning and development is the foundation of our species' remarkable ability to reach beyond our biology, to change, create, and progress. Through learning we become inventive and distinctive as individuals, groups, and cultures. It is the source of our genius as a species.

Still, the ability to reach beyond our biology through learning and development constitutes a two-edged sword, both a strength and a weakness. It can lead to extraordinary expressions of creativity and progress but also to self-destructive excess and self-defeating action. In other words, straying beyond our biology is not an infinite flexibility, but rather one bounded by our inherited needs. If we are to avoid dysfunction, we must remain true to our biology and inherited inclinations, including the need to affiliate with nature.[6]

Our inborn affinity for the natural world is, in effect, a birthright that must be cultivated and earned. For a creature of learning and free will, this is not a hard-wired outcome, but one that requires conscious and sustained engagement. To become adaptive and beneficial, our biophilic tendencies must be learned through experience and be supported by others. Too little contact with the natural world and our biophilic values atrophy. In excessive and exaggerated form, they can also become dysfunctional. One may control nature too much or too little, as well as be emotionally apathetic or love to excess. Within these extremes, an immense potential exists for distinctive expression by individuals and societies, and a wealth of opportunity for the exercise of human ingenuity and inventiveness.

The human capacity for choice thus carries the potential for self-destructive behavior and belief. In many respects, evidence of this excess exists today. The distortion of our biophilic values in modern times has led to widespread environmental degradation and increasing alienation from nature. A fundamental shift in human consciousness and the emergence of a new ethic will be required to resolve our current linked environmental and social crises. To achieve this shift we need to be motivated not by the desire to "save" nature, but rather by the pursuit of our own fundamental self-interest.

In the course of this book, we will engage various aspects of our humanity and consider how each remains contingent on the quality of our connections to the natural world. We will explore the many ways humans are inherently inclined to affiliate with nature, and how each confers a suite of physical and mental rewards. We will examine the decline in modern times of many of these relationships to nature, and the consequent loss of fitness and the potential to lead lives of virtue and fulfillment. We will delve into the challenges of childhood development, the principles of sustainable design, the practicalities of everyday life, and the usefulness of our ethics and sense of justice as a means to restore the connection between people and nature in the modern era.

Sixty years ago, Rachel Carson published a seminal book, *Silent Spring*, that conjured a horrific future absent the sounds of life and nature, silenced by humankind's ignorant, arrogant, and indiscriminate poisoning of the earth.[7] In this book I explore the opposite possibility—a future in which humans flourish through a rich and rewarding engagement with the natural world. Nature remains our magic well: the more we draw from its nourishing waters, the more we sustain the human body, mind, and spirit. The wondrous diverse beauty of the natural world remains the source of who we are and can become as individuals and societies. Like all other life, we are rooted in the earth, our health and potential dependent on our connections to the natural world of which we are a part.

The exploration of our relationship to nature confronts us with the most basic of questions: Who are we? Where do we fit as a species into the world beyond ourselves? What is our birthright and destiny? Are we just another species subject to the dictates of its biology, invariably responding to the requirements of its evolutionary heritage? Or are we altogether different, capable of escaping our biology through learning, culture, and creativity? Biophilia suggests we are both—a *biocultural* creature, the product of our inheritance yet capable of extraordinary independence and inventiveness. We may construct and create our world through learning and the exercise of free will, but to be successful, we must remain true to our biology, which is rooted in nature. If we stray too far from our inherited dependence on the natural world, we do so at our peril.

A worrisome aspect of modern life is that we have come to consider nature a dispensable amenity rather than a necessity for health and happiness. Until we achieve a fuller understanding of where we fit into the world that embraces a new consciousness and ethic toward nature, we will continue to generate environmental and social problems that no technology or government policy can ever resolve. The moral imperative of biophilia is that we cannot flourish as individuals or as a species absent a benign and benevolent relationship to the world beyond ourselves of which we are a part.

In this book I employ a mix of theory, science, and practice to delve into the complexities of our inherent inclination to affiliate with nature, and how it contributes to our physical and mental health, productivity, and well-being. In the hope of making these issues more accessible, I also employ narratives that often draw upon my own personal and professional experience. These stories are generally set apart as "interludes," which provide another kind of expression of the human relationship to nature. The first interlude follows, an imagined future in which the values, ideas, and arguments of biophilia hold sway. In it I conceive of a time when modern urban society has come to the realization that only through sustaining a beneficial connection with nature can people achieve health and the potential for happiness.

1. Are we just another creature subject to the dictates of our biology, or are we altogether different, capable of escaping our genetic heritage through learning, culture, and creativity? The idea of biophilia is that we are both, a biocultural creature who can construct and create our world through learning and the exercise of free will, but only if we remain true to our biological origins.

Interlude

A Field of Dreams—2030 and 2055

It was highly unusual back in 2030, and is still far from common today, to encounter a large ungulate—let alone a huge carnivore—in or near a city. Even now, the memory unsettles my soul. I was eight then, living with my parents and sister in Denver. Our home was in an "urban village," a relatively unusual attempt in those days to re-create an old-fashioned neighborhood within the city's core. The "village" consisted of single-family homes, attached townhouses, and a few multistory apartment buildings—also vegetable gardens; a shopping center that seemed less like clusters of stores than like a street fair with stands; a high school and a lower school, all stitched together by footpaths. The large streets and parking areas were at the rear of the complex, meaning you had to navigate the main living and shopping areas by electric cart, bike, or foot. You could see the Rocky Mountains from the complex, like some great wall looming in the distance, although my parents said that in previous years the mountains had vanished into a curtain of polluted air.

I really liked my school there, as we spent as much time outdoors as inside. Even the classrooms were full of plants and great views of the mountains, and we studied the ecology of the pond at the school entrance, especially the terraced slopes where a variety of plants were grown to treat the school's water, including the rainwater that ran down cool-looking animal-like spouts from the rooftop. The roof was also covered with solar energy panels, which along with other solar panels in the village, and a circle of great wind turbines that surrounded the city and the hydrogen fuel cell plants, supplied all our energy.

You would think a heavily populated city would offer few places for children to play. But besides our backyards, the village also had a number of small parks and playgrounds, as well as the creeks that captured the storm water and the ponds where you could see frogs and catch the fish used to cleanse water from the homes. Paths also led from the village to the city's recently established greenway system. The greenways were trails flanked by trees and bushes that linked various parts of the city to one another, to the suburbs, and, eventually, to farms and distant wilderness areas. People loved moving about the greenways by bike, foot, and even horseback. One moment you would be close to home, then downtown, then passing a shopping center, and finally, with persistence, in a national forest. The greenways became so popular that newly constructed or renovated homes along their borders were the most expensive in the city. The village kids were not supposed to venture far into the greenways, and most of the time we were content to play in our backyards and nearby parks. But occasionally, we sneaked off to the greenways, often to one in particular, where we had constructed a hideout and tree house in a large cottonwood. We worked hard at making our fort more comfortable than our parents could ever imagine; and, there we planned great battles and trips to distant lands.

One of my great pleasures was meeting Dad once a week for lunch at his office, a fifteen-minute walk from home. I loved his building. Tall and narrow, it rose like a needle, tapering at the top; from a distance, it looked like a forest because of its pyramidal shape, triangular window designs, and trees actually growing on the rooftop. The glass sides had tens of thousands of photocells, which—along with the building's fuel cells—generated most of its electricity. In addition to the trees, the rooftop held gardens, a pond, various sitting areas and meeting places, and two restaurants. The gardens and pond were also connected to the building's heating and cooling system, and the rainwater collected in the pond was used for plumbing and for irrigating the six interior gardens.

Located every tenth floor, the three-story interior gardens contained plants, aviaries, and butterfly gardens, each representing a different Colorado habitat, with an informational kiosk about that habitat. Also connected to the building's heating and cooling system, the gardens were places where you could have lunch or just sit. Dad said he did some of his greatest work in these indoor parks, where he often had meetings with colleagues. Some of the upper floors on each of the building's four sides also had ledges; here, great nests could be found where peregrine falcons raised their young and hunted pigeons. I could watch the birds all day, particularly when the nests were full or when the adults dive-bombed the pigeons at awesome speeds. The nests helped the once-endangered birds, which returned the favor by scaring away songbirds that otherwise might crash into the building's glass sides.

We often ate lunch at the office building, but sometimes we ventured to a nearby wetland. Depending on the season, we saw yellow-headed blackbirds, black-necked stilts, avocets, turtles, frogs, fish, dragonflies, cattails, lilies, and more. I particularly recall one time toward the end of winter when we were huddled behind an interpretive display, trying to keep warm while eating our sandwiches. Suddenly, we were startled by a loud splash. The critter didn't see us because we had been concealed. But when we looked up, we saw the retreating shape of a sleek gray animal sliding into the water, its sinuous body protruding before disappearing below the surface. My first thought was the Loch Ness monster, but Dad exclaimed after a moment's reflection, "I'll be darned. It's an otter!" We saw the animal one more time before it disappeared for good, its cute whiskered face holding a small fish sticking out from both sides of its mouth.

Practically unknown in the city at the time, otters were thought to avoid swimming under bridges or entering less-than-pristine waters. But wetland and creek restoration had been going on for some time. The improvement in water quality, coupled with a growth in otter populations, had led some younger otters to venture into the great metropolis. We were incredibly proud of our discovery, although we soon learned that similar sightings had been occurring elsewhere in the city. And it wasn't long before a permanent otter population became part of the Denver scene. People were excited at first, but soon some began to complain that the otters were decimating fish populations. It took some time before people learned to live with the otters while still managing to protect their property.

My best wildlife experience of all occurred along the greenways. For me as a kid, the greenways were most exciting on those frosty winter days when elk came thundering down from the mountains like a living avalanche, bursting into and through the city on their way to the warmer prairies and wet meadows on the eastern side of town. Before the greenways, the elk were not able to travel to their historic winter range because of fencing, degraded habitat, and past overhunting. By the early twenty-first century, however, elk numbers had rebounded in response to a decline in ranching, an increase in wildlife protection, and ecotourism. Still, these factors would not have brought elk back into the city if not for the greenways, which provided the migratory corridors that were needed to connect the mountains to the plains. The greenways, in effect, restitched some great connective tissue linking all those open spaces.

After the greenways were completed, few elk used the corridors at first. But then, apparently when the elk population reached some critical threshold or experienced a harsh enough winter, the small numbers became a stream, as if some great spigot had been turned on and out gushed tens of thousands of elk. The first few days, you would see only a lone animal or a small group, but soon a huge mass appeared and advanced almost as one across the city. When this occurred, thousands of people turned out to gape, some cheering even as police, fire, and wildlife officials tried to keep them quiet and at a distance. An elk or a person might occasionally be hurt, but usually the animals passed without incident, parading before the kids glowing, the adults ogling, the television commentators commenting, the merchants hawking, and the scientists studying. The migration quickly became the stuff of legend: a cause for annual celebration and a source of great pride for the city.

I will always remember one event above all others. One winter, Dad, having heard that elk would probably be passing through the city, had managed to obtain a permit allowing us to occupy a viewing blind within dark, concealing pines in a preserve at the city's edge. For four consecutive days, we arrived early in the bitterly cold mornings hoping to see elk, but nothing happened. Then, on the misty morning of the fifth day, we heard a snapping of twigs that sounded like heavy animals. Soon, barely discernible, ghostlike shapes appeared out of the cold fog, their numbers swelling until the ground nearly shook. Tawny browns and grays, bare heads and flaring spikes, massive hulks and some very large antlers left us in awe. In the weak light, they seemed like apparitions, ancient visages commingling with the present, coalescing and dissipating as they passed through our human-dominated landscape.

Then something far more improbable occurred. We had been watching the elk for perhaps an hour; most of the mature males had by then passed by, the mothers and new calves now following. Suddenly, something bolted from the pines opposite us that at first looked like a horse crossing the meadow at full gallop. The elk reacted as if a bomb had exploded, fleeing in every direction, yet one small yearling remained on the ground, pinned by the interloper. The incident had taken seconds but seemed to unfold as if in slow motion. The creature that had streaked from the forest had been fast but hardly graceful and oddly lumbering, lacking the polish and grace of a horse. Besides, horses don't run down and pounce on elk. Even my unformed mind sensed I was in the presence of something wondrous and fearsome. It was the greatest of all land predators, that enormous carnivore of arching back and unyielding determination. It was the great mythical bruin!

"Oh, my god!" Dad cried out. "A griz. But it can't be!"

As far as anybody knew, with the exception of a few hardly believed biologists, grizzly bears were not found anywhere near Denver, only a small population having been rediscovered and augmented in the San Juan Mountains in the southwestern corner of the state. Occasional grizzly sightings had been reported in Rocky Mountain National Park, not far from Denver, but these were generally unconfirmed and dismissed. Yet this was no apparition. It was probably a young bear, hungry, recently awakened from a deep sleep, that had wandered the cold mountains, caught the scent of elk, and followed the great herd—a bear just young and dumb enough not to avoid its ancient archenemy: humans. Maybe it also sensed the diminishing threat from a once-lethal species that of late had embraced a new covenant of reverence for the wild, especially for the legendary lord of the mountains.

The young bear stood on its hind feet at Dad's yell, glaring in our direction. It rose perhaps six feet tall, its round, almost humanlike face staring menacingly at us, while we gazed back too awed and frightened to flee. An electric arc of conflicting emotions passed between the bear and us like some great indigestible stew: fear, fascination, perhaps appreciation, and just possibly mutual respect. We certainly meant the creature no harm, yet Dad assumed an aggressive posture and yelled back at the bear, his first instinct being to protect his young. The bear in turn snorted and growled, his nose flaring. But he soon settled back on all fours and with great strength dragged his prey into the forest, quickly disappearing.

Dad and I felt as though we had just experienced a massive hallucination. We soon told our tale to officials, who were skeptical at first. But following careful investigation and additional sightings, it soon became known that a small grizzly bear population had reestablished itself around Rocky Mountain National Park and adjacent wilderness areas. My young boy's heart had been touched by something miraculous, something beyond amazing that would affect me for the rest of my life. If an eight-year-old can experience a transcendent moment, that was it—and I've carried it around inside me since then. I have reached back during moments of crisis and gathered strength from the memory of the bear. I can pluck the great bruin from the recesses of my mind like a constellation from the sky, retrieving some enduring meaning that somehow mutes whatever anxiety or uncertainty has befallen me.

Even now, for a middle-aged man in 2055, a day hardly passes without my recalling that singular instance of inspiration and joy. Just today, I awoke stressed by events at work and in the world. I read daily of wanton cruelties and needless destruction, circles of pain radiating from a world of indifference and greed. Perhaps I was also reacting to having just come back from being in the hospital for gall bladder surgery. It went well, and the recovery was aided by the calming effects of the beautiful and varied gardens and aquatic environments that had become common within many hospitals, since the discovery that such places greatly increase the pace of recovery. Still, like any major surgery, it was a worrisome time.

At moments like this, I remember the great bear and gather my dogs for a walk up the mountain near where I live. When I do this, the city is soon left behind as I follow a path lined with willows along a dry creek bed. Cactus wrens cry, and circling raptors appear. I move quickly, driven by the goal of reaching the summit, until a mosaic of sensations slows me down. The dogs help, reveling in their curiosities, circling about and encased in a world of smell more than sight, drawn by a multiplicity of plants, rocks, and other signs of nature. I begin to open myself to a world of endless detail. At first, I intellectualize, identifying various birds, flowers, and more. I count and classify, drawing pleasure from my

2. The grizzly bear has a long history of conflict with humans, and the preservation of this threatened species is viewed by some as the test of humanity's willingness to coexist with the natural world.

growing familiarity and seeming control. But then I soon give way to an intense appreciation of wonder, beauty, and discovery. A monarch butterfly alights on a nearby rock, and I marvel at its orange and black patterns so in harmony that they defy the narrow interpretation of a mere evolutionary fitness. I am stunned by the miracle of this creature, so flimsy that it seems weightless but able to travel enormous distances. I am awed by its supposedly inconsequential brain, which guides it to distant lands despite weather and terrain.

I finally reach the summit and look back at the city spread across the plain, admiring its immensity and creation. I look up at the clouds and imagine the shape of my childhood bear. I travel with him across the sky, carried by winds connecting me to a world greater than myself. The great bruin never leaves me, has always been a part of my consciousness. We remain fellow travelers in the grandeur of our lives. And then I am stripped of my self-absorption and self-pity, carried along by this miracle of creation.

I return to my home and office no smarter, more skillful, or healthier, but nonetheless renewed and revived. I have drawn sustenance from the bear and the butterfly, been emboldened by their accomplishment. I have become the bear, rising on its hind legs, startled, apprehensive, yet irrevocably tied to those humans who stare back with anxiety but also with reverence and devotion.

1

attraction

Who among us finds cockroaches appealing? I suspect only the most saintly and forgiving. Most of us regard these creatures with a mixture of disgust and disdain, tending to see them as repulsive. Our aversion to these insects is so deep and enduring few hesitate to destroy one, and with little hesitation or guilt, especially if it suddenly appears in a sink or a drawer. Nor are these aversive reactions confined to insects and spiders; most of us react similarly to such vertebrates as rats and snakes commonly perceived as vermin.

But cockroaches, those targets of our revulsion, are closely related to beetles, some species of which are viewed as attractive and sometimes beautiful: ladybugs, for example, and many scarabs, especially the brightly colored metallic beetles that have inspired aesthetic adornment in jewelry and other decorative forms. Beetles are also the most numerous of all animals, numbering some 400,000 scientifically described species and an estimated 1 to 2 million or more awaiting formal classification, accounting for a remarkable one-quarter of all animal species.[1] Their extraordinary numbers purportedly prompted the nineteenth-century British entomologist J. B. S. Haldane to reply, when asked by a prominent cleric what all his scientific studies had told him about the existence of God: "It appears the Creator has an inordinate fondness for beetles."[2]

Despite the Creator's beneficence and our aspirations to be in His likeness and please Him, most people view as aesthetically unappealing the great majority of beetles, as well as many other "bugs," as we imprecisely lump together insects, spiders, and other many-legged crawlers. The reason for this aversion to invertebrates is complicated, and we shall return to this subject again in chapter 3. For now, their limited appeal can be said to derive in part from their strange, alien, and fundamentally different ways, and their related lack of characteristics we hold most dear such as feeling, intellect, individuality, free will, caring, and the exercise of moral choice. These creatures seem nothing like ourselves, pursuing existences that strike us as somewhere between something

3. Most people view the majority of insects and spiders as unappealing and unattractive because they lack qualities people highly value, such as feeling, intellect, individuality, free will, and the ability to care and exercise moral choice.

fixed and lifeless and a sentient creature. This perception of invertebrates predisposes most of us to view these animals as unappealing and unattractive, apart from those exceptions we make for the likes of ladybugs, scarabs, or butterflies. In somewhat analogous fashion, most regard vertebrates like rats and rattlesnakes as repugnant and repulsive, despite our tendency to view some of their cousins—think of beavers and iguanas—as cute and sometimes cuddly.

So what, if anything, can we deduce from these few illustrations? Are there any consistent conclusions to be drawn other than that most people's aesthetic judgments about the natural world appear to be fickle, biased, and somewhat irrational? It is worth noting that most of our aesthetic likes and dislikes regarding cockroaches, rats, butterflies, beavers, and many other creatures are highly predictable and consistent across culture and history. Moreover, similarly consistent and widespread aesthetic judgments can be cited toward many inanimate environmental features: rainbows, waterfalls, flowers, conical mountains, sunrises, sunsets, or savannah landscapes.

If these widely held perspectives are universal across culture and history, they may be regarded as reflections of our biology and thus our evolution as a species. In other words, these aesthetic preferences may have become embedded in our genes, representing adaptive responses to the natural world that proved advantageous to our fitness and survival during the long course of human history. Moreover, unless we view these tendencies as vestigial—once adaptive, but no longer relevant—these aesthetic judgments may continue to render important contributions to our health, productivity, and well-being.

Skeptics argue that our aesthetic judgments toward nature are really quite subjective, easily manipulated and altered, given to fads and fashions, and greatly influenced by group pressure and bias. These critics view perceptions regarding what is attractive or unappealing in nature as fickle, superficial, and marginally important to human welfare. The conservation biologist Norman Myers, for example, argues: "The aesthetic argument for conservation is virtually a prerogative of affluent people with leisure to think about such questions."[3] More tongue in cheek, but no less indicative of the presumed limited importance of our aesthetics of nature, a *New Yorker* cartoon depicted a father and son walking through a beautiful forest glade; arm draped about the boy, the father sagely offers this piece of advice: "It's good to know about trees. Just remember nobody ever made any big money knowing about trees."[4]

Is there anything that we can conclude from these inconsistencies and doubts regarding the importance of our aesthetic judgments of nature? Is our attraction to the natural world a universal imperative or a highly malleable and marginally significant reflection of human subjectivity and bias? I will argue for the former—that our commonly held assumptions about the aesthetic value of nature reflect evolutionary forces that we encountered during our long history as a species. Moreover, I will assert that these judgments continue to be relevant to our health, development, and fitness even in today's increasingly artificial, urban, and constructed world. Indeed, I will suggest that our aesthetic judgments contribute to such essential functions as our ability to reason, imagine, create, solve problems, recognize an ideal, organize complexity, manage stress, heal, and attain sustenance and security.

The universal importance of the aesthetic attraction to nature has been advanced by two eminent biologists, Edward O. Wilson and Aldo Leopold, and their insights are worth noting. Wilson, relating nature's beauty to human fitness and survival, suggested: "Beauty is our word for the perfection of those qualities of environment that have contributed the most to human survival."[5] Leopold, reflecting on the perception of nature's beauty to an intuitive understanding of the health and integrity of natural systems, remarked: "A thing is right when it tends to preserve the integrity, stability, and beauty of the biotic community. It is wrong when it tends otherwise."[6] Both advanced a view that our aesthetic affinity for nature, particularly a sense of beauty, is central to human and ecological fitness, and just perhaps a consequence of their interrelationship.

How might this be so? The answers are complicated, and as Leopold observed: "The physics of beauty is one department of the natural sciences still in the dark ages."[7] Yet evidence mounts that our aesthetic value of nature is integral to many critical human attributes.

We might start with intellectual development and cognitive capacity. After all, the aesthetic attraction to nature is fundamentally an act of curiosity. An object or phenomenon in nature captures our attention and provokes a response, even if only a fleeting one. The aesthetic reaction causes us to observe, perhaps to reflect and act, in a process of progressive intellectual involvement. Even if this curiosity is brief and superficial, it creates the potential for more refined levels of discovery, exploration, imagination, and creative engagement. In most circumstances, we experience only a casual attraction to something superficially appealing and picturesque. But if cultivated, an aesthetic attraction can inspire deeper understanding and involvement. Moreover, with perseverance, refinement, and perhaps the guiding hand of another, aesthetic curiosity can lead to creativity and inventiveness.

Even in today's world of accumulated knowledge and powerful electronic communication, the natural world remains the most sensory-stimulating and information-rich environment people ever encounter. Consequently, the aesthetic appeal of the natural world inevitably provokes some degree of interest, urges us to examine and explore, to investigate and discover, to problem-solve and invent, all critical tools in the development of human intellect. Moreover, the opportunity to engage and exercise our aesthetic response to nature is widely accessible, for the most part found nearly everywhere, even in our largest cities.

The aesthetic appeal of nature can also encourage the perception and pursuit of an ideal of harmony and perfection. In recognizing this ideal, we are drawn to an awareness of proportion, balance, and symmetry. We see in the rainbow, the waterfalls, the flowering rose, the stately tree, the snowcapped mountain, the spreading savannah, the colorful butterfly, the rising trout, the regal crane, the antlered elk, the fleet cheetah—even the well-designed park or building whose features reflect principles occurring in nature—a sense of harmony, grace, and elegance in a world where imperfection is more the norm.

Our recognition of ideal beauty in nature often reflects prominent features of the natural world that have particularly contributed to our survival over time. Thus we encounter in the rainbow or waterfall rich sources of potable water, in lush flowerbeds the prospect of food and fruitfulness, in the sleek cheetah and powerful elk models of strength and prowess, in the stately tree or regal crane qualities of elegance and excellence.

The perception of an ideal in nature can further inspire and instruct us. Our awareness may start as a subjective impression, an intuitive sense of appealing proportion. With engagement, study, and understanding, however, we may gain a keener sense of what is outstanding, an insight into the source of this seeming perfection. At the least, the accomplishment satisfies us. At a more advanced level, we are inspired to mimic in our own lives the qualities we perceive. And if we are especially clever, we can adopt these attributes in the service of our own needs, subjecting them to the inventive hand of human creativity.

We often recognize in nature's beauty a quality of perfection that all life strives to achieve, including our own, even if it is rarely achieved. We discern in the struggle outstanding qualities to which all species aspire. This aesthetic awareness focuses our attention on notable features that have conferred a special evolutionary advantage in an organism's struggle to thrive and survive—an elk's antlers, a cheetah's speed, an elephant's strength, the symmetry and color of a rose. We admire those attributes that over time have contributed most to a creature's or even a habitat's viability and perpetuation. We identify an impulse that all organisms share. As Edward. O. Wilson suggests, "It is interesting to inquire about . . . the ideal toward which human beings unconsciously strive no less relentlessly than flycatchers and deer mice."[8]

All life constitutes specialized solutions to the particular challenges of survival faced over unimaginable time and hammered into a species' genes through repeated trial and error. Each unique adaptation constitutes the special genius of a species, its intrinsic beauty, its elusive ideal. We are inclined to respond to those qualities in creatures and landscapes that reflect this distinctive evolutionary advantage. Moreover, when this aesthetic response contributes to human fitness, it becomes biologically embedded in our own genes and reveals itself independent of our effort. Even the worst among us—for example, a psychopathic killer confined to solitary confinement for the dangers he poses to society—is typically unable to resist the aesthetic attraction of a beautiful sunset, a colorful rainbow, a bouquet of flowers, even if his response is fitful and less robust than our own.

The continuum of aesthetic attraction ranges from simple gratification at the superficially pretty to more subtle levels of recognizing harmony and perfection. With engagement and cultivation, aesthetic sensitivity to an ideal in nature becomes sharpened. We may be initially attracted to particularly spectacular settings or creatures. As we gain sensitivity, however, ordinary objects of nature can inspire wonder and deep appreciation. Even the bramble beside the road may evoke a reverence for the beauty of nature, as the following prayer by the theologian Walter Rauschenbusch suggests:

> We thank you for our senses by which we can see the splendor of the morning, hear the jubilant songs of love, and smell the breath of the springtime. Grant us . . . a heart wide open to all this joy and beauty. Save our souls from being so steeped in care or so darkened by passion that we pass heedless and unseeing when even the thorn bush by the wayside is aflame with the glory of God.
>
> Enlarge within us the sense of fellowship with all the living things, our . . . brothers, to whom you have given this earth as their home in common with us. We remember with shame that in the past we have exercised the high dominion of man with ruthless cruelty, so that the voice of the Earth, which should have gone up to thee in song, has been a groan of travail. May we realize that they live, not for us alone, but for themselves and for thee, and that they love the sweetness of life even as we, and serve thee in their place.[9]

Recognition of an ideal in nature provokes, at minimum, pleasure. But it also can relieve stress, enhance the capacity to cope with adversity, and physically and mentally heal and restore. Recognition of an ideal in nature can lead to discerning the basis of excellence in another creature or landscape, an appreciation that inspires and instructs, generating insight and understanding. It can propel us along pathways that through mimicry and simulation allow us to adopt analogous solutions into our own lives.

An aesthetic response to nature can additionally assist in ordering and organizing the complexity that confronts us in the natural as well as the human-made world. Orchestrating complexity has been important during the long course of human evolution when we have faced the challenges of navigating often overwhelming detail and variability. This profusion of information and choices confronting us occurred in the form of diverse vegetation, landscapes, geological conditions, animals, possible pathways: visual and auditory cues that together presented uncertain choices regarding the safest and most advantageous course to follow. We often dealt with this complexity by finding a particular promontory, a unique vantage point, a prominent environmental feature, an especially salient plant or animal that helped us to structure this variability by making it coherent and legible. We organized the complexity that challenged us by simplifying and thus rendering it comprehensible.

Aesthetic attraction facilitated this movement toward order and organization. By being attracted to a particular plant, animal, geological form, or landscape feature, our attention could become focused, a sense of pattern emerging from what had previously been a multiplicity of disaggregated objects. Aesthetic appeal concentrated our awareness, encouraged us to organize parts into organized wholes. Emergent patterns became revealed as we focused on a prominent and stately tree, a striking ledge, a distinctive watercourse, the edge of a forest, a cluster of bright flowers, a church spire or building façade that simulated organic forms. These aesthetically salient natural or human-made objects that mimicked nature helped us to structure our context, lending meaning and coherence to what had been too detailed, or, at the other extreme, featureless.[10]

Certain natural features especially serve as powerful sources of aesthetic attraction, often reflecting their evolutionary significance, even if particular learning and cultural circumstances result in their variation across people and societies. From a strictly biological viewpoint, these environmental features may be of limited significance. From an experiential and phenomenological perspective, however, they can assume considerable importance, helping to bring a landscape or even a built environment into organized and aesthetically attractive focus. For Aldo Leopold, for example, a single bird, the ruffed grouse, served this purpose, aesthetically transforming a landscape from a collection of disconnected objects into something possessing what he called a special "motive power," although in strictly physical terms the creature's biological importance was limited. As he wrote, "Everyone knows . . . that the autumn landscape in the north woods is the land, plus a red maple, plus a ruffed grouse. In terms of conventional physics, the grouse represents only a millionth of either the mass or the energy of an acre. Yet subtract the grouse and the whole thing is dead. An enormous amount of some kind of motive power has been lost."[11]

By helping to organize our experience, aesthetically attractive nature reduces the immense detail of a world that might otherwise be overwhelming, confusing, and even chaotic. The dark and indistinguishable forest, the thickly vegetated swamp, the landscape with too many possibilities, rather than being a source of anxiety and uncertainty can become instead familiar, safe, and navigable. In contrast, too much uniformity and plainness creates a lack of aesthetic

4. Fractal geometry is a feature of both natural and human-made objects, wherein variations on a basic theme occur at different scales. This variability of parts in relation to wholes is often aesthetically appealing and reflects a balance of complexity and organization.

appeal. We are bored by the stagnant body of water, the featureless rock, the uniform desert, the drab building, the box-shaped shopping mall, the homogenous housing development. Each dulls our senses, striking us as aesthetically impoverished, lacking variety, stimulation, and information. What we find aesthetically appealing in both natural or human-made objects are settings rich in detail and diversity, but rendered orderly and organized.

This quality of organized complexity is evident in what has been called "fractal geometry," a feature of both natural and manufactured objects we generally find attractive. The mathematician Benoît Mandelbrot defined fractals as: "Rough or fragmented geometric shapes that can be split into parts, each of which is (at least approximately) a reduced-size copy of the whole."[12] More colloquially, fractals are parts that reflect wholes, basic patterns resembling one another, but not identical copies. Fractals are variations on a theme or structure whose individual elements occur at varying scales, sizes, and shapes linked to an overall model or pattern. This characteristic is sometimes called self-similarity. Fractals are reflected in various natural and man-made phenomena: snowflakes, which, while alike, all vary in slightly distinctive ways; leaves on a tree, though similar, each differing to a degree; the patterns of grains of wood of the same tree shaped into distinctive paneling; the architectural or fabric design that mimics and simulates natural forms. This variability of parts to wholes tends to be aesthetically appealing, balancing detail and diversity with order and organization.

Our aesthetic attraction to certain species, landscapes, and environmental features has also made an important contribution to human sustenance and security over evolutionary time, and this function continues to find expression in today's world. Environmental features that have long supported our needs for safety, food, potable water, shelter, and mobility include bright flowering colors, clear flowing streams and rivers, and long views and vistas from sheltered areas. By contrast, we tend to find aesthetically unappealing natural features that increase the danger of injury or disease; thus our aversion to ticks, spiders, leeches, cockroaches, snakes, rats, dark swamps, and enclosed forests. Although these perceptions can be excessive in some people, and seemingly have lost much of their adaptive significance in the modern world, they remain functional depending on circumstance, and often assume subtle symbolic significance. These aesthetic judgments are frequently taken for granted with little consideration of their origins or continuing utility. We rarely question why we routinely bring flowers into a hospital, pay more for a home or hotel room overlooking a body of water, prefer landscapes that include meadows, canopy trees, and a streamcourse—ones, that is, which reflect relationships to nature that over evolutionary time have made us more safe and secure.

Even obscure aesthetic preferences can be linked to such beneficial and adaptive functions. For example, take our aesthetic preference for creatures with round, vaguely childlike faces, such as bears, raccoons, pandas, and seals. Aesthetically appealing childlike features include a large head relative to body size, a curved forehead, round eyes, and a short, relatively small nose and chin: all features that trigger our inclination to care for and protect the young. The aesthetic attraction to these prominent juvenile features can be linked to the vulnerability of human children, who continue to depend on adults for more than twice the period found in even our closest related primates. The similarity of these features in human children and other species is prominently exploited in such toys as teddy bears, popular conservation logos like the World Wildlife Fund's panda, or campaigns to save animals like baby seals from being killed for their fur.

An even more symbolic illustration of the aesthetic appeal of juvenile-like characteristics is the shift over time in appearance of the celebrated cartoon character Mickey Mouse. Originally a creature with small eyes and the pointy

5. Human children are born helpless and remain dependent on adults far longer than any other creature. Characteristics that trigger humans' inclination to care for children include a large head relative to body size, a curved forehead, large round eyes, and a short and relatively small nose and chin. These aesthetically pleasing features are also associated with certain species, such as giant pandas.

snout of a typical rodent, Mickey over time "evolved" into a far more aesthetically appealing character possessing big eyes, a round face, and an altogether human childlike appearance, and with this shift his appeal and popularity soared.[13]

Evolutionary explanations for our aesthetic preferences can seem like a tautology, a circular "just so" reasoning difficult to prove or disprove. But increasing evidence supports the seeming universality of these aesthetic judgments across culture and history that buttresses the claim for their biological origins. Various studies report that favored natural scenes include the presence of water, bright flowering colors, canopy-like trees, and safe refuges with long prospective views. The geographer Roger Ulrich reported, based on a review of studies in North America, Europe, and Asia: "One of the most clear-cut findings . . . is the consistent tendency to prefer natural scenes over built views. . . . Even unspectacular or subpar natural views elicit higher aesthetic preferences."[14] Nor is this a new perception: the nineteenth-century architectural critic and designer John Ruskin observed: "As far as I can recollect . . . every Homeric landscape, intended to be beautiful, is composed of a fountain, a meadow and a shady grove."[15]

Even if these aesthetic preferences for nature seem biologically rooted, are they important to the health, productivity, and well-being of twenty-first-century people, especially in urban areas far removed from nature? A room with a view may be nice, but does it confer any special advantage? Bringing flowers into a hospital is a pleasant gesture, but does it signify anything more than a pleasant kindness and caring? People may find rats and rattlesnakes repulsive and baby seals and Mickey Mouse cute, but do these aesthetic preferences constitute more than trivial considerations? Moreover, could these aesthetic judgments be mere vestiges of our evolutionary past no longer relevant in our highly fabricated and technologically sophisticated society, anomalies of history that will eventually wither away and disappear?

The psychologist Alan Thornhill explains the dynamics of a vestigial tendency, which begins as "an adaptation . . . necessarily adaptive in the environments of its evolution. . . . The relationship between an adaptation and current reproduction depends on the similarity between the environment in which the adaptation is expressed and the environmental features that generated the selection that designed the adaptation. This correlation [may] no longer exist for contemporary organisms."[16] In other words, our aesthetic preference for certain creatures, landscapes, and environmental features may reflect tendencies that evolved in an ecological context no longer meaningful in today's highly artificial and increasingly urban world. Perhaps, but mounting evidence suggests that many of our aesthetic responses to nature continue to confer significant physical and mental benefits. For example, the average office worker today toils in a windowless setting lacking natural stimulation and aesthetic appeal. Recent studies have shown that the introduction of aesthetically attractive depictions of nature, appealing plants, and commanding views to the outside can lead to lower blood pressure, less illness, reduced absenteeism, and greater attention and productivity.[17] Among hospital patients, research has found that views of nature, access to vegetation, and the presence of companion animals can result in lower stress, accelerated recovery, diminished aggressiveness, and reduced need for potent painkillers.[18] Further studies of factory workers report that attractively restored landscapes and increased interior vegetation can improve worker motivation, satisfaction, and performance.[19]

The aesthetic attraction to certain natural features may be excess genetic baggage that in today's world will eventually atrophy and disappear. The results of these studies suggest, however, that these aesthetic predilections continue to affect people's physical and mental health and well-being in significant ways. For the foreseeable future, colorful flowers, stately trees, an arresting sunset, a fast-flowing stream, a soaring eagle, or even fabrics, furnishings, and designs inspired by nature will continue to exert healing and restorative effects on the human body, mind, and spirit.

The inclination to value nature aesthetically can be related to a more general human tendency to respond to art. The philosopher Denis Dutton, in his 2010 book *The Art Instinct: Beauty, Pleasure, and Human Evolution*, explored the human biological tendency to perceive and produce art, and his work is worth briefly noting for what it tells us about people's aesthetic affinity for nature.[20] Dutton identified a number of reasons why art appears to be genetically encoded in people. Each of Dutton's factors can be related to adaptive benefits associated with the aesthetic experience of nature.

Dutton first credits beautiful objects with providing *direct pleasure*, eliciting satisfaction that motivates us to take action. One of the most consistent consequences of an aesthetic attraction to nature is the simple joyful satisfaction in confronting a colorful flower, a beach stretching endlessly to the horizon, the patterns of a butterfly, the stripes of a cat, or a bird soaring on high. Dutton also emphasizes the benefits of *skill and virtuosity* involved in producing art. Likewise, the aesthetic response to nature often reflects skillful engagement whether landscaping, gardening, flower arranging, fishing, and birding, or more deliberatively creative acts like drawing, painting, or sculpting some natural object or using nature as a template for design.

Dutton further underscores *novelty and creativity* as especially imaginative and inventive benefits of art. In analogous ways, the aesthetics of nature can elicit creative, imaginative, and innovative responses to the world around us. Dutton also stresses the role of *criticism* in the experience of art, what he calls an "evaluative conversation" involving critical thinking and reasoned judgment. The aesthetics of nature similarly extends from simple curiosity to more complex degrees of analytical reasoning, examination, and understanding. Dutton goes on to emphasize the *special focus* and *expressive individuality* of art, reflecting its uniqueness, exceptional quality, and distinctive expression. The aesthetic experience of nature also prompts us to perceive the world as singular and special, even when we confront situations experienced many times before such as a magnificent waterfall, an awesome mountain, or a majestic species.

Dutton stresses the vital benefits art confers as a consequence of the

6. Beetles are the most numerous of all animal species. They can inspire scientific fascination and aesthetic appreciation, but also fear and revulsion.

emotional saturation it provides. He argues that art engenders intense feelings like "fear, joy, sadness, anger, disgust, contempt, and surprise."[21] These feelings are also characteristic of many of our aesthetic responses to various creatures and landscapes. Finally, Dutton emphasizes the importance of the *imaginative experience* in art, what he describes as "imagination in problem-solving, planning, hypothesizing, inferring the mental states of others, or merely in daydreaming [as] virtually coextensive with normal human conscious life."[22] Nature's aesthetic appeal likewise provokes our imaginative and symbolic capacity, prompting us to explore, discover, and imagine worlds of countless possibility.

Like all our biophilic tendencies, the adaptive benefits of the aesthetic inclination to value nature rely on its functional development through experience and social support. Our aesthetic experience of nature is often provoked by a particularly moving event that becomes memorable and sometimes a seeming part of our identity. It might involve an encounter with a spectacular setting—for me, first seeing the Grant Tetons, or elephants and lions on the African savannah. But mundane paths can also take us to equally sublime places and experiences: a special backyard tree, the sun rising over cattails in a local marsh, the call of a bobwhite secreted within ferns and bayberries close to home. Even vicarious and representational encounters with the beauty of nature can be poignant and memorable, awakening our aesthetic sensibility; my first encounters with two great landscape paintings, Frederic Church's *The Heart of the Andes* and Albert Bierstadt's *The Rocky Mountains, Lander's Peak*, filled me with awe comparable to being in the locales depicted.[23]

These aesthetic encounters with nature can become "touchstone memories," what the poet William Wordsworth called "spots in time." For years afterward, they may be recalled as profound instances of intense pleasure and inspiration. Wordsworth poetically describes this quality:

> There are in our existence spots of time,
> That with distinct pre-eminence retain
> A renovating virtue . . .
> That penetrates, enables us to mount,
> When high, more high, and lifts us when fallen.[24]

For Wordsworth, a spot in time occurred during his visit to the Swiss Alps. Upon crossing a mountain pass and descending into a ravine, he spied a magnificent lake below. In a letter to his sister Dorothy, he described the importance of that experience: "At this moment when many of these landscapes are floating before my mind, I feel a high enjoyment that perhaps scarce a day of my life will pass in which I shall not derive some happiness from these images."[25]

Reflecting on the long-term effect of this experience on Wordsworth, the writer Alain de Botton remarked on the lingering glow of deep aesthetic engagement in nature. He suggests that we, too, can share this sort of Wordsworthian inspiration:

> Decades later, the Alps would continue to live within [Wordsworth] and to strengthen his spirit whenever he evoked them. Their survival led him to argue that we may see in nature certain scenes that will stay with us throughout our lives and offer us, every time they enter our consciousness, both a contrast to and relief from present difficulties. . . . Nature's loveliness might in turn, according to Wordsworth, encourage us to locate the good in ourselves.[26]

Most of us carry within ourselves spots in time when our aesthetic experience of nature exalted, comforted, and sustained us. I'm sure a recent encounter will become such a moment for me. In the fall of 2011, while vacationing on a Caribbean island, I snorkeled to see the brilliantly colorful fish lurking just below the gray and featureless sea. Donning my mask, I encountered spectacular angel, parrot, and butterfly fish, wrasse, grunts, snappers, jacks, corals, fans, and other amazing denizens of the coral community. Though I had seen these species many times before, I was stunned anew by their exquisite colors and forms: the sheer lush bountifulness totally captivated me. Eventually tiring, I exited the water brimming with wonder and awe. When asked whether it had been worth seeing, I blurted out without thinking: "If you like God, you definitely want to see it." What did I mean by this spiritual outburst? I suppose the sight of this incredible beauty left me feeling as if I had experienced a glimpse of perfection that reached beyond a narrow material utility. The lavishness of the coral reef inspired in me a desire to deeply engage cascading connections of meaning in this community of life, coral rock, and warm and dynamic sea, all and more tying me to a world beyond myself that felt glorious and inspiring.

Whether extraordinary or commonplace, aesthetic moments move us physically, emotionally, intellectually, and sometimes spiritually. Such a moment starts with a simple aesthetic attraction, but with cultivation and often the guiding hand of another, it can shift to more complex and satisfying levels of appreciation and understanding. We are encouraged to reach beyond the picturesque to more penetrating layers of engagement with the natural world. Commenting on this progression of aesthetic appreciation from the merely

7. Most of the world's crane species are rare and endangered, although the Sandhill Crane of North America is relatively abundant. The Platte River in Nebraska attracts nearly 450,000 Sandhill Cranes during their annual migration.

pretty to more complex levels of appreciation, Aldo Leopold cited the beauty of Sandhill Cranes as his portal to the nameless sublime. He observed:

> Our ability to perceive quality in nature begins, as in art, with the pretty. It expands through successive stages of the beautiful to values as yet uncaptured by language. The quality of cranes lies, I think, in this higher gamut, as yet beyond the reach of words. . . . Our appreciation of the crane grows with the slow unraveling of earthly history. His tribe, we now know, stems out of the remote Eocene. . . . When we hear his call we hear no mere bird. He is the symbol of our untamable past, of that incredible sweep of millennia which underlies and conditions the daily affairs of birds and men.[27]

An aesthetic appreciation of nature requires this deeper and sustained level of engagement. It demands that we open ourselves to the wonder, mystery, and harmony of life in all its vastness and splendor, and the underlying abiotic systems that render this achievement possible. When this occurs, we feel privileged at the chance to bask in its reflected glory, allowing ourselves the possibility to partake in its joy, and even take guidance from the beauty of the simple thornbush beside the road, as spectacular in its own way as the colorful and symmetrical rose. Conversely, when we debase or remain indifferent to nature's beauty, our senses become dull, our emotions flatten, our intellect withers, and our capacity to find meaning in our lives is replaced by cynicism and pessimism.

2

reason

If emotions represent the primary motivational entryway to our initial interest in the natural world, then intellect plays the critical guiding role, directing our choices and actions down the (presumably) wisest and most prudent path. Feelings are the wellspring for our desire to experience nature, but reason shapes these emotions. We are, after all, the quintessentially thinking animal, endowed with the seemingly unique ability for analytical and reasoned action.

As a species, we are most defined by our extraordinarily large, adaptive, and inventive brain, that anatomical feature that has distinguished us most from all other life, and allowed us to outcompete many creatures endowed with greater speed, strength, stealth, and sensory capacities. What we call the mind, including thinking and consciousness, has provided us with the remarkable ability to generate knowledge, symbolize, communicate, and create. This, in turn, has allowed us to reach far beyond our biology through the exercise of learning and culture, passed from one person and generation to another.

Underscoring the importance of intellect in human consciousness and identity, the French philosopher and mathematician René Descartes famously remarked: "I think, therefore I am."[1] He suggested that cognition takes precedence over feelings and the senses in developing our understanding of reality, asserting: "Knowledge of . . . reality derives from ideas of the intellect, not the senses."[2] The pioneering ecologist Aldo Leopold took Descartes' dictum one crucial step farther, tying the development of human intellect and selfhood to our understanding and experience of the world beyond our selves, to what Leopold called "the land." He asserted: "As a land-user thinketh so is he."[3]

In this chapter I explore why and how our intellect has always depended and continues to rely on the inherent inclination to affiliate with nature, even in the modern age. We start this exploration of the connection among intellect, our sense of reality and identity, and the experience of nature, with a brief personal interlude, about a time of stress and challenge but also growth and healing.

Interlude

Many years ago, I was in a serious automobile accident in Kenya. The accident resulted in a compound fracture to my femur that caused a life-threatening aneurism, followed by hepatitis contracted in the hospital. To-gether, these various maladies necessitated a four-month stay in Nairobi Hospital. At the time, hospital conditions in Kenya were quite simple, with few amenities: no radio, no television, and personal computers a dream on the horizon. Even books and magazines were scarce, prompting me more than once to attempt the surprisingly difficult task of reading slowly. Much of the time I was confined to bed, on a thin mattress, where I often lay immobile, experiencing considerable discomfort.

I would stare out the window a good deal of the time onto a relatively sparse landscape of shrubs, a distant forest edge with tall trees, and nearby, a worksite of construction ditches that had been started but was now suspended, though every other day a man would inexplicably appear to sweep the dirt ditches. Despite the limitations, the view to the outside became something of my lifeline, at first a distraction, but after a while an increasing absorption as I observed and studied the rocks, the vegetation, and the critters that would occasionally appear to make this landscape ever more detailed and meaningful.

I became especially interested in a hawk that suddenly arrived one day. It was a male African harrier hawk, a striking bird of prey of sub-Saharan Africa, known to eat vertebrate animals and the fruit of the oil palm, and possessed of the unusual ability to climb by using its feet and wings. The bird would often alight on a large branch in a tall and bordering tree on the edge of the open plain. There he would settle Buddha-like for long periods, to my anthropomorphizing mind seemingly content and aloof. On the contrary, he was always alert and focused, as demonstrated by his tendency to become suddenly tense, eyes focused on the ground, his binocular vision having spied some slightly anomalous but significant movement. The tension would usually dissipate after a while, and he would return to a more relaxed pose. But on a number of occasions, he sprang into action without warning, quickly flying from the tree and rapidly swooping down, disappearing into the high grass or construction ditch. More often than not, he would reemerge with a small rodent, a snake, or a songbird in his talons. He would then fly back to his branch and proceed to dismember his victim in surprisingly delicate fashion, typically consuming a piece at a time.

This hawk became my fascination, almost obsession. While he was in sight, I would observe the hawk at length, examining, studying, and reflecting upon his many qualities—his anatomy, behavior, needs, even his presumed place in the world. I became so familiar with the bird that I came to recognize his distinctive patterned hues, the complexity of his flight, the extraordinary precision of his attack, the unyielding fierceness of his predation, his habits and seeming lust for life.

The bird progressively captivated me, even if he remained sublimely unaware and indifferent to my existence. I telescoped into his world, making his reality an integral part of my own. I used the animal to develop a growing awareness, alertness, and involvement. And through this expanding knowledge and connection, I became acutely attached to the animal and his world, allowing him and it to emerge as the basis for a deepening intellectual relationship and even reverent regard.

From a clinical perspective, my immersion in the hawk's existence had the unanticipated consequence of making me feel healthier and more alive, as if I could be healed by the association. Until then, my time in the hospital had been painfully slow and laborious, days of suffering, boredom, and often self-pity. Time felt as if it accelerated, hours passing into days, days rapidly merging into weeks, as I became increasingly absorbed by the bird and his world. My energy and optimism were renewed, my lethargy was pushed aside, and my symptoms even diminished. I had somehow borrowed this creature's unrelenting vitality and made it a part of my own. I felt a renewed engagement that replaced my chronic anxiety, and my pleasure in the bird displaced my self-absorption.

The more I came to know and connect with the bird, the more he seemed to become party to my recovery. I had adopted the creature's passion for life, and through this identification revived a faith in my own. I felt as if I had been administered a therapy originating in my better knowing and understanding the creature and his world. It seemed a medicine as relevant to my health and healing as the synthesized pharmaceuticals I took for my infections and surgical recovery.

NATURE AND HUMAN INTELLECTUAL DEVELOPMENT

The anthropologist Claude Lévi-Strauss once remarked that animals are as "good to think with" as they may be to eat or otherwise utilize and exploit.[4] The veterinarian and anthropologist Elizabeth Lawrence invoked the phrase "cognitive biophilia" to underscore the role that animals and nature in general play in the maturation of human intellect and intelligence.[5] Both Lawrence and Lévi-Strauss intimated that people's inclination to understand the natural world has always served as an essential contributor to human consciousness, cognitive development, and identity.

Learning about nature is vital to developing the human capacities for understanding, naming, categorizing, analyzing, and judging, all basic to the evolution of human intelligence. Intellectual maturation, in turn, is fundamental to our ability to form language, communicate, and create, all cornerstones of the transmission of knowledge from one person and generation to another, and thus of the formation of culture. This cognitive capacity emerges from our aptitudes for empirical observation, systematic analysis, and evaluative judgment, all honed and refined by our knowledge and experience of nature.

Contact with nature is vital to human intellectual development because the natural world is the most information-rich and sensory-stimulating environment people ever encounter, particularly during the important years of childhood. Nature is an unrivaled context for learning and experience, even in an age of extraordinary accumulated knowledge and electronic communication, where vast amounts of information literally lie at our fingertips. This critical contribution of the natural world to our intellectual development is often unappreciated, obscured by its subtlety. Because nature is all around us, we sometimes take for granted our contact with it, much as a fish might be unaware of the water through which it swims or a bird the air wherein it flies. The detail, diversity, and variability of the natural world are pervasive, and there lies much of nature's significance as a source of human intellectual maturation and development.

To illustrate this point, consider the remarkable richness and abundance of life on earth, the most salient aspect of nature for us, even if during our lifetimes we come to know just a tiny fraction of all this biological diversity. Currently known species number approximately 1.9 million, although there are probably some 8 to 10 million more species awaiting scientific classification and discovery. As remarkable as this may be, it represents a tiny fraction, perhaps one-tenth of one percent, of all species that have ever existed on the planet.[6]

Moreover, each species reflects an astonishing degree of its own diversity as revealed by its distinctive populations, races, subspecies, and other manifestations of anatomical, behavioral, and geographic variability. Alluding to this remarkable variation, the Nobel Prize–winning scientist Karl von Frisch, when asked about devoting his life to the study of a single species, the honeybee, remarked that the more he explored and examined it, the more he found there was to know and discover. He suggested: "The bee's life is like a magic well: the more you draw from it, the more it fills with water."[7] My experience of the hawk was somewhat analogous, as the more fascinated I became with its many attributes, the more deeply I dipped into its fountain of seemingly endless detail and source of understanding.

A similar degree of astonishing variety confronts us when we examine the nonliving elements of the natural world: rocks, soils, water, minerals, geological formations, atmosphere, weather, stars, landscapes, even if again our exposure is only to a small fraction of this detail and diversity. The question that confronts us is the relevance to people's intellectual development of all this information richness and sensory stimulation. Can compelling and convincing reasons be offered why this diversity in nature might exert a significant effect on human cognitive growth, especially among young and inquiring minds?

We might start with the lives of average American children residing in a typical city or suburb. Looking at the world through their eyes, we encounter a remarkable degree of natural abundance and variety occurring just about everywhere. Moreover, this natural diversity is an ongoing source of richly stimulating experience relevant to children's cognitive development. Every day, children confront a flood of sensory stimulation from aspects of nature that demand recognition, response, identification, differentiation, naming, analysis, evaluation, and judgment, even if only at a rudimentary level. This intellectual engagement is prompted by a wide variety of encounters, with unmediated nature outdoors, with domesticated nature, like a potted plant or a pet, and with representational nature, in pictures, stories, or electronic media.

A typical child on a typical day encounters soil, rocks, bushes, trees, flowers, insects, birds, perhaps a worm or a fish, an occasional reptile, some mammals; and all these encounters play out within an atmosphere, perhaps of wind or various weather conditions, under clouds, sun, or stars. Consciously or unconsciously, the child responds to each natural stimulus, making distinctions within any category of environmental experience—for example: big trees and little trees, house plants and garden plants, vines and ferns, ants and flies, spiders and bees, frogs as against turtles and snakes, ducks contrasted with robins and cardinals, sparrows compared to hawks, mice in relation to bears, lions, or wolves, cats and dogs and horses, extinct and imagined creatures like dinosaurs, Pooh bears, and stuffed animals. In confronting various landscape features—hills, valleys, streams, lakes, rivers, oceans, waves, mountains—a child further learns distinctive characteristics that lend meaning to particular places. Children also respond to a world of nature transformed, whether food, furnishings, designs, decorations, or building materials, whose origins may have become obscure, but which are often still recognized as originating in the natural world.

This abundance of information and detail is relevant to children's intellectual development because it requires their cognitive engagement in recognizing, sorting, differentiating, labeling, understanding, and committing to memory all this stimulation and diversity. Moreover, this occurs on a routine and everyday basis, accessible to most children, even those living in a city or suburb.

For example, consider the important intellectual task of distinguishing and categorizing. Not only are children aware of rocks, hills, plants, animals, and other commonplace environmental features, but they also classify these into groups based on similar and analogous features of these objects. Thus an oak and a maple are clumped into trees, and recognized as different from trees whose needlelike leaves do not appear to shed. Cardinals and robins are recognized as birds, but distinct from hawks or ducks. This process is repeated across an extraordinary variety of environmental features and circumstances that require recognition, naming, understanding, sorting, distinguishing, and categorizing. This taxonomic task forms the foundation for the development of human language and our remarkable capacity to communicate.

The information richness and sensory stimulation provided by the natural world are further enhanced by its highly variable and dynamic qualities. Nature is characterized by its constant flux and change, alterations that require children's adaptation to volatile conditions and circumstances, in contrast to the relative passivity of static, lifeless, and artificial objects. Moreover, the dynamic qualities of nature are typically unpredictable and sometimes surprising, even at times mysterious. Changes in weather, a plant's appearance, an animal's behavior, landscapes shifting cyclically across the year and over time—these all challenge the child to adjust to a dynamic community of fluid experiences and relationships.

The most salient aspect of nature's unyielding attraction to children is the encounter with other life. In nature children experience and imagine other creatures' lives, which are at the same time different from their own but similar, offering a wealth of opportunity for intellectual and emotional engagement. Children confront this living diversity not only in the "real" outdoors but also representationally in stories, pictures, and symbols, all of which foster intellectual development. Living creatures possess the motivating "power" that arouses the child's interest, curiosity, and cognitive response.

To illustrate, imagine a young boy's and a young girl's respective encounters with water and trees. The young boy experiences water in the form of rain falling from the sky and recognizes that when rain occurs, it is generally cloudy, not sunny. Living in a temperate latitude, he experiences both rain in summer and snow in winter. Extrapolating from this association of rain or snow with certain meteorological conditions, he begins to form a basic understanding of weather. He further associates water with the growth of certain vegetation, and notices variations among plants in response to quantities and qualities of water. With the assistance of parents, siblings, friends, and teachers, he learns that water flow has something to do with volume, environmental context, and meteorological circumstance, and the ways in which these features affect the occurrence of streams, rivers, lakes, and other aquatic bodies. By now, he probably recognizes the difference between the fresh water of land and the salt water of the oceans, and the implications of the difference for life and his own experience. These and a multitude of other encounters with a single environmental element help the boy evolve from simple to ever more complex levels of intellectual reasoning, from sorting and classifying to the more challenging cognitive tasks of assessing, interpreting, evaluating, judging, and taking reasoned action.

The young girl lives in a suburban community, and among her first memories is an especially large tree that grows in her backyard. She plays in the shadow of this imposing tree, which she learns is a big oak; over time she becomes aware of other nearby trees, which her parents tell her are maples, dogwoods, cherries, pines, birches, and others whose names she has difficulty remembering. Although she cannot name all the trees, she recognizes variations in their size, shape, color, and leaves, and where they grow. She grasps differences between trees and bushes, shrubs and ferns, grass and plants in her mother's garden.

She notices that the oaks and maples have leaves in summer that disappear in winter, while the needles of the pine trees often remain—though she knows that they occasionally drop, because she has made a soft bed of their needles, where she also sees that hardly anything else grows. She further observes that some trees have seeds and pods, others cones, and that both properties appear connected to how trees reproduce themselves. She becomes aware that certain animals are often found in trees: insects, birds, squirrels, and other critters. She further becomes aware that dead branches and dead trees tend to foster mushrooms, fungus, and creatures like worms, termites, and woodpeckers. Her parents, friends, and teachers instruct her that people get things from trees like fruit, wood, paper; from her own experience, she knows that they also provide shelter and beauty.

Both the girl and the boy employ a simple and commonplace experience of nature to advance their intellectual capacities. They assimilate facts and understanding, they learn to name and identify, they classify and differentiate, they engage in analysis and interpretation, they evaluate and judge. They accomplish these intellectual tasks through direct encounters with nature, as well as through more indirect and symbolic means like reading and looking at pictures. Through all these experiences, they not only emerge more knowledgeable about the natural world, but, more important, they utilize nature to hone their intellectual skills and capacities through exercising the cognitive muscle of their brain.

The extraordinary detail, diversity, and accessibility of the natural world as a basis of children's intellectual development have been described by the psychologist Rachel Sebba. Sebba particularly emphasizes three characteristics of nature worth reiterating here. First, she stresses that the natural world arouses all of children's senses. Humans tend to be visually oriented, and certainly nature is a visual feast. Yet the natural world also provokes other primary senses like sound, smell, feel, and taste, as well as the secondary senses of temperature, balance, movement, pain and discomfort.[8]

Sebba further stresses the dynamic qualities of nature. The natural world continuously changes depending on time of day, weather, season, and the dynamic processes of aging, maturation, and senescence. Moreover, these changes are often unexpected, surprising, and unpredictable. These alterations stimulate a child's awareness and response, and require adaptive thinking and behavior.

Finally, Sebba emphasizes the importance of life as an especially salient characteristic of nature for the developing child. Nature is that singular place where children encounter other creatures different but analogous to themselves, encouraging their relationship and connection of what they observe to their own experience. Children personalize and identify with other life, engendering emotional attachments that motivate their intellectual interest and engagement.

The psychologist Benjamin Bloom and colleagues usefully identified six stages of cognitive development relevant to furthering our understanding of the role of nature in intellectual growth and maturation. Although this classification scheme is not universally accepted, particularly the assumption of developmental stages, these distinctions provide insight regarding the role of the natural world in children's cognitive development. The six stages progress from simpler to more advanced levels of cognitive complexity and include:

- *Stage 1, Knowledge* Learning simple facts and terms that foster basic causal understandings and classification schemes;

- *Stage 2, Comprehension*—Interpreting facts and ideas in order to extrapolate understandings to other situations and circumstances;
- *Stage 3, Application*—Applying knowledge to generate new ideas and concepts;
- *Stage 4, Analysis*—Examining and breaking down knowledge into constituent parts that enhance understanding of underlying relationships;
- *Stage 5, Synthesis*—The opposite of analysis: integrating knowledge of discrete parts to organize and structure understanding of wholes;
- *Stage 6, Evaluation*—Forming judgments regarding the functioning of parts and wholes based on examining evidence, impacts, and outcomes.[9]

Children's experience of nature is critical in the development of each intellectual stage. For example, the first stage involves the child generating knowledge of basic facts, ideas, and terms that are used to create simple classification schemes and causal understandings. This intellectual development depends on observing, identifying, sorting, naming, and categorizing. As we have seen, these capacities are facilitated by children's reactions and responses to nature's extraordinary detail, diversity, and dynamic character, which are readily accessible in most everyday circumstances. This intellectual growth is further enhanced by children communicating this knowledge and experience to parents, siblings, friends, relatives, and teachers, who in turn assist in promoting this understanding.

The intellectual ability to form ideas and learn facts and terms through the experience of nature can be developed by direct outdoor contact with nature or through more representational means such as images and stories. In this latter respect, young children's books often involve subjects drawn from nature, particularly animals, that are used to encourage the development of capacities to identify, sort, classify, name, and numerate. For example, a typical book on counting or naming might include one cuddly bear, two fat hippos, three gangly giraffes, four fearsome tigers, five big birds, six many-legged spiders, seven tall trees, eight colorful flowers, nine scaly fish, ten smiley clouds, but rarely one pencil, two paperclips, three pipes, four machines, five roads, six office towers, seven television sets, eight computers, nine telephone poles, or ten desks. One study found that nearly ninety percent of the characters in young children's books are drawn from the natural world, and when inanimate objects appear, they are often rendered lifelike by the addition of eyes, nose, mouth, or the ability to move and take purposeful action.

The first stage of cognitive development is especially important in language formation and the developing capacity for speech, both basic to human communication. The building blocks of language development are identify-ing, differentiating, sorting, naming, and classifying. The natural world pro-vides unparalleled opportunities for children to label, distinguish, and organize knowledge that in turn facilitates speech and language development. The ecol-ogist Paul Shepard, commenting on this effect and particularly the importance of animals, suggested:

> Human intelligence is bound to the presence of animals. They are the means by which cognition takes its first shape and they are the instruments for imagining abstract ideas and qualities. . . . They are the code images by which language retrieves ideas from memory at will. . . . They enable us to objectify qualities and traits. . . . Animals are used in the growth and de-velopment of the human person, in those most priceless qualities we lump together as *mind*. . . . Animals . . . are basic to the development of speech and thought.[10]

Other stages of children's cognitive development can also be tied to the experience of nature. Bloom's second stage, *comprehension*, and the third, *ap-plication*, focus on the interpretation of information and then the extrapolation and application of this understanding to other situations in order to generate new ideas and understandings. As the previous examples of water and trees sug-gested, most children's experience of nature affords them ample opportunity to understand and interpret events and to use this knowledge to advance new ideas applicable to other situations. In the case of water, children commonly recog-nize that rain occurs under certain circumstances such as cloudy and overcast days, and then they apply this understanding and expectation to other weather conditions. Or, to take another example, nearly all children are able to distin-guish a songbird from a hawk, although they realize that both animals are birds, with feathers and the capacity for flight. They use this understanding to differ-entiate a duck from a pigeon, or a bird from a flying mammal like a bat. Again, the important point is not how much children learn about nature but how the basic processes of learning are facilitated by the children's experience of nature.

Bloom's cognitive stages of *analysis* and *synthesis* involve more complex reasoning that includes the breaking down of knowledge and then its reas-sembly and integration into organized wholes. Children's contact with nature provides many opportunities to develop these complementary cognitive ca-pacities. Returning again to the example of water, many if not most children recognize that rain or snow falling in the mountains eventually flows into streams, then rivers, and usually empties into the sea. They also realize that rain is a liquid, snow a solid, and in between there exists a vaporous state found in clouds and fog, which given the right circumstances once again becomes rain or snow and falls from the sky. Through engaging the processes of analysis and synthesis, children form basic understandings of the water cycle long before being taught this phenomenon in schools. They further come to associate certain landscapes—a rainforest or a desert, for example—with rain or its absence, and by extrapolation they can deduce which plants and animals are appropriate to each setting. Once more, they use nature to shift from simpler to more complex levels of cognitive reasoning as they develop their intellectual capacity and understanding.

The final stage of Bloom's taxonomy is *evaluation*, that is, children's formation of judgments based on evidence, impacts, and outcomes, and use of this understanding to make choices and take reasoned action. The natural world provides children with a wealth of opportunity for developing this intellectual capacity. For example, most children learn that climbing onto the limb of a tree, or hanging over a cliff, or swimming in deep water increases the risk of harm and injury. They learn that stagnant and discolored water is generally not good to drink, or that throwing a rock at a bird usually provokes punishment as a wrongful and cruel act. These and other examples reveal how often children's contact with nature is used to facilitate their capacities for evaluating, judging, and making rational choices that facilitate critical thinking and problem solving.

I have argued that the inclination to affiliate with nature to foster intellectual development is an inherent and, thus, universal human tendency. As such, it should occur among all peoples independent of culture and history, even if as a learned tendency it will vary considerably among individuals and groups. Thus we should expect nature to be as much a factor in human intellectual development among so-called primitive and preliterate peoples as it might be in modern society, with its extensive formal learning and scientific orientation.

There is, in fact, limited evidence to support this thesis, based on studies of traditional hunter-gatherer societies. In this regard, we might examine research involving the Foré of tropical Papua New Guinea, and the Athabascan Koyukon of the North American Arctic.

The Foré have been the focus of studies conducted by Jared Diamond and others.[11] Diamond's investigations reveal that the Foré possess an extensive knowledge of the natural world that extends far beyond a narrow and immediate material utility. Diamond suggests that this knowledge among the Foré is often comparable to modern scientific understanding. Although the Foré lack a written language, formal education, and modern observational technology,

Diamond reports, they possess an extensive and often quite precise understanding of natural history and even ecology. He cites the following illustrations of their impressive knowledge of the natural world:

- The Foré possess 110 names for the 120 scientifically classified bird species occurring in their area.
- They can name at least 1,400 species of plants and animals.
- They can distinguish and identify very similar bird species based on slight variations in behavior and sound rather than by just physical appearance.
- They make these distinctions without the aid of binoculars, spotting scopes, or other modern technology.
- They can recall and describe rare species years afterward without the assistance of written records.

Diamond also cites other studies that report similarly impressive degrees of natural history knowledge among other Pacific Island peoples, again rivaling the understandings of modern science. He suggests that much of this knowledge exists independent of its immediate practical significance for food, clothing, medicine, or aesthetic decoration.

He poses the following critical question: "Why do New Guineans and other Pacific Islanders devote so much stored memory to the names and habits of so many plant and animal species? What do they make of all this knowledge, and why do they involve themselves so intimately in the natural world?"[12]

By way of an answer, Diamond ambiguously concludes that among the Foré and other tribal peoples there exists: "An intrinsic . . . interest and natural affinity . . . simply because the species are there." Yet this answer begs the question, offering little explanation beyond a vague reference to "intrinsic interest." A more likely explanation is that the Foré and other Pacific Islanders, like all peoples, utilize their knowledge of the natural world to advance their intellectual development, a capacity every bit as fundamental to human fitness and well-being as is the material utilization of nature. Although Diamond found that many species of interest to the Foré lack immediate practical utility, the knowledge and awareness of these species still provided them with a wealth of opportunity for distinguishing, identifying, naming, and understanding basic to intellectual growth and maturation. The Foré use their knowledge of nature, just as all people do, to foster cognitive development and the growth of the most prized of human possessions, the brain and the mind.

An analogous process is described and reported by the anthropologist Richard Nelson in his studies of a very different hunter-gatherer people, the

Athabascan Koyukon, residents of the frigid North American Arctic.[13] Based on his and others' studies, Nelson came to a conclusion consistent with Diamond's: "Traditional societies . . . have accumulated bodies of knowledge much like our own sciences."[14]

Among the Koyukon, Nelson reports extensive understanding of nature that extends far beyond its immediate material utility. Commenting on the extent of this understanding of the natural world, its origins, the subtlety of its expression, its role in the worldview of these peoples, and its impact on the development of human intelligence, Nelson insightfully remarks:

> What repeatedly struck me above all else was [the Koyukon's] profound knowledge of the environment. . . . Volumes could be written about the behavior, ecology, and utilization of Arctic animals . . . based entirely on [their] knowledge. . . . A traditional [Koyukon] plumbs the depths of his intellect—his capacity to manipulate complex knowledge. But he also delves into . . . nature, drawing from intuitions of sense and body and heart: feeling the wind's touch, listening for the tick of moving ice, peering from crannies. . . . He moves in a world of eyes, where everything watches—the bear, the seal, the wind, the moon and stars, the drifting ice, the silent waters below. . . . It fairly staggers the imagination. And it gives strong testimony to the adaptation of mind . . . a connectedness with non-human life [that] infuses the whole spectrum of their thought, behavior, and belief.[15]

Many people today harbor the belief that what distinguishes our modern world from the world of the "primitive" is our advanced intellect, revealed in particular by the contemporary practice of science. Moreover, scientific knowledge is typically assumed to be the particular province of a few formally trained for the purpose, who are set apart from the rest of society. The studies of the Foré and Koyukon instead suggest that an intellectual affinity for the natural world, even the occurrence of something akin to science, is a universal tendency of all peoples. Perhaps this seeming contradiction can be reconciled by broadening our understanding of what we mean by science.

One dictionary defines science as "the observation, identification, description, experimental investigation, and theoretical explanation of phenomena . . . Knowledge, especially . . . gained through experience."[16] All these attributes of science—observation, identification, description, theoretical explanation, knowledge gained through experience, with the possible exception of experimental investigation—occur among the Foré and the Koyukon. Even the practice of repeated observations under varying circumstances—a characteristic of experimental investigation—is widespread among these and most people seeking to advance understanding of the natural world under changing circumstances and to acquire a better ability to predict and anticipate events. In other words, what we regard as science may be more a qualitative than absolute distinction, where most if not all people perform a kind of science in advancing their intellectual development through knowledge and understanding of the world beyond themselves.[17]

The flourishing of human intellect requires curiosity, a sense of wonder, and a yearning to learn about nature's endless detail, diversity, and mystery. Even the most mundane aspects of the natural world can yield a bounty of intellectual reward. As the writer Roman Vishniac suggests, a drop of local pond water may provoke as much wonder as traveling to the most distant and remote places on the planet.[18]

But imagine for a moment a world where wild and living nature had become a rarity—where bushes and trees were an aberration rather than commonplace, where nary a bird or insect was heard or seen flying, where the landscape and all geological forms had become uniform, where weather was always the same. How might this place be viewed and experienced? I suspect it would be perceived as dull beyond belief, monumentally ugly, homogenous and stupid—a place where children largely cocooned themselves within vicarious and virtual realities, and adults had lost their power to communicate in more than technical terms. It would be a place where intellectual and emotional development had become stunted, and human interactions and relationships were impaired and fitful if not often frightening.

This chapter concludes with a more optimistic perspective, an interlude that recalls two experiences where nature helped shape my intellect, sense of wonder, and reverent appreciation of life.

Interlude

At one point in my life I was particularly interested in seeing, identifying, and naming as many birds as I could. I was especially drawn to identifying warblers in the spring, shorebirds in summer, raptors during fall, and waterfowl in winter. Although I was also attracted to the beauty of birds, my passion at the time was honing my ability to identify and classify them.

Yet over the years, I found myself moving to subtler and more complex levels of intellectual appreciation and understanding. Initially, this revealed itself in my becoming more aware of the faithfulness of many bird species to certain foods found in certain settings and habitats. This eventually led to a growing awareness of how these birds had evolved particular anatomical features well suited to exploit particular ecological niches. Through this expanding under-standing of relational dependencies, I also came to appreciate the importance of interactions among bird species and their environments, and how this played a role in their biological development.

In time, this growing awareness led me to better recognize how many aspects of modern life threatened the delicate balance and interdependence of birds and their habitats. I became cognizant of the vulnerability of many spe-cies to human-induced change that impeded their access to foods, habitats, and beneficial circumstances. I came to recognize that the relatively high rates of metabolism of many bird species made them especially vulnerable to the intrusive effects of modern life. I became as aware of the ecosystems that birds inhabited as I was of the creatures themselves, and that brought a realization of the vulnerability of other plant and animal life that occurred in these areas. I became cognizant of the destructive impacts of my own species on the species and habitats I had come to revere. With this knowledge, I emerged motivated and better equipped to advance the conservation and protection of these areas.

This expanding knowledge reflected my movement from simpler to more complex stages of intellectual development. I started with the relatively straightforward desire to see, identify, and name as many birds as possible. Yet over time I found myself moving to more subtle levels of comprehension, analysis, evaluation, and judgment of my own and others' behaviors, assump-tions, and values. I never abandoned my passion to experience the pleasures of seeing and identifying ducks in winter, raptors in fall, warblers in spring, or seabirds in summer. But I layered onto these interests a growing aware-ness, appreciation, and concern for the floodplains and swamps, the wooded slopes and littoral zones, the high mountain ridges and hidden valleys where these species dwelled. I found that they contained a fountain of life and nonlife bound together into a great chain of being that miraculously included my own. Through this circle of widening connection, I came to know my avian kin bet-ter, and gained a deeper affiliation with an encompassing universe of creation.

Likewise, I conclude with the tale of a tree that also helped me to achieve a more advanced intellectual understanding and appreciation. The story starts some years ago on a walk in a forest near where I live. There I encountered a huge tree, called a tulip tree, whose magnificent features just about stopped me in my tracks. I was at the base of a great cliff not far from a nearby river. Like most large tulip trees, it rose like an arrow to well over one hundred feet, its great limbs branching only about halfway up the tree.

The bark of a mature tulip is especially arresting, deeply furrowed and dark brown. The tree's leaves are also unusual in having four lobes that, rather than being pointed, are truncated, giving the leaf a squarish heartlike shape. The leaves sit at the end of long stems that flutter in the slightest wind. On sunny days, the glossy leaf surfaces catch and toss the sunbeams, making them shimmer and flash in the reflected light.

The aesthetic beauty of the tulip tree is capped by its blossoms, which give the tree its name. Strikingly colorful, the blooms seem to belong in a flower garden rather than on a wild tree. Tulip tree flowers are big and showy, pale yellow with a touch of green, an orange band, and a dash of red like frosting on a cake. They seem delicate from afar, but up close they are stiff and waxy, rarely drooping even in the hardest rain and strongest wind.

It is not surprising that I, like others, was initially attracted to the tulip tree because of its extraordinary aesthetic features. Yet as I have come to know this tree better, I have found myself progressively moving into expanding realms of curiosity and understanding. I have learned that although the tree thrives not far from water, it is oddly intolerant of being inundated, unlike other trees found near the floodplain. I also came to recognize that despite being a forest dweller, the tree thrives on sunlight, its great height depending on being at the edge rather than interior of the forest. I have also learned that the tulip tree is a member of the magnolia family, a taxa more common to southern areas than to where I live.

My growing appreciation of the tulip tree has led me to study its relationship to people and its historic uses. I have learned that its wood is not especially strong, but has long been used to make furniture, panels, and boxes. Yet its relatively lightweight and smooth wood can be easily worked and precisely finished, qualities that have made tulip wood especially suitable to the construction of organ pipes and valves. I further became aware that the tulip tree is a great favorite of bees, which produce a prized honey. I also came to appreciate that the great size of the tulip tree made it a good home for various other insects, birds, and mammals.

My intellectual odyssey started with the simple attraction to an especially arresting tree. It expanded over time to ever widening and satisfying reaches of understanding and admiration. I still relish seeing this particular stately tulip tree, especially when in blossom. But I now have a deeper affiliation with tulip trees, immersing myself in a multiplicity of values that intellectually extend my horizons, better connecting me not only to this tree but to a broader realm of awareness and relationship to the natural world.

3

aversion

Above all, we humans pride ourselves on our intelligence, the basis of our ability to make rational decisions and the foundation for our vaunted science and technology, which have propelled our species to its overwhelmingly dominant position on the planet. Most people consider the enemy of rational choice to be succumbing to emotions, especially "irrational" feelings like dislike, hate, and fear. Conservationists decry, for example, the hostility and loathing that historically have contributed to the harm and even destruction of such animals and habitats as snakes, wolves, insects, spiders, swamps, and deserts.

Why, then, would we extol the value of aversion toward and even fear of nature? On the contrary, should not our focus be on encouraging a rational, caring, and affectionate relationship, and on replacing negative emotions with reason and admiration? Understanding and appreciating the natural world is, of course, essential to its conservation. But aversion to nature is also critical to human health and well-being, and has always been a cornerstone of the fitness and survival over time of any species, including ours. Moreover, a certain apprehension is a necessary component of feelings of awe and respect for nature that ultimately form the basis for a deep, reverent regard for powers greater than our own. These sentiments in turn inspire ethical restraint when we exploit nature—preservation rooted in keeping a healthy distance. Our examination of this subject begins with a personal interlude, a time when I experienced panic so pronounced it bordered on terror, but that also included a deep appreciation and respect for the source that provoked this anxiety.

Interlude

This experience involved my encountering in the wild a legendary creature of fear and sometimes loathing, the wolf. I had until then known wolves largely through books and research, although I was fascinated with the animal and involved in its conservation. I was also sympathetic with the plight of this animal, given its long history of persecution, especially in the United States, that had brought the animal to near extinction in the forty-eight contiguous states. Perhaps I was also motivated by my affection for the most beloved of creatures, the domestic dog (*Canis lupis familiaris*), whose biology is nearly identical to that of the gray wolf (*Canis lupis*), though the two animals are generally perceived in fundamentally different ways.

Eliminating the wolf had once been a norm among Western nations, especially in the United States and across much of Europe. Indeed, the North American effort to extirpate the wolf continued well into the twentieth century. This effort at exterminating the wolf was so unrelenting that the writer Barry Lopez called it a form of genocide or, more accurately, "specicide," the deliberate extinction of a species.[1] Antipathy toward wolves became so widespread in America that even the pioneering conservationist President Theodore Roosevelt referred to the wolf as the "beast of waste and desolation."[2]

I had read extensively about this animal and knew a fair amount about its biology, history, and conservation. I had also encountered live wolves in zoos and in a simulated wild setting on a multiacre enclosure in the Rocky Mountains. I had further conducted several investigations of human relationships with wolves, including a study of the animals' possible reintroduction and recolonization to areas where they had been extirpated, and I had served on a National Academy of Sciences committee involving wolf management and conservation in Alaska. I admired the species' intelligence and social ecology, and was committed to improving its imperiled status through much of the animal's historic range.

Still, my knowledge of wolves remained largely secondhand, mainly derived from books, research, and encounters with captive animals. Thus I jumped at the chance when asked to accompany one of the world's most renowned wolf biologists, David Mech, on a trip to northern Minnesota, where he had been conducting studies of wolves in the wild for many years. At the time, this area included the only free-roaming wolf populations in the contiguous United States.[3]

We flew by floatplane to a part of northern Minnesota colloquially known as the boundary waters area, a place of extensive rivers, streams, lakes, and wetlands. We were seeking radio-collared wolves using transmitters from the plane. We did find a small pack and pursued it down an old logging road. After landing, we tranquilized a large male and obtained blood samples, extracted a tooth, and gathered data that allowed estimates of the animal's age, health, size, and overall condition. Although exciting and in the field, the experience remained relatively safe, aloof, and insulated.

The next day, another prominent wolf researcher, Fred Harrington, joined our camp. Fred's specialty was the study of wolf vocalizations, particularly the animal's legendary howl. Fred also asked whether I wanted to join him later that evening, when he planned to collect data in the field, and I again jumped at the opportunity.

At the time, the wolf's howl remained largely a mystery, its function attributed to various possibilities including communicating its location, reinforcing pack solidarity, signaling prey availability, and other theories. Fred sought a clearer understanding of the wolf's howl through studies in the wild, particularly gathering information during the crepuscular hours between day and night when wolves tended to be most vocal and active. He would play recordings of wolf howls, and then when the live animals responded, note their vocal and, if feasible, behavioral responses.[4]

Fred and I departed close to midnight, driving for perhaps an hour down old logging roads through dark, thick, and overhanging evergreen forests. We finally arrived at a heavily wooded area where Fred had successfully called wolves a few weeks before, and where he set up his sound and recording equipment. He played a series of wolf howls for the next hour, but none elicited a response. Meanwhile, the silence and darkness of the heavily wooded area cast a surreal quality. Fred would periodically play wolf howls, then long intervals of silence would follow, as he and I listened intently, although I often found myself drifting into a day- (or, more accurately, night-) dream. After a while, I resigned myself to nothing happening, thinking that we would soon return to camp.

Then, unexpectedly, from what seemed like a long distance away, I heard a sound so faint that initially I thought it more the product of my imagination than something real. Fred's affirmative nod confirmed that it was a wolf calling in response to the recording. Fred then played the recording more frequently and turned the volume higher. This time the responses became more audible and frequent, although still from what seemed like a long distance. As the cycle of sound recording and live response continued, it became apparent there was more than one wolf howling, although it was difficult to determine how many. Fred and I communicated by gesture rather than words, not wanting to alert the wolves to our presence. The wolves were clearly coming closer, although their howls still seemed distant.

I was excited by their proximity, even though the combination of high technology and Fred's scientific and unemotional approach lent to the experience a quality of remoteness and security. Then a wolf howl suddenly rose without warning from not far away, and then another wolf howled, answered quickly by others. It was clear that the wolves had encircled us and were nearby, although they remained hidden in the woods.

Their calls were so loud and startling that my reaction was spontaneous and visceral. What had been a few moments earlier a largely intellectual engagement, almost a kind of entertainment, had suddenly become deeply anxious, atavistic, and discomforting. I was consumed with a dread that bordered on terror, and it shook me to my core.

The wolves' howls increased in frequency, multiplying and surrounding us in the darkness. The evening had begun to lighten into shades of charcoal gray. I was at the edge of panic, acutely aware of my total exposure and seeming defenselessness. I could not smell or see as well as wolves, and the animal possessed a strength, ferocity, and predatory prowess that reduced me, at least in my mind, to little more than edible meat foolish enough to render itself easily available for the taking. For the first time in my life, I experienced the reality of the cliché about the hairs on the back of one's neck standing on end, and I fought a desire to burst into the classic "fear and flight" of the prey animal. All my knowledge about and sympathy for the wolf had become irrelevant, subordinated to my mounting insecurity and dread. I was hardly comforted by reminding myself that wolves rarely, if ever, attack people.

Fred also seemed uncertain and tense, though perhaps that was just my projection. Still, he gestured for us to move away slowly in the direction of the pickup truck. We cautiously backed toward the vehicle, leaving the equipment. To my immense relief, we finally reached the safety of the truck. I looked back and before entering thought I could see the grayish outline of two skulking wolves at the edge of the woods. Upon entering the truck, I uttered a loud sigh of relief, realizing that all the while I had been holding my breath. I lay back against the seat, trembling in excitement, trying to restore my calm and self-confidence. I peered back at the lengthening shadows of the new dawn and thought I could see the shape of a large wolf staring in my direction. I imagined a fiery glow in his or her eyes, one of curiosity, or perhaps hungry disappointment.

We sat for a good long time in the truck until confident the wolves had retreated into the forest. We then exited and collected the equipment, lingering anxiety prompting me to look more than once over my shoulder into the dark woods. Finally, we drove back to camp, largely quiet, as if words would disperse the magic of the moment. I felt embarrassed by my fear and near panic. Yet I

8. Eliminating the wolf was once a widely held goal in the United States. The attempted extermination of this animal has been called "specicide," the deliberate extinction of a species.

was thrilled at having been in the presence of something majestic, awesome, and, in a strange way, joyful.

The power of the wild wolf had become personal and poignant. I had engaged in a dance of intimate association, even if it was prompted by terror, and I came away with a far deeper appreciation and admiration for this creature. That moment was burned into my memory, a spot in time that lingered with me for years. I felt a reverence that comes when fear mixes with wonder and deep appreciation for a power greater than one's own. My respect and veneration for the wolf had moved from the abstract, intellectual, and sentimental to something more meaningful and lasting.

THE INHERENT FEAR OF NATURE

Our fear of and aversion to nature is as much a reflection of our biology as any other inborn tendency toward the natural world. Although biophilia is

Latin for love of life, the concept, as noted, also includes other inherent inclinations to affiliate with nature that reflect adaptive functions developed over
evolutionary time, including an aversion to nature. Indeed, some of our most
hard to resist reactions and responses to the natural world reflect fears and anxieties that evolved under historical conditions when rapid response to dangerous features in nature was vital to our survival. As a consequence, many of our
reactions to such creatures as spiders, ticks, leeches, wasps, mosquitoes, sharks,
snakes, and large predators or such environmental conditions as fierce lightning, strong winds, steep slopes, dark forests, thick swamps, polluted water,
decaying bodies, large waves, wildfires, or open deserts are easily provoked and
frequently difficult to suppress or extinguish. Only when given sufficient time
to anticipate and adjust are people more likely to react somewhat rationally to
these species and conditions.

The aversion to such perilous aspects of nature is involuntary, prompting
distancing responses and sometimes destructive behaviors. These anxieties and
fears can at times be excessive and counterproductive. They can give rise to
some of our most common phobias, such as paralyzing dread of snakes, spiders,
thunder and lightning, caves, heights, and open spaces. Yet excessive fear of
and aversion toward nature is no more intrinsically dysfunctional than extreme
expressions of any biophilic value, including exploitation, dominance, or even
the excessive love of nature. Conversely, an insufficient fear of and aversion
to threats in nature can be equally injurious and self-defeating: one who has
"no fear" of steep mountain passes, large predators, strong storms, flood-prone
areas, volcanoes, or large waves often courts disaster. On balance and over time,
an aversion to nature emerged as an inherent inclination because it has served
us well.

The emotion researchers Michael Jawer and Marc Micozzi suggest that all
great emotions "impel a person to action." The inborn inclination to avoid and
fear nature has especially encouraged defensive actions that rapidly mobilized
the abilities of a terrestrial human primate of limited speed, strength, stealth,
stamina, sight, smell, and hearing. Jawer and Micozzi identify five benefits of
strong emotions like fear of and antipathy toward nature that have contributed
to human fitness and survival over time, and each can be usefully connected to
our inherent aversions of the natural world.[5]

First, they emphasize: "Emotions enable individuals to discriminate us versus them."[6] An aversion to nature—a snakelike movement in the grass, dark
storm clouds gathering overhead, a thick and impenetrable swamp, the presence of biting and stinging invertebrates—all prompt quick judgments regarding safe as against threatening circumstances, friend versus foe, where we ought

or ought not to be. Jawer and Micozzi further stress: "Emotions enable individuals to react quickly and expeditiously to changes in [their] environment."[7] Many risks encountered in nature occur suddenly and without warning, are highly volatile, reflecting shifting circumstances that require our expeditious response to threatening circumstances. Jawer and Micozzi also suggest: "Emotions enable individuals to communicate something of importance to one another."[8] Many fears of the natural world are easily recognized through vocal responses and facial expressions that signal anxiety and fear: shrieks, grunts, sweating, wide and bulging eyes, goose bumps, or hair standing on end. These universal reactions are often far more effective than words, communicating dangers that lie ahead, and almost always elicit a response.

Jawer and Micozzi additionally assert: "Emotions cement bonds between people."[9] Throughout history, people have forged some of their strongest bonds when they commonly confronted such significant environmental threats as floods, earthquakes, predators, vermin, or inauspicious habitats like swamps and deserts. In fall 2011, for example, I returned home as a hurricane was about to hit and encountered an extraordinary and unusual camaraderie otherwise lacking in my community. Finally, Jawer and Micozzi note: "Emotions are integral to memory and learning."[10] Many of our most powerful memories and stories originate in existential threats occurring and, equally important, resolved in nature. Such narratives prominently occur in such classics as the *Odyssey*, *Beowulf*, and the legend of King Arthur, and in many modern stories, including the *Lord of the Rings* trilogy or the *Star Wars* and *Indiana Jones* movies.[11]

The inherent inclination to fear aspects of the natural world has also been revealed in studies conducted by the Swedish psychologist Arne Öhman and his colleagues. In one investigation, participants encountered subliminal glimpses (fifteen to thirty milliseconds) of snakes, spiders, handguns, and frayed electric wires. Almost all the subjects reacted aversively to images of snakes and spiders, few of them to the modern dangers of guns and worn wires. Moreover, once the aversive responses to snakes and spiders had been aroused, they were slow to dissipate.[12] In another investigation conducted by other researchers, the innate fear of snakes among primates, including humans, was demonstrated by laboratory-raised monkeys: although the monkeys had never before seen a snake, they responded with fear and even panic when suddenly exposed to these reptiles.[13]

This evidence says nothing about the continuing relevance of these fears of nature in our modern urban society. As we have seen, any inborn tendency can become obsolete or "vestigial" if the historic context in which it evolved is no longer applicable to current conditions and circumstances. Inborn tendencies that no longer confer any particular biological advantage will probably atrophy and disappear over time. The studies cited suggest an inherent human tendency to fear and avoid creatures like snakes and spiders, but they do not demonstrate any continuing adaptive significance of these aversive responses.

Still, many of our fears of and anxieties about the natural world continue to be adaptive under varying circumstances, and some that are remain powerful symbols that influence our language, art, and design. Where would Hollywood and much of the advertising industry be without our anxious response to the likes of snakes, spiders, sharks, and swamps? More pragmatically, when we lose our fear of nature, we often act foolishly and imprudently; we might not try to hug a half-ton bear or lift a colorful viper, but we court greater disaster by constructing highways on landfills, homes on floodplains, or nuclear reactors on seismic faults.

Both the functional and the dysfunctional inclination to fear nature may be usefully illustrated by our historic and current treatment of two kinds of animals—arthropods, a large group of creatures that includes insects and spiders, and, as previously touched upon, the wolf.

Arthropods comprise an incredible number and diversity of species, from insects and spiders to scorpions, centipedes, crustaceans, and others. They make up the greatest proportion—roughly eighty percent—of animal species. For most people, however, the arthropods, particularly the insects and spiders, are collectively the "bugs." This label reflects the widespread aversion and fear most people often harbor for these creatures.

Most of us perceive bugs as strange, even bizarre; they prompt discomfort at best, contempt at worst. Bugs are alien and otherworldly, defying our deeply held assumptions about what is right and normal. Among their more disturbing qualities is the seeming absence of feeling and reason that distinguishes people as individuals and as a species. Arthropods implicitly reject the significance of such feelings as affection, caring, love, morality, freedom, and even fear as a basis for existence. The bugs also appear to deny the relevance of individual selfhood and identity. All they seem to have in common with us are vaguely familiar body parts and a passion to survive and reproduce.[14]

It should not be surprising, then, that arthropods are often associated with words and symbols of abnormality and even insanity. The psychologist James Hillman notes in this regard: "Bug-eyed, spidery, worm, roach, blood-sucker, louse, going buggy, locked up in the bughouse—these are all terms of contempt supposedly characterizing inhuman traits. . . . To become an insect is to become a mindless creature without the warm blood of feeling."[15]

The enormous populations of arthropods also negate assumptions about the seeming worthiness of a single or individual life. Most people find disturbing the reality that a single ant colony can contain millions of organisms, that an acre of soil can harbor more arthropods than there are humans in the largest of nations, that the world's population of insects and spiders is beyond imagining and perhaps even counting. As Hillman further remarks: "Imagining insects numerically threatens the individualized fantasy of a unique and unitary human being. Their very numbers indicate insignificance of us as individuals."[16]

Most insects and spiders appear indifferent to our presence and presumed dominance of the earth. Instead of routinely fleeing at our presence, as do most vertebrates, many arthropods fail even to take notice. They routinely take up residence in our homes and workplaces, and most of us shudder when informed that during our lifetime we will rarely be more than five feet from a spider.

Consequently, the average person dislikes and avoids the "creepy crawlies"—

9. Antipathy toward many invertebrates is easily aroused in most people, with few showing much sympathy, compassion, or affection for these animals. While aversive emotions toward these animals are typically strong, they can also be positively channeled into fascination, curiosity, and exploration.

spiders, ticks, lice, leeches, locusts, scorpions, crabs, centipedes, cockroaches, flies, wasps, ants, termites, mites, mosquitoes, and more. Moreover, our anxieties and aversions toward these creatures are often excessive. Few harbor much guilt when squashing a mosquito, stepping on a spider, extinguishing an ant, spraying a cockroach. We rarely have sympathy or compassion for bugs, or see them as worthy of moral consideration, let alone sacrifice in the name of conservation or protection. Quite the contrary, our antipathy and destructive actions toward these creatures are easily provoked.[17]

But our attitudes and behaviors toward arthropods, excessive and irrational though they may be, were internalized for largely functional reasons: fear of disease, injury, pain, pollution, and property damage. Moreover, our inherent inclination to dislike and avoid many insects and spiders can sometimes be constructively channeled. Under the right circumstances, often when we are guided by the right mentors, these strange and otherworldly creatures can prompt our curiosity and our sense of wonder, and can encourage our fascination and the desire to know and explore more fully the nonhuman world.

This more enlightened path is increasingly evident in our shifting, though still ambivalent, relationship to the wolf. Of course, this large predator is very different biologically and culturally from the arthropods. Quite unlike insects and spiders, the wolf reminds us of ourselves, and is nearly identical genetically with our most favored of all companion animals, the domestic dog.

As noted, before the twentieth century the wolf in North America and much of Europe was largely the focus of what has been called a "pathological hatred," which resulted in its widespread elimination. Efforts to eradicate the wolf in the United States were typically rationalized by the goals of livestock protection, personal safety, and a view of wolves as competitors for game such as deer, elk, and bison. Wolves were also the victims of guilt by association, identified with the wilderness that the American nation sought to tame and convert to a largely agrarian landscape.[18] Summarizing this volatile combination of factors, the writer Barry Lopez remarked: "It was against a backdrop of taming wilderness, law of vengeance, protection of private property, an inalienable right to decide the fate of animals, and the conception of man as protector of defenseless creatures that the wolf became the enemy [and] the object of pathological hatred."[19]

As a result, a de facto "war on wolves" prevailed, with every means of extermination employed, including indiscriminate shooting, trapping, poisoning, even collective wolf hunts in which entire communities celebrated their shared antipathy toward this presumably "evil" creature. Eliminating wolves began with the American colonies: the first official act of wildlife control in the New World was a 1630 bounty on wolves in Cape Cod, Massachusetts. Antiwolf passion proceeded to roll across the American landscape with settlement; the routine practice of killing these animals continued well into the twentieth century.[20] Long after the wolf had ceased to be a practical threat, elimination of this animal remained official government policy. For example, Edward Goldman, the founding head of the Federal Bureau of Biological Survey, the precursor of today's United States Fish and Wildlife Service, remarked at the start of the twentieth century: "Large predatory animals [like wolves], destructive of livestock and game, no longer have a place in our advancing civilization."[21]

Even well-known advocates of wildlife and wilderness protection viewed the wolf with disdain, as we have seen in the views of President Theodore Roosevelt. William Hornaday, the founder of the New York Zoological Society, and ironically a virulent opponent of the leg-hold trap, the device generally used to capture wolves, proclaimed: "Of all the wild creatures of North America, none are more despicable than wolves. There is no depth of meanness, treachery, or cruelty to which they do not cheerfully descend."[22]

Widespread killing of wolves reflected the goal of annihilating the creature altogether, an outcome viewed as ethically and morally justifiable. Destroying this animal would presumably rid the world of something intrinsically unworthy and malevolent. The intensity of these feelings appeared to be representative of a cultural bias, as Barry Lopez suggests:

> The motive for wiping out wolves proceeded from misunderstanding, from illusions of what constituted sport, from strident attachment to private property, from ignorance and irrational hatred. But the scope, the casual irresponsibility, and the cruelty of wolf killing were something else. I do not think it comes from some base, atavistic urge, though that may be a part of it. I think it is that we simply do not understand our place in the universe.[23]

Yet during the second half of the twentieth century, attitudes toward the wolf began to shift dramatically. More appreciative and sympathetic views became widespread throughout much of the Western world. Many factors prompted this change, not least the wolf's becoming endangered across much of its historic range. This species came to symbolize for many not just an animal in peril, but more broadly the disappearance of American wildlife and wilderness. In addition, a growing understanding and appreciation of wolf biology and the species' ecological value contributed to a more positive perception. A more tolerant and appreciative attitude toward wolves was also characteristic of an increasingly educated and urban society, where such traditional rural activities as livestock production and hunting, for which the wolf represented a threat or competition, were in decline.[24]

Foreshadowing this change, the pioneering ecologist Aldo Leopold experienced a radical shift in his views of the wolf during the early part of the twentieth century. Like most of his contemporaries, Leopold had viewed wolves as vicious killers of livestock and game. Following graduation from the Yale Forest School in 1909, Leopold worked in the Gila National Forest of New Mexico, and rarely passed up a chance to kill wolves. Yet his growing understanding of wilderness and the ecological connections between predators and prey encouraged Leopold to think more positively about wolves. During one incident of wolf killing, he experienced an emotional and intellectual epiphany that marked a profound shift in his outlook on wolves, and more generally, on nature.[25] The year was 1912, and Leopold describes the dying wolf that changed him forever:

> We were eating lunch on a high rimrock, at the foot of which a turbulent river elbowed its way. We saw what we thought was a doe fording the torrent, her breast awash in white water. When she climbed the bank toward us and shook out her tail, we realized our error: it was a wolf. A half-dozen others, evidently grown pups, sprang from the willows and all joined in a welcoming melee of wagging tails and playful maulings. What was literally a pile of wolves writhed and tumbled in the center of an open flat at the foot of our rimrock.
>
> In those days we had never heard of passing up a chance to kill a wolf. In a second we were pumping lead into the pack, but with more excitement than accuracy. . . . When our rifles were empty, the old wolf was down, and a pup was dragging a leg into impassable side-rocks.
>
> We reached the old wolf in time to watch a fierce green fire dying in her eyes. I realized then, and have known ever since, that there was something new to me in those eyes—something known only to her and to the mountain. I was young then, and full of trigger-itch: I thought that because fewer wolves meant more deer, that no wolves would mean hunters' paradise. But after seeing the green fire die, I sensed that neither the wolf nor the mountain agreed with such a view.[26]

Leopold's realization presaged a broader societal shift in sentiment toward wolves that gathered force as the century progressed. Most Americans today view the wolf in largely sympathetic terms and as a symbol of the country's wildlife and wilderness. Yet ambivalence remains, particularly among those living in close proximity and in a more competitive relationship to the wolf. Surveys reveal that rural and resource-dependent residents in areas close to wolves are significantly more likely to dislike and fear this animal, in marked contrast to far more positive sentiments among educated and urban Americans.[27] Illustrative of these differences are contrasting comments of those strongly in favor and opposed to wolf reintroduction into Yellowstone National Park:

"Only a fool would not agree to the reintroduction of this beautiful and essential animal."

"The wolf is like a cockroach and will creep outside of Yellowstone and devour wildlife."

"Restoring the wolf to Yellowstone will be like planting the flag at Iwo Jima."

"Only a brain dead son of a bitch would favor reintroduction. It's like inviting the AIDS virus."[28]

What has remained constant is the wolf's capacity to elicit intense inherent feelings and to serve as a barometer of attitudes toward the natural world. Views of the wolf reveal how often emotions take precedence over intellect in guiding our actions toward nature. For example, studies reveal the greatest knowledge of wolves occurs among those strongly in favor of and those strongly opposed to wolf conservation and restoration. It is as if members of each group use their greater knowledge of the wolf to rationalize and support their feelings rather than as a basis for reexamining their biases toward this animal.[29]

Like perceptions of insects and spiders, the wolf's emotional salience originates in deeply held anxieties about the natural world. Similar to our relationship with arthropods, these feelings can at times be channeled in more positive and beneficial ways. At a moment in our history when people appear more separated from nature than ever before, perhaps strong feelings toward the wolf can be used to encourage and promote greater awareness and appreciation of the natural world.

Moreover, our innate aversion to aspects of nature remains largely adaptive even in our modern society. Denying its legitimacy invites a different kind of dysfunction and self-defeating perspective. The natural world continues to pose many practical threats including: hurricanes, floods, earthquakes, steep mountains, biting and stinging invertebrates, wildfires, sharks, rats, and sometimes even snakes and large terrestrial predators.

For our adaptive relationship with nature to continue to function, it must be robust and balanced. The cavalier assumption that fear is a weakness or a sign of cowardice is, at best, shortsighted and, at worst, an invitation to disaster. On the contrary, failure to maintain a healthy distance from dangers occurring in the natural world is foolish, even disrespectful. Ignoring nature's awesome power can encourage irrational behavior, inviting harm and even death. This ignorance was evident in the destructiveness of the 1994 Los Angeles earthquake, the 2005 Hurricane Katrina, the 2008 Iowa floods, and other instances when people remained indifferent and arrogant toward the powers of the natural world. When we no longer fear nature, we often engage in such self-defeating acts as building in floodplains, channelizing rivers, or filling wetlands.

The fear of nature also reminds us of forces greater than our own. We behave with restraint when we respect the strength and power in the world beyond us. The anthropologist Richard Nelson refers to this as recognizing the "luminescence of power" in all of the natural world, which may be seen in the mightiest of rivers, the most fearsome of predators, but also the smallest of creatures, and the tiniest of atomic elements.[30] Respect for nature is partly a derivative of appreciating its immense power. A healthy fear of nature is reflected in the dictionary's definition of awe: "an emotion of mingled reverence, dread, and wonder inspired by something majestic; . . . respect, tinged with fear, for authority."[31]

Nature utterly mastered and tamed rarely inspires respect, deep appreciation, or awe. A tiger, lion, or wolf completely controlled and incarcerated behind bars, manically pacing within its barren cage, invites little more than condescension. Moreover, when we lack respect and reverent regard for the natural world, we seldom act as good environmental stewards. We protect and preserve that which we admire; an ethic of stewardship derives as much from a deferential respect for powers greater than our own as from strong affection, aesthetic appreciation, or informed understanding. The chapter concludes with a personal interlude that explores the complicated connection between fear, awe, and respect for the natural world.

Interlude

Some years ago, I participated in a wilderness canoe trip in Canada's Northwest Territories. To get there, we flew first to Whitehorse in the Yukon Territory, and from there by small float plane to a remote part of the northern reaches of the Northwest Territories. Our flight required hours over a vast and undifferentiated wilderness, the thousands of lakes and rivers below lacking even a name. Gazing down from the floatplane, all we could see was a limitless expanse of wildness and stunted trees that filled us with a mix of excitement and anxiety.

The plane landed and then departed, and we found ourselves in an area that seemed totally isolated and unsettling. The virtual absence of human settlement soon became evident as we confronted unrelenting and tormenting blackflies and mosquitoes, continual rain and permanently saturated ground, and occasional predators like grizzly bears and wolves. Our ostensibly high-tech rain gear became soaked, and we settled into a state of perpetual dampness, cold, and discomfort.

In time, however, we also came to appreciate this magnificent unspoiled and beautiful wilderness. We became enthralled by its many thousands of waterfowl, shorebirds, caribou, even the fearsome bear and wolves, which, apparently never having seen humans before, seemed more curious than ferocious. The days were still long in late August, with only a few hours of darkness, although we rarely saw the evening sky given the near-constant rain and overcast.

On the sixth night, it finally cleared. And, as the brief hours of darkness fell, something splendid and miraculous occurred that I had intellectually known about but had never witnessed before. In some ways it was really quite ordinary, just the evening sky, something I experienced each and every day. Yet that evening I made my first acquaintance with the northern lights, aurora borealis.

I was enchanted and lay there for hours watching the vaporous ribbons of light and color swirling in sinewy ghostlike shapes, constantly shifting from hues of yellow, green and blue to red, magenta, and purple. The shapes were continuously changing, evanescent and fleeting, morphing into new forms. Altogether, it was magnificent, inspiring, beyond words, beautiful, and miraculous, and impossible to fully convey.

It was also unsettling and, in its way, paradoxically frightening. It was just the sky—a reality I knew well and took for granted. But tonight it had become something altogether different, something otherworldly. My assumptions of normality had been ripped asunder. I was humbled, my complacency replaced by a wonder and newfound respect for the commonplace. I had intellectually known about the northern lights, and had anticipated seeing them on this trip. But the reality I encountered was far from what I knew abstractly, and it left me with a fresh, awe-filled, and reverent respect for the sky I had never known before.

It also reminded me that the average city child today sees only a few dozen stars in an average nighttime sky.[32] I speculated about ancient children and the deep appreciation they must have felt on beholding the spectacle of a sky filled with thousands of stars, forming constellations and associated stories of godlike beings. I left Canada's Northwest Territories with a newfound respect and admiration for the sky, and with it the resolve to work toward a world where children might connect with the miracle of everyday creation.

4

exploitation

More than anything else, modern society is inclined to value nature as a source of material goods and services. Most people readily appreciate that forests provide wood for building materials and paper; that fossil fuels power most of our transportation and energy; that soil is responsible for growing crops and grass for feeding our livestock; that surface water and underground aquifers provide our drinking supplies. These and other common uses of nature reflect how people in modern society often perceive nature as primarily a "natural resource."

Yet this narrow outlook often undervalues nature's contribution to our physical, emotional, intellectual, and even spiritual health and well-being. Moreover, its emphasis on current modes of exploitation and economic markets tends to reflect a limited appreciation of the natural world's role in our material welfare. Despite a bias to value nature for its material benefits, few recognize the practical importance of ecosystem services: "components of nature . . . used to yield human well-being."[1] These ecosystem services include waste decomposition, crop pollination, seed dispersal, pollution control, soil remediation, nutrient cycling, oxygen and water production, or the provision of wild foods and medicines. Moreover, few people today recognize the future promise of extracting goods and services from nature as our knowledge and technology expand, assuming we do not first irreversibly damage this potential before it has come to fruition.

Despite these underappreciated benefits obtained from exploiting the natural world, modern society remains inordinately inclined to value nature materially over all other environmental values. Indeed, this bias is so excessive and out of balance that it has rendered us dysfunctional in many ways. We start with a personal interlude that highlights the tension between our inclination to exploit nature for its goods and services while slighting other important values of the natural world.

Interlude

I often gather my dogs in the early morning for a walk in a nearby forest. This area is part of a four hundred–acre park in the moderate-sized city where I live. I enter the park by passing through a restored wooden covered bridge that some three centuries before marked the beginning of the stagecoach road that led to the state capital thirty miles to the north. Once across the bridge, the dogs and I follow a path that parallels the river. We are also at the base of a large and looming three hundred–foot traprock cliff, all that remains of an ancient volcano following the erosion of the softer surrounding sandstone.

This walk is during the early spring, the frozen ground just beginning to thaw after the long winter. The swamp at the interior side of the path is saturated, looking like a giant mud pie. As is often true at the start of our walk, I am lost in a fog of concerns, preoccupied with commitments, worries, and plans. Soon enough, the sights and sounds of the forest and river begin to lift me out of my self-absorption.

I begin to take greater notice of the surroundings as we continue along the path wedged between the river and floodplain. Then, a strange movement stops me, something odd going on in the mucky swamp. At first it looks like a weird pulsating bladder ball, roundish in form, slowly expanding and contracting. Astonished and even a bit anxious, I am also amused by its bizarre shape and clownlike movement. I pause to take a closer look and realize that it's a living creature. The animal is mottled brown, beige, black, and white, so effectively camouflaged that it practically blends into the surrounding leaves and mud. I recognize its features as those of a moderate-sized, fattish bird, eyes on both sides of its head, and a long narrow beak. It is working hard at pushing its head and beak into the muddy but still partially frozen ground. With a kind of "eureka," I realize that I have encountered a relatively rare treat, one of the forest's most beguiling creatures, the American woodcock. Although technically a shorebird, this species mainly occurs in woods and interior swamps rather than along the shore like most of its relatives, the sandpipers and plovers. Its nickname, "timberdoodle," has always amused me as both appropriate and funny, and I smile now at the thought of how perfect its name seems today.

I suppose the bird is hungry following the long winter, and is probing the recently thawed ground for its favorite food, the juicy earthworm. Because the woodcock has eyes on both sides of its head, it can see in two directions at once. It is also famed for its spring "sky dance." This mating ritual begins with the male flying high into the air, perhaps three hundred feet, in a roughly vertical spiraling flight, wings atwitter along the way. Upon reaching the top of its lofty flight, the woodcock rapidly descends in a zigzag dive, chirping on its way down, ideally landing near a suitably impressed mate. The sky dance caused a reporter for the usually dispassionate Audubon Society to write: "Many birds attract a mate with their colorful feathers, but the woodcock's dull plumage does not seem to be attractive even to other woodcocks. Instead of looking great, male woodcocks show off through incredible mating displays each spring."[2]

The ecologist Aldo Leopold, lamenting more than seventy years ago the lack of appreciation for woodcocks and their sky dance, commented:

> The drama of the sky dance is enacted nightly on hundreds of farms, the owners of which sigh for entertainment but harbor the illusion that it is to be sought in theaters. They live on the land, but not by the land. The woodcock is a living refutation of the theory that the utility of a game bird is to serve as a target, or to pose gracefully on a slice of toast. No one would rather hunt woodcock in October than I, but since learning of the sky dance I find myself calling one or two birds enough. I must be sure that, come April, there be no dearth of dancers in the sunset sky.[3]

Encountering the woodcock this morning was a delight for me, as I found myself enchanted by the surprising sight of a rare and fascinating creature. Like Leopold, I also pondered the value of this odd bird, in my case imagining its appeal to a more urban and suburban citizenry increasingly disconnected from nature.[4]

I supposed that seeing this critter would be a thrill for the average birder, but despite a rise in popularity, I recognized that bird-watching remained an interest of only a relatively small number of urban people. For the more scientifically inclined, I thought the woodcock's adaptation to the interior swamps and forests would provide a satisfying understanding. I also imagined for a larger group of persons interested in natural history that an encounter with the bird and its unusual behavior could prompt both fascination and curiosity, perhaps encouraging some to learn about its ecology and conservation. For those with a more practical outlook, I thought they would find appealing the species' contribution to the cycling of the forest's nutrients and its role in enhancing the productivity of timber and pulp trees. I was confident that those who deliberately sought the chance to see woodcocks in the wild—whether birders, naturalists, or hunters—would experience the satisfaction that derives from mastering a challenge and being a successful predator. For most people, witnessing the woodcock's sky dance could provide a bounty of aesthetic enjoyment and even inspiration. I also imagined encountering this beguiling bird following the harshness of winter would yield emotional and spiritual rewards that come with the promise of a reviving spring.

Like a cultural kaleidoscope, the woodcock embraces a multiplicity of values that offer different pathways of connection, discovery, and utilization of nature. Each extends beyond simple material exploitation, each carrying the potential to expand our sense of who we are and how we can find worth in our lives. The bird viewed from the outlook of any single value, such as its material significance, can be easily marginalized and rendered irrelevant when set against more tangible land uses that generate a clearer practical and economic return. Yet when seen in the context of values that reflect a broader spectrum of relationships, this bird emerges as more worthy of our affection and respect.

Through a fuller engagement with the woodcock, we build a narrative of connection with the world beyond our selves. We may never lose our aversion to the swamp where it lives or the inclination to choose one creature and habitat over another, but a deeper affiliation emerges that diminishes the tendency

10. The American woodcock is a shorebird found in the woods rather than along the shore. An odd duck, so to speak, the woodcock has eyes on both sides of its head to see in different directions.

to undervalue life and the habitats that sustain it. When this occurs, we tend to be more inclined to take responsibility for the care of this creature and its habitat. The woodcock becomes another portal for deepening our sense of self-hood and membership in a broader community, enriching both our personal and our collective lives.

THE MATERIAL BENEFITS OF NATURE

As suggested at the beginning of the chapter, most people readily recognize that the natural world offers a bounty of goods and services, especially the raw materials and natural resources that contribute so much to our materially secure and comfortable lives. These benefits provide us with routine access to substantial quantities of food, fuel, fiber, medicines, and construction materials, and a wealth of consumer products. We are proud of the accomplishment measured in terms of shelter, longevity, health, and the highest economic standard of living the world has ever known, despite the poverty and inequality that remain.

People have historically utilized an estimated one hundred thousand different plants and animals, and a wide variety of inorganic resources such as minerals and metals, and once-living organisms, such as fossil fuels of oil, coal, and gas.[5] Most of us recognize that the material exploitation of the natural world underlies much of contemporary agriculture, energy production, transportation, building, and manufacturing.

Despite this awareness, the public remains largely unaware of the extent of our material reliance on the natural world. This lack of awareness tends to be encouraged by modern packaging, processing, production, and marketing, which often obscures the natural origins of many products. The role of nature in the generation of many goods and services is frequently disguised by the likes of meat wrapped in cellophane, vegetables frozen in casseroles, wood compressed into particle board, oil converted into plastics, compost distilled into chemical fertilizers, or medicinal plants processed into pills. Even food grown on the land is typically seen as the product of human invention more than as something originating in the natural world when a single genetically modified crop is produced in enormous quantities on huge geometric fields, subject to massive applications of fertilizers and pesticides, and irrigated by water drawn from distant sources. The lack of "source knowledge" distorts an appreciation of the natural origins of food and other environmental goods and services.

Modern medicines illustrate this tendency to credit human invention and ingenuity more than nature. An estimated one-third to one-half of all pharmaceuticals today originate in a wild plant, animal, or microorganism.[6] Yet, most people view modern medicines as largely the creation of laboratory science and synthetic production, a notion reinforced by modern packaging and marketing that masks the natural origins of these products. The disconnection of modern medicine from the natural world is also encouraged by the emphasis on anti-septic and sterile medical settings, based on the assumption that suppression and elimination of other organisms is essential to fighting disease and protect-ing public health.

Many people are largely unaware of how much society continues to depend on exploiting nature for many common goods and services. Material benefits derived from exploiting the natural world include not only a wide variety of medicines and foods but also oils, lubricants, paints, papers, pesticides, plastics, clothing, cosmetics, and building materials. We also rely on many wild species to help control pests that compete with us for resources we extract from nature. For example, many bird and bat species control insects that would otherwise consume a good proportion of our crops. We further rely on many wild species in crossbreeding and genetic engineering that reinvigorate domestic plants and livestock.

An example of our continuing material dependence on nature for food is illustrated by our harvest of products from the sea. Indeed, our exploitation of seafood from the wild is thought to "exceed that of cattle, sheep, poultry or eggs [as] the largest source of either wild or domestic animal protein for the world's . . . human populations."[7] Half of this wild seafood is actually inverte-brate life such as shrimp, clams, crabs, lobster, and other "shellfish."

Unfortunately, many of these marine species have been harvested at unsus-tainable rates due to more efficient and environmentally destructive technolo-gies and ineffective government regulation and management. Considerable damage has also been inflicted on important marine habitats such as tidal wetlands, coral reefs, and mangroves. The decline of the exploitation of wild seafood has resulted in an increasing reliance on domestically raised fish and shellfish. Indeed, for the first time in human history, a majority of the world's seafood has become the product of "aquaculture."[8] As a consequence, we are currently witnessing the demise of the last great form of commercial hunting of wild free-roaming species. Still, the harvest of seafood continues to be a power-ful illustration of our continued dependence on materially exploiting nature for a product as basic as food.

Our dependence on wild creatures as a source of food and other material benefits is also illustrated by the honeybee. The nectar obtained from bees has long been an important sweetener. Today, the global honey trade generates an estimated one billion dollars annually, involving some three hundred flowering

11. Bees illustrate well the utility derived from exploiting nature. They are a source of honey, but also important pollinators of agricultural crops that account for nearly one-third of all U.S. agricultural production.

plants as the source of the pollen needed for production. In addition, the pollinating activities of bees remain vital to the production of many agricultural crops. In the United States alone, bees as pollinators are responsible for approximately one-third of all agricultural production, including apples, alfalfa, almonds, blueberries, cherries, cranberries, cucumbers, melons, plums, pears, squash, strawberries, and many other crops.[9]

From an economic perspective, our current material dependence on wild plants and animals is said to account for fifteen percent of the global economy, amounting to trillions of dollars.[10] In addition, people materially benefit from a wide range of "ecosystem services," not easily converted into monetary measures or exchanged in economic markets. These services include oxygen and water supply and regulation, soil formation, erosion control, nutrient cycling, climate regulation, plant pollination, seed dispersal, the breakdown of biological wastes, the remediation of pollutants, and others. For example, people and their livestock in the United States annually produce an estimated 150 million tons of organic waste, nearly all this organic material broken down by microbial organisms, leaving us to wonder what we would be up to our eyeballs in if not for the labors of these microscopic allies.[11] The monetary value of this and other ecosystems services is difficult to gauge, but one 2010 estimate suggests a value in direct and indirect benefits of $30 trillion.[12]

The contribution of the natural world to human health and material well-being is likely to be substantially greater in the future as a consequence of the exponential growth in our knowledge, technology, and ability to exploit nature. Any plant or animal species has the potential to yield material benefits once we sufficiently understand and extract the distinctive physical, chemical, and biological properties hammered into the organism's genes by countless episodes of evolutionary trial and error. Such unique characteristics constitute the peculiar genius of any life form, the product of the inventive hothouse of reproductive fitness and survival. We have scientifically identified only an estimated fifteen to twenty-five percent of all species, let alone examined them for their potential material importance. The rapid growth in knowledge of other life and the technology to exploit this understanding are reflected in significant advances in genetics, molecular biology, and bioengineering. An unprecedented and revolutionary expansion of this knowledge, all but inevitable in the not too distant future, will be an enormous boon to the world's standard of living and economy. This revolution depends, of course, on our not preempting it through shortsighted environmental destruction that results in the extensive elimination of other species. Unfortunately, current rates of extinction could result in the disappearance of one-quarter of all species during the next half-century if we continue our current course of habitat destruction, overexploitation, chemical pollution, and atmospheric degradation.[13]

The problem of undervaluing the future material benefits to be obtained from nature is related to the challenge of estimating the monetary worth of ecosystem services. Both reflect the limitations of modern economics. Without question, money is a powerful tool for assessing value, especially in a highly materialistic market-oriented society such as ours. Yet monetary measures often fail to capture the many contributions that nature offers for human health and fitness. Moreover, modern economics tends to discount the future, regarding it as largely an unknown that can be addressed by future technologies and changing markets. For example, the depletion of a species is often viewed by modern economics as a problem that can be resolved either through the substitution of a depleted creature by a closely related species, or through the invention of some technology that serves the same purpose. An illustration of this distorted logic is the plight many whale species once faced. As these animals were being driven nearly to extinction, their overexploitation was economically rationalized by the substitution of depleted species by more abundant ones, the development of new technologies like fossil fuels, and the reinvestment of surplus profits from whaling into other areas of economic endeavor. This economic bias not only represented a moral failure but ignored the many other important values whales provided to human physical, emotional, intellectual, and spiritual health and well-being.

This broader contribution of nature to human welfare, not easily captured by economic measures, is reflected in the undeniable contribution of the natural world to people's character and personality development. Beyond monetary gain, materially exploiting the land and its creatures can yield a bounty of physical and psychological reward. Activities such as gardening, the gathering of wild foods, firewood collecting, beekeeping, camping, fishing, or hunting often provide satisfactions that foster physical fitness, problem solving, critical thinking, independence, self-confidence, and self-esteem.

Recreational hunting and fishing offer an interesting and controversial illustration. The hunting of birds and mammals has become a matter of strong debate in modern times, fishing much less so even though it may be viewed as just another form of hunting of a different vertebrate class. Studies suggest that hunting can result in significant physical and mental benefits, including satisfactions associated with harvesting meat, learning about nature, acquiring various skills, and demonstrating competence and prowess in the wild. Recreational hunters also report important satisfactions obtained from being an active participant in nature, outcompeting another creature endowed with keener senses and familiarity with its environment, and demonstrating craft and cunning in the wild. Some hunters also report considerable satisfaction from being a part of a natural cycle, the transformation of energy and matter from life to death and back to life again, through harvesting wild animals and consuming the food.[14] The following interlude provides a personal illustration of these physical and mental rewards involved in materially exploiting nature through hunting, at the same time addressing the moral controversy associated with this activity.

Interlude

I went hunting in fall 2009 for Rocky Mountain elk in wild country in the Big Horn Mountains, a chain extending from north central Wyoming into Montana and separated from the better-known Rocky Mountains by hundreds of miles of short-grass prairie. The day after I arrived, my guide and I rose before dawn and, following a quick breakfast, mounted horses, and, bringing a pack mule, rode up into the foothills before climbing to the surrounding higher mountains in search of our quarry.

We rode in semidarkness, mostly in silence that for me seemed almost like a sound, contrasted with my more normal urban existence. At one point, I looked up into the still-dark sky filled with so many stars in the high and clear mountain air that I could hardly make out the more familiar constellations. Occasional shadows of rapidly darting jackrabbits and mule deer were startling. At first, I tried to guide my horse, but soon I gave up, trusting in the darkness to the animal's far superior sure-footedness. For nearly twelve hours that day and the next, we rode, walked, and climbed in search of elk, with little success until the close of the second day. It was often challenging and exhausting, yet always gratifying. Sometimes we came on elk, and a number of times saw animals that might have been taken, but some fled as we approached too close, others remained too far away for a good shot, and I passed up opportunities to shoot young males or females in favor of the larger and older bull I sought.

Toward the early afternoon of the second day, we stopped for lunch on a high rock rim, and following lunch took a brief nap, having risen at four that morning. After waking, we scanned the horizon with our binoculars, barely making out in the distance two scattered elk herds roughly eight miles distant. We set off to take a closer look, and for the next five hours rode up and down precipitous terrain before descending into a relatively flat wet meadow. We rode partway across, then dismounted and slogged farther, approaching the elk herds as quietly as we could.

It was late afternoon by this time, the sun drifting toward the horizon, the good light beginning to fade. We came within sight of the first herd and saw that it consisted mostly of females and fawns. We set off for the second herd and found that it included some males, but mostly small and young ones, with many breeding years ahead of them. The day was rapidly waning, and we had a long ride back to camp, mostly in the dark, so we turned to leave. We started up the trail to the higher plateau, but then as we rose to a better vantage point, we saw another smaller elk herd on a distant mountainside. We had been hunting for more than twelve hours, and I was physically and mentally exhausted, caked in dirt, my eyes stinging from fatigue and dust. I was very much looking forward to a hot meal, the comforts of camp, and a shower. But as we studied the herd, we thought we glimpsed a large, mature bull, partially hidden by the surrounding vegetation and other elk.

We rode closer for a better look. As we approached, we dismounted, moving quietly up the steep slope in hopes of not spooking the herd. We struggled up the mountainside—well, I did; my guide, seemingly part billy goat, never seemed to tire. Not having fully acclimated to the thin mountain air, I sucked oxygen into my exhausted lungs. I pushed my sadly out-of-shape body to its limits. But slowly we came closer, trying to calm the now alert and restless animals by walking in single file, my face up pushed near to my guide's rear in an attempt to simulate the look of just another innocent four-legged creature.

Finally we came within some four hundred yards of the herd. We scanned them with our binoculars, my eyes glassing from tears of tiredness. Partially obscured by the herd and surrounding pines and junipers was a massive bull. I watched him with my riflescope for nearly twenty minutes, until finally I had a clear and unobstructed shot that would not wound any nearby animal. I was exhausted, cramped with strain and immobility, yet I maintained a focused attention and intensity, a near total immersion in the moment. I was rooted in my place in both space and time, all my senses attuned, not just sight, but also a palpable sense of hearing, smell, touch, even taste. It had been this way throughout the hunt, though this moment was the keenest: the world of the prey animal had become my own. This was no longer a picture, a fantasy, a spectator sport, a vicarious reality, but something intimate and integral to the here and now, my feeling fully engaged with the elk and its natural community. It called to mind something the Spanish philosopher José Ortega y Gasset had said:

> When one is hunting, the air has another, more exquisite feel as it glides over the skin or enters the lungs; the rocks acquire a more expressive physiognomy, and the vegetation become loaded with meaning. All this is due to the fact that the hunter, while he advances or waits crouching, feels tied through the earth to the animals he pursues. . . . A sensing and presentiment . . . that leads the hunter to perceive the environment from the point of view of the prey, without abandoning his own point of view.[15]

With a clear line of sight, I shot the animal. I prided myself on being a good marksman, and I had practiced extensively before coming west. The elk died quickly, the rest of the herd rapidly fleeing. We then climbed up to where he lay, and in the waning light of day, cleaned and quartered the animal, packed the meat onto the mule, and began the long ride back to camp that lasted well into the night. The next day we took the meat to a processor, who some weeks later shipped more than one hundred pounds of various cuts to me, which I shared and enjoyed with family and friends. The creature had lived off the fat of the land without the aid of steroids, antibiotics, or the confined cruelty of the crowded feedlot and conventional slaughtering. I then lived off the elk,

12. Controversy reigns regarding the morality of hunting not justified by necessity. Some view this activity as the exercise of skill and prowess in being a harvester; others see it as an anachronistic exploitation of nature, the cause of needless loss, and the cruel infliction of suffering on innocent others.

making this magnificent creature, its health and vitality, a part of myself, and in the process I took in a bounty of physical, psychological, and spiritual reward.

I had been responsible for this creature's death, and felt then and now sadness at having inflicted this loss. But his death had given me many tangible benefits and intangible satisfactions: I was a successful harvester, feeding myself and others; I proved my stamina and strength, my perseverance and skill; I had become intensely and intimately tied to the animal and the beauty and bountifulness of the land. I cherished my immersion in his world and the feeling of time slowing, making me one with my surroundings, allowing me to incorporate the elk's existence into an actual and symbolic part of my own. The creature I hunted had lived a fine life, he was a magnificent representative of his kind, and I felt emboldened by the reality of making his essence a part of myself.

I was and remain keenly aware that others will view this nonessential killing of a wild creature as cruel and destructive, a gratuitous infliction of needless death on an innocent other. The rationalizations of blood sport ring hollow and unconvincing to these opponents of hunting. They also point to the long list of victims of overhunting and lament the destruction of creatures like the great auk, the tiger, the American bison, and many others. They might cite the passenger pigeon, perhaps the most abundant bird species of all times, estimated to have numbered at least five billion animals at the time of the European settlement of North America.[16] The scale of the destruction of the passenger pigeon is difficult to fathom, but a glimpse may be discerned through the eyes of the ornithologist and painter John James Audubon, recounting a single hunt during the mid-nineteenth century:

> Suddenly, there burst forth a general cry of "Here they come!" The noise which they made, though yet distant, reminded me of a hard gale at sea, passing through the rigging of a close-reefed vessel. As the birds arrived, and passed over me, I felt a current of air that surprised me. Thousands were soon knocked down by polemen. The current of birds, however, still kept increasing. The fires were lighted, and a most magnificent, as well as wonderful and terrifying sight, presented itself. The Pigeons, coming in by thousands, alighted everywhere, one above another, until solid masses, as large as hogsheads, were formed on every tree, in all directions. Here and there the perches gave way under the weight with a crash, and, falling to the ground, destroyed hundreds of birds beneath, forcing down the dense groups with which every stick was loaded. It was a scene of uproar and confusion. I found it quite useless to speak, or even to shout, to those persons nearest to me. The reports, even of the nearest guns, were seldom heard. . . . No one dared venture within the line of devastation. . . . The uproar continued . . . the whole night. . . . Toward the approach of day, the noise rather subsided. . . . It was then that the authors of all this devastation began their entry amongst the dead, the dying, and the mangled. The pigeons were picked up and piled in heaps, until each had as many as he could possibly dispose of, when the hogs were let loose to feed on the remainder.[17]

The last of the passenger pigeons died at the Cincinnati Zoo in 1914. Aldo Leopold—ironically, an avid hunter who had written eloquently about the virtues and benefits of hunting—offered these insights at the dedication of a monument to honor "Martha," the last passenger pigeon:

> We grieve because no living man will see again the onrushing phalanx of victorious birds sweeping a path for spring across the March skies, chasing the defeated winter from all the woods and prairies. . . . There will

always be pigeons in books and in museums, but these are effigies and images, dead to all hardships and to all delights. Book-pigeons cannot dive out of a cloud to make the deer run for cover, or clap their wings in thunderous applause of mast-laden woods. Book-pigeons cannot breakfast on new-mown wheat in Minnesota, and dine on blueberries in Canada. They know no urge of seasons; they feel no kiss of sun, no lash of wind and weather. . . . Our grandfathers were less well-housed, well-fed, well-clothed than we are. The strivings by which they bettered their lot are also those which deprived us of pigeons. Perhaps we now grieve because we are not sure, in our hearts, that we have gained by the exchange. The gadgets of industry bring us more comforts than the pigeons did, but do they add as much to the glory of the spring?[18]

Confusion and controversy reign regarding the morality of hunting not justified by necessity. Some view hunting as a beneficial exercise of skill and prowess, as a chance to become intimate with and immerse oneself in the land, as a way of learning about and materially utilizing the natural world at a time

13. The extinction of the passenger pigeon, estimated to have numbered five billion birds at the time of the European settlement of America, illustrates the effects of overhunting. In 1914 the last of the passenger pigeons expired at the Cincinnati Zoo.

when modern society is increasingly separated from nature. Others see recreational hunting as anachronistic, a dangerous form of exploitation of nature, the cause of needless loss, and the cruel infliction of pain and suffering on innocent others.[19]

My experience intimates that a meaningful harvest of physical and psychological reward can be obtained from the personal exploitation of nature beyond a narrow material or monetary reward. Practical gain is certainly obtained through activities such as hunting, fishing, gardening, wild plant collecting, firewood harvesting, and other outdoor pursuits. But just as important, we may harvest physical fitness and craft, the exercise of skill and perseverance, a sense of independence and autonomy, and the feeling of joyful immersion in nature and its fundamental processes. It has been said that death makes the spark of life glow more brightly measure for measure, and this elusive reward can be a part of the material harvest and exploitation of nature.

AN INORDINATE FONDNESS FOR MATERIALISM

Even though most people have an insufficient appreciation for the full range of material benefits we derive from nature, our modern world still tends to regard the exploitation of the natural world as vastly superior to all other environmental values. Prevailing cultural norms and a narrow market-oriented economy encourage this skewed emphasis. This imbalanced modern focus on the material value of nature has become so extreme that it has become dysfunctional, contributing to widespread environmental degradation and a diminished capacity to reap other important environmental benefits.

This unfortunate situation does not devalue the importance of materially exploiting nature, but rather suggests that such exploitation, like any biophilic value, must not be excessive and out of balance with other critical values of nature. The inherent inclination to materially utilize the natural world does not inevitably lead to environmental degradation. Our extraction of goods and services from nature inevitably transforms it, and many other species do the same, from elephants, alligators, beavers, and otters to coral polyps and termites.[20] All these creatures fundamentally alter their environments, sometimes deleteriously, in the process of materially utilizing it. In most instances, their utilitarian exploits contribute to the productivity of the landscapes they occupy. People can similarly exist in compatible relation to the land, living in mutually beneficial association with nature, while pursuing the extractive activities of our species.

But such a benign outcome demands a more moderate and balanced exploitation of nature than prevails today. It requires that the cultural bias equating progress and civilization with the material subjugation and transformation of nature be overturned. Most people today still adhere to the assumption that the historian Lynn White described: "The daily habits of action [of modern people] . . . are dominated by an implicit faith in perpetual progress. . . . No item in the physical creation [is seen] as [having] any purpose save to serve man's [material] purposes."[21]

This exaggerated material value of nature, and the related assumption of people's superiority to the natural world, has become an article of faith in modern society. Few lament the destruction of a habitat or species if substantial material benefit and economic progress occur. Rather than critically examining this underlying value bias, we have relied on Band-Aids applied to its symptoms mainly involving government regulation and technology to mitigate its harmful effects. Material exploitation of the natural world is a fact we must accept and even applaud, but it needs to be moderated by recognition of the necessity of a balanced relationship with other equally important values of nature. To deny the legitimacy of a material value of nature or a free-market economy is to risk replacing one distortion with another. But to allow the material exploitation of nature to occur in unfettered fashion is also to invite our dysfunction and decline.

Moderation of the inherent inclination to value nature materially, accompanied by a balanced relationship to other essential biophilic values, is the basis of a more sustainable society and economy. The exploitation of nature includes a variety of land uses that produce food, energy, fiber, shelter, water, recreation, and an array of ecosystem services. Problems arise when the exploitation becomes unsustainable, for example, emphasizing maximum short-term extraction of resources that discounts the future and ignores and undermines other environmental values.

A more sustainable approach should stress a multiplicity of land uses and environmental values managed to yield a bevy of benefits over the long term. But can this approach prevail in a free-market economy? In such an economy, the focus on a single land use maximally exploited over the short term almost always outcompetes a single sustainable land use. An alternative model capable of competing with the single land use approach might instead focus on multiple sustainable land uses that collectively outperform a single conventional land use over the long term by generating multiple income flows and retaining a better ability to adapt to the inevitable economic and environmental changes that occur. This "multilayered sustainable land use approach" would embrace a wider range of environmental values that yield a greater breadth of physical and psychological rewards to people and society. For this model to succeed, it requires a large geographic scale to accommodate a multiplicity of land uses implemented over long periods of time in complementary and productive relation to one another.

This multilayered sustainable land use approach is illustrated by a project I have been involved in with others on a Pacific island archipelago. This island chain currently imports almost all its energy, mostly in the form of fossil fuels transported thousands of miles, resulting in high energy costs, extensive greenhouse gas emissions, and widespread chemical pollution. Agricultural production on these islands has also relied on large-scale production of single crops like sugar and citrus fruit, which are exported thousands of miles to distant markets, while the islands import more than eighty percent of their food in the form of largely processed food products. This agricultural system has resulted in widespread habitat destruction, introduction of invasive species, depleted soils and aquifers, and the extinction and endangerment of much of the islands' unique plant and animal life. Yet the islands possess outstanding wind and solar energy potential, and a wide variety of local organic and fresh food products could grow in their rich volcanic soils and warm tropical climate.

An alternative multilayered sustainable land use approach has been proposed for approximately two hundred thousand acres on sites located on two of the archipelago's islands. These sites have historically been the focus of unsustainable single-crop agriculture production that has resulted in depleted soils, deforestation, saltwater intrusion, widespread pollution, and subsequent large-scale tourism that was equally unsustainable and culturally inappropriate, and which soon failed. The proposed multilayered sustainable development alternative instead emphasizes renewable wind energy production, organic and grass-fed livestock production, biological wastewater treatment, ecologically oriented community development, and nature-based tourism. The initial economic driver is the extraordinary wind energy potential of the area, which could generate one-fifth or more of the archipelago's energy needs at significantly lower economic and environmental costs. A compact, pedestrian-oriented, mixed-use village would provide for the community's energy needs and recycle its wastes on less than two percent of the total land area. Restoration of the soils, wetlands, forests, and biological and cultural resources would rebuild the economic and environmental infrastructure of the land and the heritage of its people.

Like all land use development, this project emphasizes the material exploitation of nature. Yet it attempts to do so in a way that encourages a complementary relationship between nature and humanity, resulting in richer, more productive, and healthier human and natural systems. It offers a model of development under which all biophilic values occur in balanced and respectful relation to one another. The long-term result is a more productive and aesthetically attractive landscape, and a sounder and more enduring economy and society. This approach does not sacrifice human needs to "save" nature, but rather promotes long-term human self-interest by striving to create a healthier and more fruitful natural system in which people can lead more physically, mentally, and spiritually rewarding lives.

5

affection

At one time or another, most of us have expressed strong affection for particular creatures and places. Sometimes these feelings become so strong—for a pet dog or cat, or a special beach or mountain that has become important to us, or a garden we have worked long and lovingly to cultivate—that we pronounce our "love" for these creatures and places. We also find ourselves spontaneously exclaiming our strong affection for dramatic manifestations of nature, like a breathtaking waterfall, a beautiful rainbow, a colorful hummingbird, flowers blossoming in the spring. We utter: "I just love this place! That dog is as dear to me as a member of the family! I am so fond of this valley, it would break my heart if it were gone!"

Should we view such declarations of affection for nature as equivalent to the emotional attachments we hold for other people? Or, should we regard them as rhetorical flourishes rather than authentic expressions of strong feelings and even love? The dictionary definition of love—"a deep, tender feeling of affection and solicitude toward a person, such as that arising from kinship or a sense of oneness"—suggests a restricted approach to the question confined principally to people and not the nonhuman world.[1]

Yet I can recall, as I suspect most people can, occasions when I felt possessed by deep and tender feelings of affection, solicitude, and caring for certain plants, animals, and places. My pets readily come to mind, particularly my dogs that have become my companions over the years. As I write this, Mario, my basset hound, and Pascal, half basset, lie close by, sharing my home with me. I believe my affections toward them are a form of love. If suddenly they disappeared or were harmed, I would feel a profound sense of loss and a sorrow akin to grief. Moreover, I value their seemingly unreserved affection for me, and I am just delusional enough to believe that they regard me with something that seems reminiscent of love.

Thinking about such arcane matters, I recall a joke I heard on the radio program *Prairie Home Companion* that asked: "How can you tell your dog loves you and is your best friend?" It went something like this:

> Well, you put your dog and your wife, husband, or some significant other in the trunk of your car, and then drive about for ten minutes. Then, you stop and open your trunk. And, who will be happy with joy and affection to see you, and who will be inclined to smack and perhaps kill you?[2]

At least with respect to my pets, I take deep and sustained emotional satisfaction from giving to and receiving from them strong affection and believe it to be the rough equivalent of love. I especially relish their exuberant expressions of affection when they see me, particularly at times when I am feeling anxious and stressed. Still, the special emotional bond between people and pets, or "companion animals," may be viewed as exceptional and not necessarily indicative of more general feelings people have for the natural world. Indeed, a pet may be viewed as a kind of "humanized" creature adopted into people's households and made a part of the family.

This kind of relationship and emotional attachment is, of course, very different from our connection to more remote aspects of nature, such as a wild plant, animal, or landscape. Yet I can recall instances when my feelings for certain wild creatures and settings were so intense that I also expressed strong affection and sometimes love for these critters and places. I recall exclaiming: "I just love bears! I adore these mountains! This beach is among the dearest places I have known! I can't imagine living in a world without flowers and beautiful sunsets! My love for nature is among the strongest feelings I have! If I died in this lovely place, I would die a happy man!"

I recall one time when I had this overwhelming sense of affection and kinship with nature, although this is just one dramatic example among many. On this special occasion, I was looking down from the great rim of the Ngorongoro Crater in Tanzania. I peered into that deep, wide basin with my binoculars and became aware of the incredible numbers of wildebeest, zebra, antelope, giraffe, and elephant spread across the plain, small groups of lions and cheetah interspersed among them. On the far side of the crater was a lake shimmering with the movement of thousands of slightly swaying flamingoes, white clouds and a bright blue sky reflected on the water's surface seemingly captured within its depths. I spontaneously exclaimed my love for this place, but more generally for nature. I knew the emotional intensity of the experience would be burned into my memory, become a part of my identity, something that I would recall for years to come, and that, even more remarkably, would somehow help and sustain me.

Again, this experience might be viewed as exceptional and thus not generalizable to our more typical affections for nature. Yet I recall analogous feelings under more mundane circumstances. Not long ago, I was depressed by the burden of a long winter and mounting concerns. As often when this occurs, I took a walk beside a river in a nearby forest. There I encountered wood ducks pairing up for the breeding season, migrating warblers returning from the south, early-blossoming trillium and colt's foot, the intense green of new leaves budding on the trees. I felt a deep affection and emotional attachment for these and other elements of the forest and river, uplifted and restored by this reviving life. I experienced a love for the broader world beyond myself that nurtured and sustained me.

Yet is it accurate to equate these affections with the love we might feel for other people, especially since these objects of nature are incapable of reciprocating the emotions? Perhaps it is when we recognize that the vitality of these natural features underlies and enhances our physical, mental, and spiritual selves. Perhaps we realize that in nurturing these feelings toward nature, we build this emotional capacity in ourselves and thus our ability to extend these feelings to other people.

Affection for nature underscores the importance of emotions in human existence, as well as the role these sentiments toward the natural world play in developing these emotional tendencies in our own species. Affection and attachment toward nature have been so significant in building this emotional capability in people that it is reasonable to contend that it emerged as an inherent inclination contributing to our species' fitness and survival. At the beginning of this book, the term *biophilia* was translated from the Latin as "love of life." As we learned then, the psychologist Erich Fromm coined the term to emphasize the need people have to love one another as a basis for mental health. Although Fromm's emphasis was on the relation of people to each other, at one point he more broadly described biophilia as a "passionate love of life and of all that is alive . . . whether in a person, a plant, an idea, or a social group."[3] Our perspective of biophilia emphasizes a wider range of physical, emotional, and intellectual affinities for nature than just love. Yet the inclination to feel a strong affection and even love for nature remains a critical aspect of our inherent affinity for the natural world.

As suggested, feelings are central to human existence, even if reason and intellect are needed to make critical choices and guide our emotions. Indeed,

emotion and intellect are almost always intertwined—strong emotions motivate us to seek knowledge and understanding, while reason guides and moder-
ates our feelings. Our highly social species depends on the assistance and caring
response of others, especially family, friends, and community, particularly during early childhood. Strong emotional attachments facilitate and encourage
this degree of caring and nurturance, and our unusual capacity to give and
receive affection has been a key to our species' survival.[4]

The development of these emotional capacities depends on close and intimate associations among people. But these affective abilities are also fostered
by strong feelings of attachment to the natural world. Other animals, in particular—especially those that most remind us of ourselves—have been critical
in this regard, and are the most typical recipients of our caring, affection, and
love. These creatures include dogs, cats, horses, and other domestic animals,
but also at times wild mammals, especially closely related species such as bears,
whales, elephants. Depending on situation and circumstance, other mammals,
as well as lower vertebrates such as birds, amphibians, reptiles, and fish, can
also become the subjects of strong affection and emotional attachment. Moreover, certain plants, landscapes, and places can further arouse our affection and
caring response.

A growing body of evidence indicates that these emotional attachments
to nature can significantly affect people's physical and mental health and well-
being. Much of this research has focused on pets or companion animals, although wild animals, plants, and landscapes have also been featured.

The term *companion animal* underscores the emotional bond that can exist between people and other creatures, although the word *pet* emphasizes the
important tactile experience that often encourages this affection when people
stroke and caress another animal.[5] Companion animals are frequently the recipients of strong feelings and treated as friends, members of the family, and
sometimes subjects of our love. The historian Keith Thomas cited three characteristics of pets: they are given names, we allow them into our homes, and,
perhaps most important of all, we don't eat them.[6] Reflecting the largely tacit
significance of the last attribute, I was once asked by students to contribute to
a poor African country facing famine. I responded that we could save money
and do more practical good by shipping millions of abandoned "surplus" cats
and dogs to this hungry nation as food than by "wastefully" incinerating them.
The somewhat offended stares I elicited suggested that my "modest proposal"
might have been viewed more as a recommendation of cannibalism than as a
practical solution.[7]

The enormous emotional appeal of companion animals today is suggested by some seventy-two million dogs and eighty-two million cats in the United States alone. People clearly own companion animals for many reasons, including work, hunting, protection, and aesthetics. But by far the most frequently cited reasons in surveys conducted on the subject are affection and companionship.[8]

Research also reveals that companion animals can exert a wide range of physical and mental benefits, including reduction of stress, healing and relief of illness, improved verbal and social skills, enhanced self-confidence and self-esteem, and other effects.[9] The psychiatrist Aaron Katcher and colleagues at the University of Pennsylvania have conducted a number of especially informative studies of these impacts. Katcher, working with the veterinarian Alan Beck and the biologist Erika Friedmann, found that sick children exposed to a pet dog had significantly lower blood pressure when compared with otherwise similar children who lacked this contact.[10] In another study of adult patients recovering from heart surgery, the researchers matched subjects according to illness symptoms and demographic characteristics, then exposed half to companion animals. They reported that contact with companion animals substantially enhanced the speed and efficacy of healing and recovery.[11] They specifically reported: "Mortality rates among people with pets [were] one-third [those] of patients without pets."[12] Concluding their study with a quotation from the Samuel Coleridge poem "The Rime of the Ancient Mariner," they emphasized the role of a love of nature in human physical and psychological health:

He prayeth well, who loveth well
Both man and bird and beast.

He prayeth best, who loveth best
All things both great and small;
For the dear God who loveth us
He made and loveth all.[13]

Katcher and colleagues further explored the healing benefits of exposure to lower vertebrates such as aquarium fish. They reported significant reductions in blood pressure and stress relief when sick children were exposed to fish.[14] In another investigation, they found substantial reductions in stress and superior coping responses among adults confronting dental surgery when exposed to a fish tank.[15]

In a 1993 investigation, Katcher, collaborating with Gregory Wilkins, conducted a study of boys suffering from attention deficit hyperactive disorder

(ADHD). The researchers sought to determine the relative therapeutic effect of exposing the boys to companion animals compared with a non-animal nature experience. They divided the boys into two groups, one of which cared for companion animals while the other participated in an outdoor challenge activity that involved hiking, canoeing, and rock climbing. Midway through the study, they switched the boys from one activity to the other to avoid the testing effect of exposure to only one type of nature experience. Although both activities had significant therapeutic effects, consistently stronger and more lasting impacts were associated with caring for companion animals. These greater effects included improved speech, better attentiveness, more effective control over impulsive and disruptive behaviors, and superior school performance. The researchers concluded that emotionally bonding with companion animals resulted in significantly greater stress relief, improved social ties, enhanced empathy, and better task and school performance among ADHD boys.[16]

Many reasons have been cited why emotionally bonding with companion animals might lead to an array of physical and mental benefits, including better health, improved coping ability, and enhanced self-esteem. The veterinarian Dr. James Serpell, having conducted an extensive review of the research literature, identified a number of potential factors, concluding:

> By seeking to be near us and soliciting our caresses, by their exuberant greetings and pain on separation, by their possessiveness and their deferential looks of admiration, pets persuade us that they love us and regard us highly. . . . People need to feel liked, respected, admired; they enjoy the sensation of being valued and needed by others. . . . Our confidence, our self-esteem, our ability to cope with the stresses of life and, ultimately, our physical health depend on this sense of belonging. . . . Pets don't just substitute for human relationships. They complement them and augment them. They add a new and unique dimension to human life.[17]

The research reviewed suggests that emotional attachment to pets and other elements of nature can be therapeutic, fostering physical and mental well-being. Yet emotional attachment to animals can also be excessive and dysfunctional. Serpell's defensive reference to pets as "substitutes for human relationships" acknowledges this possibility, a criticism some have directed at what they view as an exaggerated emphasis on companion animals in modern society. These critics argue that the inordinate focus on pets is indicative of a contemporary world that uses these creatures to compensate for flawed human relationships and increasing alienation from nature. The ecologist Paul Shepard has strongly remarked in this regard:

14. The dog is among the most favored of companion animals, and has been domesticated for 15,000 years. Yet, the dog is almost genetically identical to the gray wolf, an historically reviled species nearly eliminated from the contiguous United States. There are 70 million pet dogs in the United States.

Less than kindly euphemisms for "companion animals" come to mind—crutches in a crippled society, candy bars, substitutes for necessary and nurturant others of the earth. . . . My concern here is not the destiny of these lumpish, hand-licker-biters among humans who are desperate for the sight of nonhuman creatures because they touch some deep archetypal need. . . . My focus is the effect of the replacement of domestic for wild animals in our psychological development. . . . Animals and their representations constitute essential elements of human mental life. . . . The substitution of a limited number of genetically deformed and phenotypically confusing species for the wild fauna may, through impaired perception, degrade the human capacity for self-knowledge.[18]

Like any biophilic tendency, emotional attachments to nature, including companion animals, can occur in both functional and dysfunctional ways. We may bond with and love nature and animals to excess, just as we can view nature with emotional indifference and disdain. An exaggerated emotional bond with nature hardly invalidates the benefits derived from our affection for the natural world when it occurs in balanced and adaptive fashion. Intimacy with and love for nature have served humans well over the ages, and these tendencies will continue to function as a foundation for developing our capacities for emotional attachment and a sense of belonging.

Emotional connection with other life and landscapes can be especially healing and restorative for the sick, stressed, lonely, and infirm. People throughout the ages have sought the therapeutic effects of particular creatures and places, whether dogs, cats, and horses or seashores, hot springs, mountain retreats, and other powerful elements of the natural world. Bonding with another animal and place can at times offer a less complicated and ambiguous relationship than our interactions with other people.

Granted that affection and emotional attachment to nature can encourage human health and development, the question remains whether these feelings further the goals of environmental conservation or, conversely, might work at variance with these objectives? Some skeptics argue that feelings are marginally relevant to conservation and, worse, frequently harmful when involving controversies about difficult policy and economic choices. These critics argue that the great conservation challenges of our time, such as large-scale species extinction, chemical pollution, and climate change, require objective, empirical, and technical approaches that are undermined by emotional biases. The following personal interlude reflects this tension, an experience when I confronted a prevailing prejudice among fellow conservationists that feelings of affection and love of nature are largely irrelevant, inappropriate, and counterproductive to the goals of environmental conservation.

Interlude

The incident occurred at a symposium in spring 2009 at the Yale University School of Forestry and Environmental Studies that honored the pioneering ecologist and ethicist Aldo Leopold, who had graduated from the school a century earlier. Each speaker discussed some aspect of his or her conservation work and related it to Leopold's life and ideas. One speaker after another stressed some legal, regulatory, scientific, technical, or economic approach deemed necessary to mitigate one or another contemporary environmental challenge, including endangered species recovery, chemical pollution, declining fisheries, greenhouse gas emissions, and environmental injustice. Among the proposed solutions were increased energy efficiency, expanded renewable energy production, more sophisticated cost-benefit analysis, greater scientific study, new laws and regulations, wider application of economic tools for valuing ecosystem services and, of course, educating an ignorant and emotionally biased public.

Scarcely a word was heard about the utility of affection for, emotional attachment to, or love of nature in marshaling support or rationalizing the value of environmental conservation. Yet ironically, the focus of the symposium, Aldo Leopold, had stressed emotions, especially love, as essential to achieving the goals of nature conservation, particularly in developing an ethic of duty and responsibility for caring for the land and its creatures. One of Leopold's most quoted statements makes this point explicit:

> We can be ethical only in relation to something we can see, feel, understand, love, or otherwise have faith in. . . . It is inconceivable to me that an ethical relation to land can exist without love, respect, and admiration for land and a high regard for its value.[19]

Perhaps the symposium participants were implicitly rejecting Leopold's argument regarding the importance of love, feeling, faith, and admiration for the land. Possibly they viewed his words as more rhetorical, strategically intended to market the conservation message to an emotional public, than something to be taken literally or too seriously, especially by scientists and policymakers. Maybe they feared that once the emotional gates had been opened, those opposed to conservation would be better able to exploit emotional messages and obstruct the goals of environmental protection. Trained as scientists, scholars, economists, and policymakers, perhaps they were reluctant to admit that their own motivations to protect the earth had once been and maybe still were influenced by feelings of affection for and even love of nature. Whatever their motivation, despite their professed allegiance to Leopold, the participants behaved as if emotional attachments to nature were irrelevant, inappropriate, and not particularly useful when confronting difficult environmental policy choices.

The symposium took place on a stormy day on the top floor of a recently constructed building. I had been involved in the planning and design of the building, for which both "low environmental impact" and "biophilic design" were important objectives. Low-environmental-impact design means avoiding or minimizing adverse environmental impacts by stressing the likes of energy efficiency and renewable energy production, reductions in pollution and waste, recycling and reuse of materials, and other strategies intended to mitigate environmental damage. By contrast, biophilic design is meant to enhance human health and well-being by fostering connections between people and nature in the built environment. Low-environmental-impact design is widely accepted as a conservation strategy, but we regarded biophilic design objectives as just as important to achieving the overall goal of sustainability.[20]

Our building did accomplish its low-impact environmental goals, reflected in its receiving the highest U.S. Green Building Council LEED Platinum rating in recognition of its energy efficiency, waste minimization, and absence of toxic effects. The building also accomplished its biophilic design objectives, with such features as extensive natural lighting, natural ventilation, views to the outdoors, restored landscapes, inside-outside connections, courtyards, colonnades, naturalistic landscaping, water features, natural materials, and interior designs that mimicked natural shapes and forms.

The symposium took place in a large room on the building's top floor that included a great vaulted ceiling, arched spaces, extensive natural lighting, floors and walls clad in wood harvested from the school's forests, the fractal geometry of complementary wood grains, views to the surrounding trees and courtyards, interior vegetation, natural material furnishings, the information richness and organized complexity that one encounters in nature, and other biophilic design features. It was a contemporary construction in an environmentally transformed city using some of the most advanced forms of modern technology. It was also a building that, by definition, is an inanimate object. Yet most people described the building as feeling "natural, not artificial," and many professed a strong affection and even love for the facility, especially its top floor, where the symposium took place.

The storm that raged that day cast a dark pall over the room. Views to the outside were obscured, the surrounding oak trees were enveloped in mist, a cold wind blew through the leafless branches. Nonetheless, I asked the symposium participants how they felt about the building and this particular space. Did they think Aldo Leopold would have enjoyed working there? Did they personally like being there? Did they view it as a good place for the meeting? Despite the poor weather conditions, all the attendees enthusiastically expressed their affection for the building and especially for this room, and they thought that Leopold would have felt the same way. I then asked them to imagine a time long after the energy-efficient solar rooftop collectors or other low-environmental-impact features had become obsolete, inevitable in a world of rapidly evolving technology. At that future time, I asked, would the building's occupants be motivated to renovate and restore the facility? The participants expressed the view that the building's occupants would want to preserve this facility because of their strong affection for and allegiance to it.

15. Kroon Hall, a new building at the Yale University School of Forestry and Environmental Studies, received the U.S. Green Building Council's highest LEED Platinum award, attesting to its low-environmental-impact features. The building was also designed to include biophilic design features meant to enhance occupant comfort, productivity and well-being through connection to nature.

Without realizing it, the participants had acknowledged the importance of emotional connections to nature not just as a fundamental basis for personal satisfaction, but as an underlying motivation for environmental conservation, including preserving a building. The dictionary defines sustainability as the quality of "keeping something in existence." If we are always building something new to be sustainable, this objective remains elusive if not impossible. Our focus that day was not on a pet dog, a favored wildlife species, a special landscape, or a valued ecosystem. It was a lifeless human-made construction. Yet the symposium participants implicitly agreed that its conservation decades from now would depend not on its technical achievements but on people coming to cherish, emotionally identify with, and even love this structure, whose abandonment would be seen as ethically abhorrent and irresponsible.

Aldo Leopold's famous quotation underscores the importance of love for and faith in nature. Reminding the participants of this quotation and the importance of emotions in sustaining even a building elicited some nodding agreement. Yet it was not long before the discussion that followed returned to the more "serious" business of analytical, technical, and policy solutions to the great environmental challenges of our day. The participants' hasty retreat to the more comfortable confines of rational and technical discourse called to mind another Leopold observation that in trying to make conservation easy by making it scientifically and economically acceptable, we risk the possibility of making it trivial.[21]

THE CHALLENGE OF ANTHROPOMORPHISM

The unease many environmental scientists and policymakers have regarding the role of emotions in resource conservation and management reflects in part an aversion to projecting human feelings onto the natural world. This emotional projection is sometimes referred to as anthropomorphism, defined as "the attribution of human motivation, characteristics, or behaviors to inanimate objects, animals, or natural phenomena." Antipathy for anthropomorphism appears regularly in debates regarding the management of high-profile species and habitats.[22]

An often-cited example is the "Bambi syndrome," a controversial effect observed after a Walt Disney movie portrayed a mother deer and her fawn menaced by hunters and experiencing a kind of terror humans might feel under similar circumstances. *Bambi* has been vilified by wildlife managers for the effect of its distortions on the attitudes of laypersons and cited as an illustration of emotion undermining the principles of rational resource conservation.

Critics also see the Bambi syndrome coloring debates about such issues as the control of feral horses and swans, seal conservation, whale regulation, the harvesting of redwood trees, the use of fire as a management tool, and sport hunting. Wherever it arises, these scientists complain, the Bambi syndrome shows why we need to eliminate subjective feelings in favor of more rational, scientific, and economic analyses in conservation policy and resource management decision making.

But without strong emotional attachment to nature, will people ever care enough to protect and sustain the natural world? Effective environmental stewardship relies as much on emotional conviction as it does on intellectual understanding. Reason and emotion must complement each other to preserve and protect the land, as well as function as a basis for people's physical and mental health and fitness. We will view other species, landscapes, or even our constructions as worthy of protection and stewardship only when we possess strong emotional attachments to them, and recognize how much their condition is interwoven with our own health and well-being. The care and love of nature motivates us to sustain these creatures and places not as an act of charity or altruism, but from a profound realization of our own self-interest.

When we stunt or deny our emotional connection to the natural world, we inevitably diminish our physical and mental potential. When humanity emotionally disassociates itself from nature, it invites its demise from what the anthropologist Richard Nelson called an "imperiling loneliness." Decrying this disconnection from nature as a growing affliction of modern life, Nelson remarked:

> Probably no society has been so deeply alienated as ours from the community of nature, has viewed the natural world from a greater distance of mind, has lapsed to a murkier comprehension of its connections with the sustaining environment. . . . Yet an affinity for other life may be as vital to us as water, food, and breath; may be so deep in us that only by a centuries-old malaise of drifting away have we come to the point of thinking about it. . . . [E. O.] Wilson asks: "Is it possible that humanity will love life enough to save it?" Surely there is no more important question. . . . But it seems nearly certain that throughout most of history, humans did love life.[23]

A love of nature often begins with a special fondness for a particular animal, plant, or landscape that has become the subject of our emotional attachment. This frequently occurs when we become intimate with a piece of ground or a certain creature. Initially, we struggle to become familiar and comfortable with our focus. Yet over time and with patience and perseverance, we form strong emotional and intellectual connections with particular localities and creatures. When this happens, we make these places and species a part of our selves, our identities, and even our spirit. We take physical and mental possession of these natural features, and they take possession of us. We become co-participants in our shared world and the ecological processes that underlie and sustain them and us. We become members of a community of relations, and we feel more alive, at peace, and in love with the earth of which we are a part.

6

dominion

All species seek to control and master their environments. This occurs among the largest carnivores and the smallest insects, and in all habitats from the terrestrial to the marine. Certain creatures, sometimes referred to as "keystone species," are especially adept at reshaping their world; among the better known keystone species are elephants, termites, sea otters, beavers, alligators, and termites. But no other creature has so mastered and controlled its environment as have modern humans, arguably to an excessive and dysfunctional degree. Contemporary society's mastery of the planet has become so dominant and transformative that it has precipitated a global environmental crisis reflected in large-scale losses of biological diversity, widespread pollution, and significant alterations to the earth's atmosphere, and potentially to its climate.

The urge to master nature is a normal and adaptive tendency in all life forms, including our own species. Lacking the inclination to control our environment, humanity would become weak and ineffectual, deficient in qualities essential to long-term fitness and survival. The grave uncertainty of the modern world is whether or not the human urge to master nature can occur in an adaptive and balanced fashion, given a population of seven billion people, the large-scale impacts of modern technology, and current rates of per capita consumption of energy, space, and materials. As with any biophilic tendency, the question is not the intrinsic worthiness or legitimacy of a particular inclination to affiliate with nature, but rather its adaptive and functional expression.

An inordinate desire to control nature is said to be a characteristic of Western society, particularly its Judeo-Christian religious traditions that have encouraged human domination of the natural world. This outlook has tended to identify human progress and civilization with the spiritually justified subjugation of nature.[1] As the historian Keith Thomas suggested, from this perspective: "Human civilization . . . is virtually synonymous with the conquest of nature. . . . Man's dominion over nature [is] the self-consciously proclaimed ideal. . . . Yet, despite the aggressively despotic imagery . . . of 'mastery,' 'conquest' and 'dominion,' they [see this] task . . . as morally innocent."[2]

The historian Lynn White linked the urge to master nature with a Judeo-Christian outlook, which he described as "the most anthropocentric religion the world has seen . . . [supporting] a view of nature [as having] no reason for existence save to serve [people]."[3] Although it may be argued how much this Western religious tradition has by itself resulted in the modern domination of nature, there is little doubt that the urge to master nature is characteristic of free-market economies that rely heavily on contemporary science and large-scale technology to control the natural world. It would appear that the combination of Western cultural and religious ideals, a free-market economy, and modern science and technology has been a combustible mixture that fueled the contemporary inclination to subjugate the earth, and is at the root of today's global environmental crisis.[4]

The Judeo-Christian religious perspective has stressed a view of people as uniquely created in God's likeness, and capable of achieving spiritual salvation through subjugating and transcending nature, and thus escaping our biological origins as just another animal species. To attain this state of grace, humanity is instructed by God to take dominion of the earth and use it for God and his purposes. The biblical Book of Genesis reflects this perspective when it proclaims:

> The fear of you and the dread of you shall be upon every beast of the earth, and upon every fowl of the air, upon all that moveth *upon* the earth, and upon all the fishes of the sea; into your hands are they delivered. Every moving thing that liveth shall be meat for you. (9:2–3)[5]

If God gauged these things, he would be proud of humanity's accomplishment. Measured in population numbers, *Homo sapiens* has multiplied exponentially. At the time when God's presumed son was upon the earth some two thousand years ago, the human population was an estimated fifty-five million. By 1500 this figure had climbed to four hundred million. Just four hundred years later, in 1900, the human population had reached its first billion. In the single century since, humanity's numbers have swelled to an astonishing seven billion. People now occupy nearly every terrestrial habitat on the planet, with the exceptions of Antarctica and some remote desert, tropical, and high mountain areas. Moreover, humans have taken dominion over nearly all the planet's creatures, with the possible exception of a few recalcitrant arthropods and microbes.[6]

A more quantitative measure of modern society's hegemony over the earth is reflected in the proportion of the life-sustaining energy generated by the sun that has been appropriated by humans. This energy equivalent is referred to as "net primary productivity," defined as "the amount of energy left after subtracting the respiration of primary producers (mostly plants) from the total amount of energy (mostly solar) that is fixed biologically." The biologists Peter Vitousek, Paul and Anne Ehrlich, and Pamela Matson estimate that people today consume twenty to forty percent of the earth's net primary productivity. This consumption involves humanity's direct exploitation of the earth for food, fuel, and fiber, as well as the indirect uses for urban development and transportation.[7] This appropriation of the earth's energy resources has been tied to the projected loss of one-quarter to one-half of all nonhuman life measured in number of species and biomass (the weight of living matter) during the next half-century.[8]

Human mastery over nature is most profoundly reflected in the design and development of the modern city. The prevailing approach to the construction of contemporary urban areas has largely relied on the subjugation and transformation of nature, including its soils, waters, geology, vegetation, and animal life. Moreover, in modern society, the city has become the "natural habitat" of the majority of people; three-quarters of the human population in economically advanced nations now resides there, and, for the first time in history, a majority of the world's population is urban.[9] One of the most significant challenges of the modern era is how to design and develop the modern city in ways that neither excessively dominate nor unalterably degrade the natural world, and do not separate and alienate people from their need for beneficial contact with nature, a subject I shall address in the final chapters.

As we have seen, the modern tendency of humans to exercise mastery over nature is merely a manifestation of an impulse shared by other species to dominate and transform their environment.[10] As mentioned, keystone species—"whose presence and role within an ecosystem has a disproportionate effect on other organisms within the system"—are particularly adept at controlling their environments.[11] Well-known keystone species include elephants on a savannah, alligators in a swamp, sea otters in a kelp bed, prairie dogs on a grassland, starfish in the ocean, or humans in a modern metropolis. Yet people today have exercised unprecedented control over nature. We have tended to equate progress with the transformation of the natural environment, and with the aspiration to escape our biology.

But we should not automatically equate the excesses of modern life with the inherent inclination to master nature, or view that impulse as intrinsically wrong or inappropriate. Indeed, the urge to exercise mastery and control over the environment remains a key to people's health, productivity, and fitness, whether as individuals or collectively. For example, this tendency is reflected in the development of so-called mastery skills, which have been linked to various aspects of character development and human well-being. These skills include, among others, physical strength, coordination, and balance; attentional capacity and mental concentration; and coping and competitiveness.[12] These mastery skills are also instrumental in problem solving and critical thinking, in generating feelings of independence and autonomy, and in shaping a sense of personal identity and self-confidence.

Acquiring these mastery skills has always relied on people's experience and contact with nature, especially during childhood. For young children, this frequently involves outdoor play in settings relatively close to home. Among adolescents and young adults, the development of these mastery skills has often been associated with outdoor activities in wilder settings where a significant degree of challenge, coping, and adventure is encountered. Studies of adolescents and young adults who participate in outdoor adventure programs illustrate this impact. These activities often require participants to leave the comforts and conveniences of modern life to spend extended periods of time in relatively primitive settings in the company of peers. The challenges encountered and their contrast with modern life are reflected in the following remark by one participant:

> I was unsure how to contribute, not being particularly strong or experienced in the outdoors. In the past two weeks, I've faced the physical challenge in unexpectedly cold conditions. I've faced emotional challenges of overcoming my pride at being presumably not especially physically able, and of having my most deeply held beliefs about human interactions and our modern world challenged at almost every turn along the way. [13]

Despite the deprivations encountered, this teenage girl deliberately left her safe, secure, and largely indoor existence to be physically and mentally challenged in a wilderness setting. She hiked long distances, climbed steep terrain, camped and cooked under primitive conditions, and experienced diverse hazards and threats. She experienced aches, pains, soreness, discomfort, bites, and the need to cope with various adversities. Yet, like most other participants, she reported extraordinary rewards, including increased physical strength, coordination, and skill; enhanced problem solving and critical thinking; improved cooperativeness and interaction with others; expanded feelings of independence and autonomy; and a growth in her self-confidence and self-esteem. These and other mastery skills are reflected in the powerful testimonials of the following participants:

> My [outdoor experience] occurred at a pivotal point in my life. It gave me the opportunity to take a risk. It strengthened my sense of self. It gave me a feeling of purposefulness, self-respect, and strength that I had never had before. . . . [It] was the most amazing, awe-inspiring, thought-provoking, and challenging experience of my life. It helped me to believe that if there is anything I really want to do in life, I have the ability to do it. . . . It helped me to realize who I was and how I fit into the world around me.

> Being in nature gave me an unbelievable confidence in myself. I found a beauty, strength, and an inner peace that I never knew was present. It made me more confident, focused, and self-reliant. . . . I learned about respect, setting goals, working to my maximum and past it. These are skills I consider to be important to everything that I do, and I feel they will help me continue to be successful throughout my life.

> The experience while isolated and out of the realm of everyday life is applicable to everything that I do. Because everything was such raw emotion and the outer events so simple, the . . . challenges faced and overcome were within myself. Much of what I faced had to do with my own fears and weaknesses. Overcoming them changed me as a person. When I now face a more "complex" problem in the [ordinary] world, I need only to go back to see what solution I came to when it was just me against myself surrounded by simplicity and the answer becomes clear. [14]

The forester Alan Ewert reviewed a wide range of studies of outdoor adventure programs and activities and summarized frequently observed psychological, sociological, and physical benefits resulting from participation in these activities (Table 1).[15]

My colleague Victoria Derr and I also conducted a large-scale study of participants of three outdoor programs. This research involved more than eight hundred participants of programs offered by Outward Bound, the National Outdoor Leadership School, and the Student Conservation Association. Data was collected from participants before, immediately following, and six months after the outdoors experience, as well as from other persons who participated in one of these programs during a previous twenty-year period.

This longitudinal and retrospective investigation found that three-quarters of participants regarded the program experience as among the most important and influential in their lives, and that it significantly affected their personal

TABLE 1

PSYCHOLOGICAL BENEFITS	SOCIOLOGICAL BENEFITS	PHYSICAL BENEFITS
Self-concept	Compassion	Fitness
Self-confidence	Cooperation	Skills
Self-esteem	Respect	Strength
Actualization	Communication	Coordination
Well-being	Friendship	Exercise
Values clarification	Belonging	Balance

and character development. Dramatic improvements were reported in self-confidence, self-worth, and self-esteem. The great majority of participants indicated significant improvements in feelings of independence, autonomy, optimism, and the ability to cope with stress. Striking improvements were also reported in the abilities to work with others, solve problems, show resourcefulness, and make difficult and complex decisions. Most participants further indicated that the experience contributed to a far greater appreciation of, respect for, and spiritual connection with nature. In effect, this study found that immersion in relatively undisturbed outdoor settings in the company of peers typically resulted in the acquisition of a wide range of mastery skills that greatly enhanced the participants' lives and coping abilities.[16]

This impact may be especially noteworthy in a world where young people increasingly feel a lack of control over their lives and are constantly reminded of their dependence on others for such basic needs as food, energy, shelter, security, and mobility. By contrast, participants of these programs report that their experiences offered them the chance to feel independent, self-reliant, and competent, while enhancing their character development and sense of personal identity. Reflecting on the particular role of challenge in nature in fostering these mastery skills, the sociologist Richard Schreyer remarked: "While not unique in its ability to afford self-concept enhancement, wilderness possesses many attributes well-suited to the development of self-concept, especially the presence of obstacles, challenges, opportunities for solitude, freedom from social forces, and enhanced ability to focus on self."[17]

16. Most participants of outdoor programs report that these experiences foster self-discovery and character development. The natural environment can be a vital medium for developing mastery skills critical to personal growth and maturation, whether encountered in a wilderness setting, a suburban backyard, or a city park.

These outdoor programs are relatively rare, and unavailable to most young persons. Still, outdoor activities accessible to children even in the largest cities have been found to contribute to character development and to the acquisition of various mastery skills. Whether experienced in a wilderness setting, a suburban backyard, or a city park, the natural environment continues to offer a vital medium for self-discovery and an enhanced sense of self-worth and personal identity.[18]

The question remains whether modern society has taken the inclination to master nature to excessive and dysfunctional lengths, especially given the impacts of our population of seven billion people, the expanding use of powerful technologies, and the contemporary per capita consumption of energy, space, and materials. In other words, has the desire to subdue the earth become a luxury we can no longer afford in a highly materialistic, human populated, and globally oriented world economy? Or do we risk in denigrating the urge to master nature a self-defeating lurch in the opposite direction, losing sight of the continuing need to exercise some degree of control over nature as a necessary basis for human physical and mental health, fitness, and development?

As is often the case, the answer is a bit of a muddle. We need to exercise some measure of control over nature as a matter of both survival and character development. Yet we must neither diminish nor degrade the productivity of natural systems, and ideally we should even enrich them. This possibility— fantasy, some would say—was usefully articulated by the Pulitzer Prize–winning biologist and pioneering conservationist René Dubos. Inspired by the Indian poet and writer Rabindranath Tagore, Dubos invoked the words "wooing of the earth" to suggest that humans could both control and enhance nature for human benefit. As he remarked: "The phrase 'wooing of the earth' suggests that the relationship between humankind and Nature [can] be one of respect and love rather than domination. . . . The outcome of [this] wooing can be rich, satisfying, and lastingly successful only if both partners are modified by their association so as to become better adapted to each other."[19]

Dubos recognized that the human inclination to master nature is characteristic of all species and is neither biologically wrong nor culturally regrettable. But he believed that we must bring wisdom, restraint, and respect to bear on our efforts to control the natural world. In so doing, he wrote, we can not only serve human interests but also enhance the health and productivity of natural systems, although some alteration to nature is inevitable. Like elephants on the savannah, humans can master the natural environment and thereby transform it, but the outcome, according to Dubos, can be, as with elephants, a more ecologically productive natural system measured by such parameters as species diversity, biomass, vegetative growth, nutrient cycling, soil productivity, and hydrological regulation.[20]

Yet for people to live in mutually beneficial relationship with the natural world, while still seeking to control it, we must conduct our interventions with humility, knowledge, reverence, and respect. At the least, this means seeking to understand more about the distinctive biological, geological, and ecological characteristics of any land or aquatic area we seek to master. Even then, our knowledge will inevitably fall short, and thus we must proceed with caution and ethical restraint. This informed yet humble approach to mastering the land is far more likely to yield outcomes in which nature and humanity achieve a mutually productive and sustainable relationship.

Dubos's confidence that this could occur is encouraged by his reading of history. He observed many successful adaptations of nature and humanity that led to ecologically productive and culturally viable landscapes. Moreover, these mutually beneficial human-nature relationships resulted in distinctive geographies that possessed aesthetic and vernacular qualities that elicited affection, loyalty, and stewardship among their human inhabitants. He cites in this regard his native Île de France region, the Cotswolds of England, the terraced rice slopes of Southeast Asia, and the stucco cliff dwellings of the American Southwest. These cherished landscapes were all significantly transformed as a consequence of human intervention and development, yet remained ecologically productive and appealing to residents and transients alike. As Dubos writes:

Every part of the world can boast of humanized lands that have remained fertile and attractive for immense periods of time. From China to Holland, from Japan to Italy, from Java to Sweden, civilizations have been built on a variety of ecosystems that have been profoundly altered by human intervention. . . . The reciprocal interplay between humankind and the earth can result in a true symbiosis . . . a relationship of mutualism so intimate that the two components of the systems undergo modifications beneficial to both. The reciprocal transformations resulting from the interplay . . . determine the characteristics of the people and the region, thus creating new social and environmental values.[21]

For much of history, these mutually beneficial associations of people and nature tended to emerge slowly and iteratively, involving trial-and-error processes of reciprocal adjustment. Unfortunately, this rarely occurs today, given the enormous spatial scale, rapid pace, and far-ranging technological impacts of modern development. Moreover, a growing reliance on national and global markets and financial flows further encourages decision making far from where the developments occur, with such decision making generally ignoring local environmental and cultural conditions. As a consequence, the dominant paradigm of modern large-scale development typically encourages profound environmental and social perturbations, the production of enormous wastes and pollutants, and a growing separation of people from nature.[22]

The greatest challenge of our time is whether or not a very different kind of development paradigm can prevail, one in which nature and humanity exist in mutually beneficial and complementary relation. Such a profound shift will be difficult to achieve, although the widespread adoption in the early twenty-first century of what has been called "sustainable development" is an encouraging step. So far, this approach has fallen short of its promise, relying mainly on limited technical solutions that seek to minimize environmental damage but fail to effect a more positive, nurturing, and beneficial relationship between nature and humanity.

Still, I share Dubos's conviction that the human need to control nature, even in the modern world, can be shaped so as to sustain and even enrich nature. One expression of his confidence anticipated the idea of biophilia, rooting this change in the biological needs of our species:

> With our knowledge and sense of responsibility for the welfare of humankind and the Earth, we can create new environments that are ecologically sound, aesthetically satisfying, economically rewarding, and favorable to the continued growth of civilization. . . . This process of reciprocal adaptation occurs in ordinary life through continuous minor changes in the people and their environment, but a more conscious process of design [can] take place. . . . [This] can be successful only if . . . [the design is] ecologically viable and also satisfies instinctive needs that human nature has derived from its evolutionary past.[23]

A mutually reinforcing relationship between nature and humanity in a particular geographical context typically leads to strong emotional and intellectual attachments between people and the places where they live. When this occurs, people feel an intimate bond with particular localities that become integral to their individual and collective identities and a source of their sense of safety and security. Dubos viewed this need for intimate connection to place as reflecting a basic need. He remarked:

> People want to experience the sensory, emotional, and spiritual satisfactions that can be obtained only from an intimate interplay, indeed from an identification with the places in which [they] live. This interplay and identification generate the spirit of the place. The environment acquires the attributes of a place through the fusion of the natural and the human order.[24]

The need to affiliate and identify with particular places reflects an evolved human territorial tendency. For much of human history, our species' survival depended on a high degree of familiarity and knowledge of local conditions and environments. By mastering and controlling particular environments, we enhanced our chances of locating resources, finding shelter, moving successfully across landscapes, avoiding danger, and understanding the complexity of complicated natural systems. We are, of course, far more mobile and transient today. Yet most of us still yearn for intimacy and familiarity with particular places that we call home, and which remain critical to our identity and self-hood, especially during childhood. Moreover, lacking this degree of physical, emotional, and intellectual connection to particular places, we often neglect and degrade them. As the poet and conservationist Wendell Berry observed: "Without a complex knowledge of one's place, and without the faithfulness to one's place on which such knowledge depends, it is inevitable that the place will be used carelessly, and eventually destroyed."[25]

In order to achieve the mutually advantageous relationship with nature that is our goal, in controlling nature, we must paradoxically surrender to it, recognizing and respecting its independent powers and autonomy. Two illustrations suggest this symbiotic potential. The first focuses on an urban park that, by definition, is a product of human creation and construction. The second is the practice of modern forestry, in which trees are deliberately managed and harvested to serve a variety of human needs.

The park is New York's Central Park, a nineteenth-century design by Frederick Law Olmsted and Calvert Vaux. Like Dubos, Olmsted also used the phrase "spirit of place" to emphasize people's need to identify with particular places as a basis for personal and collective identity. Olmsted further suggested that the experience of nature is essential to human physical and mental health, even in the modern city. He remarked: "The charm of natural scenery is an influence of the highest curative value; highest, if for no other reason, because it acts directly upon the highest functions of the system, and through them upon all below, tending, more than any single form of medication we can use, to establish sound minds in sound bodies."[26]

Olmsted viewed the experience of nature as especially critical to healthy living in the city, where people are so often separated from the natural world. This could be achieved, he thought, by constructing parks in relative proximity to people. He advocated the creation of "greenbelts," "emerald necklaces," and what he called "parkways," which could be interwoven into the lives of urban dwellers and located relatively short distances from where they lived and worked.

His and Vaux's most famous creation, Central Park, is an 883-acre expanse of open space that has become as much a landmark for this famous city as its museums and skyscrapers. After 150 years, the park continues to be highly esteemed, valued by residents and visitors alike as a source of beauty, recreation, and physical and mental restoration. Yet, like most urban parks, it reflects a mastery and transformation of nature.

Central Park has clearly benefited people, but has it done so at the cost of degrading the natural environment that preceded it? Studies of the park's ecology and biota offer a mixed answer, although on balance the natural environment has flourished in many ways. The most obvious environmental benefit has been the amount of preserved open space, despite the extraordinary monetary value of the land if developed. From a biological perspective, Central Park has retained attributes of a productive, if diminished, natural system. Plant studies reveal a number of species today roughly equal to when the park was created. A slight majority of these plants, however, are invasive species, and several native plant species have been extirpated.[27] Animal studies also yield mixed results. Many terrestrial species, especially large mammals, have been eliminated or greatly reduced in number. More mobile species, like birds, have largely thrived since the park's creation. Of the estimated 888 bird species found in the United States and the 459 in New York State, 275 occur in Central Park.[28] This unusually large number of bird species in an area this size prompted the National Audubon Society to identify Central Park as "one of the nation's top 14 birding areas, [comparable] . . . with the Everglades and Yosemite."[29]

For people, Central Park continues to embody both the spirit and genius of New York, lending a treasured beauty and identity to this urban location. It has become a focus of affection, aesthetic appreciation, and reverent regard by most of the area's inhabitants. Its vigorous stewardship reflects a deep attachment to place, and a willingness to defend the park's interests with passionate resolve. There persists an interest in enriching this place both culturally and ecologically, and its relative success suggests people and nature can coexist in mutually beneficial relation even in a modern urban setting.

What about modern forestry, where the desire to exert mastery over nature has often resulted in extensive environmental degradation? The subjugation of forests for commercial purposes has been linked to a particularly Western attitude toward trees. Lynn White described this view as seeing trees as little more than a physical fact whose exploitation can proceed largely with a "mood of indifference" to the rights of these plants.[30] Viewed from this perspective, trees are mainly regarded as an insentient element of nature and a largely undifferentiated mass. One tree seems very much like another, and their exploitation requires little moral consideration beyond how it might affect other people. As a former governor of California is said to have remarked: "When you've seen one redwood tree, you have seen them all."[31] Or, as a businessman responds to the passionate defense of a particular tree in the popular film *Avatar*, "What the hell have you people been smoking out there? They're just goddamn trees."[32]

This attitude has encouraged a view and practice of forestry in which trees are treated as little more than a harvestable commodity. Yet commercial forestry can be conducted with affection, humility, and respect, even while exploiting trees. The forester Bob Perschel offers this alternative outlook, describing an ethical approach to commercial logging:

As a forester, you spend all day weaving your way back and forth through the . . . forest, examining each tree in turn and deciding whether it should live or die. You repeat this each day, considering 30,000 or 40,000 trees and selecting about three hundred of them to mark with a blue paint spot. Each decision involves factors such as age, size, health, soil, aspect, economic value, competition, potential growth, wildlife value, and so on. You calculate all these in your forestry-educated brain. You raise your paint gun to deliver the death sentence, and then something unnamable crawls up from your belly and asks, "Is this the right thing to do?" "How well does this action fit into the natural flow of the forest?" "What harm is this causing?" "What does this have to do with me?" . . . "What is your relationship with this entity you call a tree?" "Is this a loving act, or a purely selfish one motivated by your need and the landowner's desire to earn money?" You squeeze the trigger, or don't squeeze the trigger, and move on to repeat the process again and again, thousands of times each day, day after day, season after season, year after year. This is work that can change you—if you open yourself to the hard questions that are about your Self: Who are you as a human being, and what is your purpose, your responsibility, your role in and relationship with the natural world?[33]

A forest, like any ecosystem, is not technically alive, but it gives rise to and sustains life and is thus lifelike. It is a fountain of mass and energy uniting life with nonlife. When impoverished, its regenerative capacity and ability to produce are diminished. When healthy and productive, it yields not only trees in abundance but also a wealth of biota, productive soils, nutritious waters, clean air, and a rich and fruitful environment. It also provides an attractive and healthful place for people to come for their own growth and regeneration. Its responsible management can be a bounty for humans and nature alike, promoting not only a forest that is ecologically resilient but also a medium for the flourishing of the human body, mind, and spirit.

7

spirituality

People's lives are enriched by the belief that their existence has meaning and value. This feeling of meaning, in turn, encourages the conviction that life is worth living beyond mere survival, and often motivates us to aspire to some higher end. At the least, it suggests that we are more than a random speck of matter existing for a moment in space and time. When shared with others, this faith in the meaning of life engenders a sense of community based on common beliefs; when formally organized, these beliefs give rise to religion. On balance and over time, these spiritual inclinations have contributed to human fitness and survival and become embedded in our biology. Under normal circumstances, these beliefs enhance our sense of self-worth and encourage us to bond with others. In times of crisis, the conviction that life possesses meaning and value helps us cope with adversity and can be comforting and healing.

This feeling of significance comes in part from the sense of being connected to a world beyond ourselves that seems coherent and even purposeful. These beliefs arise from and are enriched by a feeling of connection to nature or, writ large, creation. As the philosopher Holmes Rolston remarked: "Nature is a philosophical resource, as well as a scientific, recreational, aesthetic, or economic one. We are programmed to ask why and the natural dialectic is the cradle of our spirituality."[1] The connection between nature and spirituality is illustrated by the interlude that follows, focusing on the life of the German theologian and physician Albert Schweitzer.

Interlude

Albert Schweitzer lived from 1875 to 1965, a time of political, moral, and spiritual upheaval in Western society. He was torn by what he viewed as the ethical barrenness of his age. He was particularly frustrated by the reductionist philosophical and scientific perspectives that prevailed during this period that viewed life as merely an empirical and material phenomenon that could be deduced and understood simply through objective study. Schweitzer chose missionary work in Africa not only to do good but also in hopes of finding a better moral and spiritual compass, one that revealed meaning and purpose in life.[2] The answers he discovered gave rise to his philosophy of "reverence for life," an understanding that imbued existence with value and purpose, and whose articulation resulted in his being awarded the 1953 Nobel Prize.[3]

The idea of reverence for life emerged in reaction to Schweitzer's frustration with the prevailing philosophical and scientific biases of his age, which asserted that only through reason, empiricism, and logic could we understand humanity and the workings of the universe. From Schweitzer's perspective, this inordinate reliance on intellect and objectivity reflected an excessive materialism characteristic of modern society that fostered alienation, a dangerous cynicism, and a spiritual and ethical void.

Schweitzer's experiences in Africa, particularly his immersion in its wildness, beauty, and lush diversity, encouraged him to view life in a far different way as worthy, purposeful, and warranting reverent regard. The incredible vitality and fecundity of the African bush both thrilled and instructed him. He encountered there a passionate will to live that led him to believe in an underlying force that motivated and united all life, humans included. By contrast, the sterility of prevailing philosophical and scientific emphases on materialism, empiricism, and quantification largely ignored and denigrated this living wonder, beauty, and exuberant striving and creativity of all life. He describes the moment of his great awakening, as he traveled upriver into the continent's interior:

> All that I had learnt from philosophy about ethics left me in the lurch. I felt like a man who has to build a new and better board to replace a rotten one that's no longer seaworthy. . . . While in this mental condition I had to undertake a longish journey on the river. . . . Slowly we crept upstream. . . . Lost in thought I sat on the deck of the barge, struggling to find the elementary and universal conception of the ethical which I had not discovered in any philosophy. . . . Late on the third day . . . at sunset, we were making through a herd of hippopotamuses, there flashed upon my mind, unforeseen and unsought, the phrase, *Reverence of Life*.[4]

This epiphany provided Schweitzer with the beginning of a philosophical perspective that imbued existence with meaning and purpose and from which he eventually derived an ethical and moral framework for action. From that moment on, he viewed all life as sharing a fundamental commonality. This underlying connection caused him to view existence with reverence and a faith in its intrinsic meaning. It motivated Schweitzer to adopt an ethic that encouraged people to do all that they could to enhance, nurture, and protect life. It also inspired in him the conviction that creation possessed a divine and purposeful direction.

A more expansive translation of the phrase *reverence for life* is "to be in awe of the mystery of life." This broader definition underscores Schweitzer's belief in the intrinsic power and inscrutability of existence, one that is both magnificent and enigmatic and perhaps unknowable. Schweitzer believed in a basic life force that was embedded within the universe, which gave it meaning and spiritual significance. He viewed the affirmation of this life force as an ethical good and a moral responsibility.[5] As he remarked:

> Reverence for life affords me my fundamental principle of morality, namely, that good consists in maintaining, assisting and enhancing life, and to destroy, to harm and to hinder life is evil. . . . Affirmation of life is the spiritual act by which man ceases to live thoughtlessly and begins to devote himself to life with reverence in order to give it true value. To affirm life is to deepen, to make more inward, and to exalt the will to live.[6]

Schweitzer recognized that all life depends on ending other lives, and that life and death, the animate and inanimate, are engaged in a continuous and unyielding exchange. Rather than viewing this inevitability as tragic, he believed that, among conscious humans, it necessitates our deliberate and ethical choice regarding how and when to inflict death and exploit other life. This need for conscious reflection and thoughtful action provided Schweitzer with a moral stance for guiding human behavior. For Schweitzer, what distinguishes humans from other life is our capacity to make ethical choices that knowingly affect the world around us and affirm its meaning and value. As he explained:

> Standing, as all living beings are, before this dilemma of the will to live, a person is constantly forced to preserve his own life and life in general only at the cost of other life. If he has been touched by the ethic of reverence for life, he injures and destroys life only under a necessity he cannot avoid, and never from thoughtlessness. Ultimately, the issue is not whether we do or do not fear death. The real issue is that of [doing so with a] reverence for life.[7]

Schweitzer believed that all creatures strive not just to survive but to find a kind of fulfillment in their existence, something he viewed as the equivalent of the pursuit of happiness. Any action that denied or denigrated the aspirations of other life to find satisfaction in its existence was for him wrong and even evil. He argued:

> What shall be my attitude toward . . . other life? It can only be of a piece with my attitude toward my own life. If I am a thinking being, I must regard other life than my own with equal reverence. For I shall know that it

17. Albert Schweitzer derived his ethical framework for action from the philosophy of reverence for life. He viewed all life, human and nonhuman, as sharing a fundamental commonality.

longs for fullness and development as deep as I do myself. There, I see evil in what annihilates, hampers, or hinders life. And this holds good whether I regard it physically or spiritually. Goodness, by the same token, is the saving or helping of life, the enabling of whatever life I can to attain its highest development. . . . We find sympathy to be natural for any type of life . . . so long as we are capable of imagining in such life the characteristic we find in our own. That is, dread of extinction, fear of pain, and the desire for happiness. . . . The important thing is that we are part of life. We are born of other lives; we possess the capacities to bring still other lives into existence. So nature compels us to recognize the fact of mutual dependence, each life necessarily helping the other lives, which are linked to it.[8]

Schweitzer viewed other life as essentially our kin. As he remarked, "Nature compels us to recognize the fact of mutual dependence." We are connected to other life, and the understanding of the unity of existence instills in us a reverent awe for the miracle and mystery of life.

NATURE AND SPIRIT

Schweitzer's sense of the connection of life and creation was, of course, not unique to him. Indeed, across history, we encounter similar understandings among diverse philosophers and religious figures, and today even among some scientists. This commonality is reflected in the insight of the Nobel Prize–winning writer John Steinbeck, who describes an analogous awareness of the unity of existence among diverse historic figures. As he eloquently observed:

It seems apparent that species are only commas in a sentence, that each species is at once the point and base of a pyramid, that all life is related. . . . And then not only the meaning but the feeling about species grows misty. One merges into another, groups melt into ecological groups until the time when what we know as life meets and enters what we know of as non-life: barnacle and rock, rock and earth, earth and tree, tree and rain and air. And the units nestle into the whole and are inseparable from it. . . . Most of the feeling we call religious, most of the mystical outcrying which is one of the most prized and used and desired reactions of our species, is really the understanding and the attempt to say that man is related to the whole thing, related inextricably to all reality. . . . This is a simple thing to say, but a profound feeling of it made a Jesus, a St. Augustine, a Roger Bacon, a Charles Darwin, an Einstein. Each of them in his own tempo and with his own voice discovered and affirmed that all things are one thing and that one thing is all things—a plankton, a shimmering phosphorescence on the sea and the spinning plants and an expanding universe.[9]

This sense of the commonality of life and its connection to a larger universe is a reflection of how an understanding of nature and our place in it can engender spiritual meaning and purpose. Two aspects of this relationship bear emphasis. First, this spiritual perspective sees in the natural world a fundamental order, organization, and structure. There is a belief that an underlying relationship and integrated wholeness is characteristic of nature, despite its extraordinary variability reflected in tens of millions of species on Earth or billions of stars in the universe. This perception of a basic unity that characterizes the natural world has historically been rationalized by philosophy and religion, but in today's world is increasingly reflected in the understandings of science. Most people share this intuition, guided by their feeling that life, notwithstanding its remarkable diversity, shares many similar properties. These include analogous bodily structures and metabolic processes that in basic ways render alike a spider on the ground, an alligator in a swamp, a fish in the sea, a bird in the air, or a person in a modern metropolis. This sense of kinship that unites all life is reflected in the scientific observations of Edward O. Wilson, when he remarks: "Other species are our kin. . . . All higher eukaryotic organisms, from flowering plants to insects and humanity itself, are thought to have descended from a single ancestral population. . . . All this distant kinship is stamped by a common genetic code and elementary features of cell structure."[10]

Second, the spiritual perspective that links nature, life, and humanity also leads to the belief in a meaning and purpose to existence. The universe is viewed as coherent not chaotic, connected rather than random, logical not absurd. Moreover, life and the universe are posited as possessing a trajectory, a kind of directional path through space and time, reflected in the evolution from simpler to more complex states of organization. This belief encourages a view that nature and humanity share a common meaning in their unified pursuit of fulfillment and perhaps harmony.

These notions of an underlying unity connecting nature and humanity, and the intrinsic meaning and purpose of existence, were characteristic of Schweitzer's notion of reverence for life, as well as many philosophies and religions throughout the ages. These insights are also found in the imagery of poets like Walt Whitman, whose reverence for the unitary miracle of life is reflected in his monumental poem "Song of Myself":

I believe a leaf of grass is no less than the journey-work of the stars,
And the pismire is equally perfect, and a grain of sand, and the egg of the
    wren,
And the tree-toad is a chef-d'oeurvre for the highest,
And the running blackberry would adorn the parlors of heaven
And the narrowest hinge in my hand puts to scorn all machinery.
And the cow crunching with depress'd head surpasses any statue,
And a mouse is miracle enough to stagger sextillions of infidels.[11]

This sense of connection with the universe is a characteristic of all great religions. Religion is the organized expression of spiritual belief revealed in formally articulated principles and practices shared by a group of people. Enormous variability, of course, is found among the world's religions. Still, they all appear to share in the belief that there exists an underlying order in the universe, and a sense that humanity is connected with the rest of creation, despite differences in how this unity and connection are rationalized and its moral implications for people's behavior. The writer Aldous Huxley referred to this similarity among the world's religions as a "perennial philosophy," which he described in this way:

> [It is] the metaphysic that recognizes a divine Reality substantial to the world of things and lives and minds; the psychology that finds in the soul something similar to, or even identical with, divine Reality; the ethic that places man's final end in the knowledge of the immanent and transcendent Ground of all being; the thing that is immemorial and universal. Rudiments of the perennial philosophy may be found among the traditional core of primitive peoples in every region of the world, and in its fully developed forms it has a place in every one of the higher religions.[12]

The world's religions share in the perennial philosophy that humanity is connected and related to the world beyond itself in purposeful and meaningful ways. The religious scholar Mary Evelyn Tucker identified four paths the world's religions have taken to connect the experience of nature to spiritual revelation and understanding. These include:

- *Nature as metaphor*, offering a path or stepping-stone to the divine.
- *Nature as mirror*, a reflection and expression of the divine.
- *Nature as matrix*, the place where people experience the divine.
- *Nature as material*, the means for being in touch with the divine.[13]

The world's religions variously utilize these pathways in nature to enrich people's sense of spiritual meaning and purpose. This may be seen in a cursory examination of four great religious traditions—Hindu-Buddhism, Judeo-Christianity, traditional tribal religions, and what has been called a contemporary nature worship. While diverse, each of these religious perspectives shares the conviction that humans are meaningfully connected to the natural world, and that this connection gives order and purpose to existence and assists in ethically guiding people's actions and behaviors.

Hindu-Buddhist religion, for example, emphasizes a commonality and unity that connects human and nonhuman life with a broader universe of creation. All living beings are viewed as sharing endless cycles of birth, death, and rebirth that occur both within and between species. All species share a similar state of being. All life is seen as participating in endless cycles of existence, ceaselessly striving after peace and enlightenment. Even plants partake in this possibility, and can become fulfilled, as the following adage suggests: "All beings, even the grasses, are in the process of enlightenment."[14]

By contrast, Judeo-Christian religion poses a different view of the relationship between nature and humanity. From this religious perspective, humans are seen as uniquely capable of achieving enlightenment, exercising moral judgment, and attaining salvation. Judeo-Christian theology affirms a single omnipotent God responsible for all of creation and governing humans and nonhumans alike. People are fundamentally different from the rest of creation in having been chosen by God and created in his likeness, and therefore are uniquely capable of salvation. In achieving spiritual attainment, people transcend their material and bodily existence and thus biological dependence on the natural world.[15]

Despite this basic separation of people from nature, the Judeo-Christian outlook does not denigrate the importance of nature or minimize human responsibility for its nurturing care. Nature, like humanity, is the product of God's purposes. Because God fashioned the world, people have a moral obligation to be good stewards. As Tucker notes, from a Judeo-Christian outlook: "Creation is sacred because God created it. Creatures are valuable because they are created by God, and humans are particularly significant because they are formed in the image and likeness of God."[16] God may have given humans the right to rule the earth, but with this power come responsibilities. As the theologian John Passmore explains, people must be a good and loving overseer of the Lord's creation: "Genesis . . . tells man that he is . . . master of the earth and all it contains. But at the same time it insists the world was before man was created, and that it exists to glorify God rather than to serve man."[17]

A traditional tribal outlook offers yet another perspective on the relationship between spirituality, nature, and humanity. There are many traditional tribal religions, making generalizations difficult. Moreover, few traditional cultures have codified their religious traditions in formal scripture and canon. Still, studies of traditional tribal religions describe a fundamental unity seen in the relationship between nature and humanity. This has sometimes been called animism, the belief that people, other animals, plants, and even the nonliving elements of water, rocks, and air possess spirit and an elemental life force. All are seen as imbued with consciousness, identity, and awareness.[18]

As the anthropologist Richard Nelson suggests, from this vantage point humans exist among "watchful beings in a watchful world."[19] Moreover, this perspective does not distinguish between the physical and spiritual worlds. People and nature are merely derivatives of the same whole rather than independent or different. All elements of nature, both living and nonliving, possess spirit and awareness, and are capable of moral judgment. This intermingling of humans with the rest of creation is reflected in Nelson's elucidation of the tribal hunter-gatherer outlook:

> Among hunting-gathering peoples, the intricate weaving together of nature and culture is like the exchange between living cells and their surroundings: the vital breathing in and out, the flux of water and nutrients, the comminglings of outer world and inner flesh. . . .
>
> Humans and animals are bound together in [countless] ways. . . . Elements of the "nonliving" environment—earth, mountains, rivers, lakes, ice, snow, storms, lightning, sun, moon, stars—all have spirit and consciousness. The soil underfoot is aware of those who bend to touch it or dig into it.[20]

Drawing on the work of the anthropologist Robert Redfield, three characteristics of the indigenous religious worldview are emphasized by Nelson:

> First, humanity, nature, and the sacred are thoroughly conjoined. . . . Second, relationships between humans and environment are based on orientation rather than confrontation: people do not aspire to control or master their surroundings; rather they seek to work with them through placation, appeal, or coercion. And third . . . : "Man and Not-Man are bound together in one moral order. The universe is morally significant."[21]

Finally, we may cite a contemporary nature worship as illustrative of the connections between nature, humanity, and spirituality among the world's religions. Like the traditional tribal outlook, this more contemporary perspective is a spiritual outlook rather than a formally organized religion. Nonetheless, the religious scholar Bron Taylor, referring to it as "Dark Green Religion," identifies three beliefs as characteristic of this spiritual perspective, including:

- Nature as sacred;
- Nature as intrinsically valuable;
- Nature as requiring reverence and care.[22]

In this spiritual outlook people and nature are viewed as fundamentally alike and tied together into a shared ecological and moral order. Nature and humanity are seen as varying expressions of an integrated system of interdependent and mutually reinforcing parts. All creation, humanity included, reflects similarly governing physical, biological, and ecological principles that connect one another through interlocking webs of interdependence and interrelationship. Humans are merely one of many life forms bound into an organized universe.

Intimate immersion in nature provides people with the means for finding spiritual fulfillment and a life of meaning and purpose. This connection imbues humanity with the obligation to respect, protect, and, when diminished, restore nature to its wildness and diversity. Adherents of contemporary nature worship often cite the views of John Muir for inspirational support, as illustrated by his writings on various occasions:

> Wonderful how completely everything in wild nature fits into us, as if truly part and parent of us. The sun shines not on us but in us. The rivers flow not past, but through us, thrilling, tingling, vibrating every fiber and cell of the substance of our bodies, making them glide and sing. The trees wave and the flowers bloom in our bodies as well as our souls, and every bird, wind song, and tremendous storm song . . . is our song.

> The pines spiraling around me higher, higher to the star-flowered sky, are plainly full of God. God is in them . . . the infinite abundance and universality of Beauty. Beauty is God.

> This glorious valley might well be called a church, for every lover of the great Creator who comes within the broad overwhelming influences of the place fails not to worship as he never did before.

> Every dome and peak with their forests and sculpture proclaiming God's glory in tones of human love none can fail to understand.

> No dead dry box buildings however grandly spired and colored, will ever bring us into the true and healthy relations with the creator as will these bold wilderness groves.[23]

18. The nature writer John Muir is a hero to many who see spiritual salvation in their relation to nature. Through intimate immersion in the natural world, Muir believed, people can achieve spiritual fulfillment and a life of meaning and purpose.

The inclination to value nature spiritually became biologically encoded because on balance and over time it advanced human fitness and well-being. Like all biophilic tendencies, this is a weak genetic inclination subject to the shaping influence of learning, culture, and experience. A spiritual value of nature can assume many expressions across individuals and groups, and be revealed in both functional and dysfunctional ways. Still, people over time have largely benefited from a spiritual affinity for nature. The foregoing discussion has intimated various adaptive functions that have resulted from this connection, including:

- A view of life as meaningful and purposeful;
- A heightened sense of personal and collective identity and self-worth;
- A feeling of connection and kinship with the natural world;
- An enhanced inclination to conserve and be good stewards of nature.

As we have seen, from a spiritual perspective of nature the universe appears coherent and organized, with features of a structured and interrelated whole. The natural world is consequently viewed as intrinsically meaningful and worthy. By living in right relation to nature, people can achieve lives of purpose and fulfillment. Under normal circumstances, this outlook can encourage contentment, joy, and peacefulness. At times of adversity, this connection and meaningful relationship to the world beyond ourselves can be physically and mentally restorative.

A view of nature as intrinsically worthy can also enhance our sense of self-worth and self-esteem. We see in our relationship to the natural world a clearer understanding of who we are and where we fit into the world. Our personal and collective identities are affirmed, and we are encouraged to persevere and seek a life of satisfaction and fulfillment through our relationship to nature and creation. We feel bound not just to humanity but also to an encompassing universe, a sense of oneness that enhances our seeking after spiritual enlightenment.

This feeling of connection to nature enlarges our understanding of community, as we intuit ties that extend beyond the parochialism of an isolated humanity. Through a spiritual affinity with the natural world, we enlarge our sense of membership in a broader community and with it our moral obligation to sustain it. We emerge as stewards of nature motivated by an expanded appreciation of our personal and collective self-interest. Desecrating nature becomes not just materially unwise but, more important, spiritually and morally culpable. This motivation for conserving nature has historically been a far more powerful and effective force for environmental conservation than have the formally enacted laws and regulatory edicts of modern governments. This chapter concludes with a final interlude that illustrates the relationship between nature, spirituality, and conservation, as reflected in the modern practice of ecological restoration.

Interlude

Ecological restoration illustrates how the connection between nature and spirituality can both enhance and be an outgrowth of a modern conservation practice. Ecological restoration has largely been rationalized in secular and scientific terms. But this activity also possesses a powerful spiritual dimension that both motivates people to participate in it and enhances the experience. The spiritual dimension of ecological restoration often stems from its emphasis on renewal and revival of nature. Moreover, the repair of natural systems is typically motivated by the need to redress harm inflicted by people. Ecological restoration can be seen as the practical expression of Schweitzer's reverence for life, and an attempt to atone for past grievous wrongs.

The restoration of damaged natural systems is often rationalized as the repair of a degraded environmental feature or function. Such activity includes recovering an endangered species, restoring a damaged habitat, or reviving an ecological function or service. Successful restoration is tied to such empirical measures as a species' population level, eliminating invasive species, reducing soil erosion, improving water quality, accelerated rates of decomposition, or biogeochemical flux. From this vantage point, ecological restoration is seen as little more than a secular, technical process, promulgated by experts and largely motivated by scientific objectives.[24]

On closer examination, however, participants in ecological restoration, laypersons and scientists alike, not unusually reveal motivations and sentiments of spiritual growth and aspiration. Restoring a species, habitat, or ecosystem can also result in an ethical and moral awakening. Moreover, through the act of reviving nature, the participants' sense of self-worth and connection to the world beyond are often enhanced and enriched. This practice can restore the human spirit as much as it can improve the productivity of the land.[25] This more expansive understanding of ecological restoration is reflected in the findings of the religious scholar Gretel Van Wieren, who observed:

> In a deeper sense, ecological restoration is the attempt to heal and make the nature-human relation whole. In its metaphysical understanding of the fundamental interconnectedness of nature and culture and in its practice, which provides a material bridge between people and land, ecological restoration is viewed . . . as providing a promising, and moral, model for human living with the natural world. In the actual practice of repairing degraded lands—reintroducing, reforesting, revegetating . . . —persons and communities are, in an important sense, restored to land. . . . Ecological restoration as a healing practice is understood as a form of restitution for past (and present) unjustified destruction. . . . The restorationist experiences an enlargement of the self. . . . Alongside feelings of sorrow, lament, and even guilt and anger in relation to land's degradation, a sense of fulfillment, satisfaction, hope, amazement and wonder [occurs] at the healing capacities of land and the human spirit.[26]

Ecological restoration offers the participant the chance to deepen his or her spiritual understanding and reverence for nature. It encourages feelings of connection to the natural world, and can contribute to the health, healing, and beauty of the land and its people. By helping to revitalize the earth, the restorer assists in its rebirth, and enhances his or her feelings of personal renewal and atonement for past wrongs. Often the participant experiences spiritual satisfaction when both the healer and the land are restored. Van Wieren reflects on these more spiritual effects:

> For the restorationist a type of wholeness in the midst of brokenness [occurs]. . . . There is a sober celebratory spirit of trust and hope among restorationists that communion and belonging in relation to land is in fact possible. . . . Our spirits, our hearts can be transformed and renewed in the midst of fragmentation and degradation. We really can "touch the sacred with our hands."[27]

These spiritual and ecological consequences are reflected in the experience of Freeman House, working to restore Chinook salmon to the Mattole River in northern California. House grieves at the damage inflicted by the salmon's extirpation, the degradation of its watershed, and its uncertain remediation. Yet he is comforted by a sense of spiritual renewal and moral purpose derived from seeking to restore the salmon, a species symbolic of nature's importance, both materially and spiritually, to the Pacific Northwest.[28] He describes the spiritual awakening he experiences one evening while struggling to restore salmon to the river:

> On [this] mind-blown midnight in the Mattole I could be any human at any time . . . stunned by the lavish design of nature. The knowledge of the continuous presence of salmon in this river allows me to know myself for a moment. . . . Gone for a moment is my uncomfortable identity as part of a recently arrived race of invaders with doubtful title to the land; this encounter is one between species, human and salmonid. . . . Salmon and I are together in the water. . . . It is a large experience . . . at once separate and combined, empty-minded awe.[29]

House's experience reminds us of Schweitzer's realization of reverence for life as he traveled upriver into the African continent. Through their deep affiliation with nature, both Schweitzer and House engaged feelings of profound and meaningful relation to the world beyond. They found an inner strength to persevere, the confidence to affirm their connection with creation, and a sense of participation in the larger community of life. By revering life and its restoration and rebirth, they found solace, peace, and fulfillment.

8

symbolism

Above all else, what makes humans distinctive is our use of symbols to represent reality. Indeed, our lives are largely lived via symbols, which provide the basis for our language, speech, and ability to communicate, as well as our capacity to imagine, create, and form culture. While literalists view symbols as somehow less than real, these representations of reality are among the most defining characteristics of our species, and a critical dimension of the human mind. Our ability to symbolize is a fundamental aspect of human learning and development, especially during childhood.

The human capacity for creating symbols relies heavily on our relationship to the natural world. Whenever we deal with the real in nature, we almost always simultaneously create a symbolic image and representation of it. We transform actual objects into their imagined form, shifting from the empirical to a more vicarious reality. This inclination to symbolize draws on all our inherent affinities for the natural world—affection, attraction, aversion, control, exploitation, reason, and spirituality. Each provides a spectrum of relationships with nature that helps funnel the real into its symbolic form.

Commenting on the importance of symbolizing nature as a basis for human thought, E. O. Wilson remarks:

> Human beings live, literally live, if life is equated with the mind—by symbols, particularly words—because the brain is constructed to process information almost exclusively in their terms. . . . To explore and affiliate with life is a deep and complicated process in mental development. . . . Life gathers human meaning to become part of us. . . . [Living organisms are the] agents of nature translated into the symbols of culture. . . . Culture . . . in turn . . . is a product of the mind, which can be interpreted as an image-making machine that recreates the outside world through sym-

bols arranged into maps and stories. . . . Organisms are the natural stuff of metaphor and ritual.[1]

Symbolizing nature takes many forms: names, images, stories, decoration, and design. It is revealed in our metaphors, our myths, and our dreams. It is manifest in our language, our everyday discourse, our poetry—even our advertising and marketing. The origin of these symbols in nature can sometimes be quite obvious, though at other times it is obscured and disguised in the etymological roots of words, in figures of speech, in turns of phrase. We often employ images and metaphors of nature to communicate a particular meaning. These can be quite mundane:

wise as an owl;
clever as a fox;
busy as a beaver;
industrious as a bee;
powerful as the mighty wind;
brave as a lion.

Or, sometimes they take less obvious forms, as when the poet asks:

Shall I compare thee to a summer's day?
Thou art more lovely and more temperate:
Rough winds do shake the darling buds of May,
And summer's lease hath all too short a date;
Sometime too hot the eye of heaven shines,
And often is his gold complexion dimmed;
And every fair from fair sometime declines,
By chance of nature's changing course untrimmed:
But thy eternal summer shall not fade,
Nor lose possession of that fair thou ow'st,
Nor shall death brag thou wand'rest in his shade,
When in eternal lines to time thou grow'st.
   So long as men can breathe or eyes can see,
   So long lives this, and this gives life to thee.[2]

The ubiquity of images and symbols drawn from nature in our language and culture is suggested by the writer Richard Mabey, who observes:

Nature is the most potent source of metaphors to describe and explain our behaviors and feelings. It is the root and branch of much of our language.

We sing like birds, blossom like flowers, stand like oaks. Or then again we eat like gluttons, breed like rabbits and generally behave like animals. . . . It is as if in using the facility of language, the thing we believe most separates us from nature, we are constantly pulled back to its, and our, origins.[3]

Nature as symbol often involves focusing on particular forms of life, most frequently animals, whose physical and behavioral attributes are borrowed from the empirical world and then transformed into their representational form in the service of human interests and needs. Tens of thousands of species are employed for this purpose, varying across culture and history, although certain creatures and landscapes figure most prominently because of their special relevance in human evolution.

Three animals that illustrate this propensity are the elephant, the butterfly, and the snake. Although biologically diverse, each has a long history of inspiring the inherent inclination to symbolize nature as a means of advancing human communication and thought.

As the largest of all land mammals, the elephant stands twice as tall as a man and weighs as much as fifteen thousand pounds. The elephant is also a long-lived creature, with an average life expectancy of seventy to eighty years. Moreover, the elephant is exceptionally intelligent, possessing a complex social life and a remarkable ability to communicate. Among the elephant's most distinctive physical characteristics are its long trunk and tusks. Elephant tusks have long been coveted; they are used to make artwork, signature seals, and musical instruments; and ivory, like gold, has often been employed as a measure of wealth. Elephants have at times been the focus of intense exploitation, their populations depleted and extirpated in certain areas. The unsustainable exploitation of African elephants during the latter part of the twentieth century led to restrictions and bans on their harvest, and remains controversial today.[4]

The attributes of the real elephant inform its symbolic function. Its image and representation occur throughout the world in folklore, mythology, art, and marketing. The elephant as symbol has been used to signify strength, wisdom, wealth, loyalty, longevity, good fortune, and uniqueness. Examples abound, from the Hindu god Ganesh, to the storybook elephants Horton and Babar, to elephants used in commercial promotions of everything from credit cards and electric appliances to soda pop. While recently walking through an airport, I was surprised to confront the image of an elephant riding a surfboard upon a large wave, his nimbleness somehow connected to the work of a computer software company.

By comparison, butterflies are wee little creatures. I have uselessly calculated that perhaps fourteen million medium-sized butterflies would equal the mass of an average pachyderm. Despite its exponential difference in size, the symbolic significance of the butterfly in many ways rivals that of the mighty elephant.

Butterflies are largely daytime creatures and, as a consequence, tend to be highly colorful as a reflection of their role as important plant pollinators. Despite the frequent benefit to humans of pollination, butterflies in their larval caterpillar stage are sometimes associated with extensive tree and crop damage. Butterflies are rarely credited with great intelligence, yet some species, like the North American monarch, precisely navigate distances of some three thousand miles from their summer to wintering areas.[5]

Color is an important reason why people find butterflies aesthetically appealing, making them among the few insects attractive to humans. The transformation of an ungainly caterpillar into a delicate and beautiful flying creature has contributed to the butterfly's appeal and made it a source of mystery and legend. These and other attributes of the real butterfly are reflected in its symbolic form, used to signify beauty, fertility, harmony, creation, transformation, transience, fragility, freedom, resurrection, and divinity. Butterflies figure prominently in folklore, art, religion, and advertising throughout the world. In our modern age, butterflies have been recruited to promote such products as cars, food, insurance, electronics, and candy. The entomologist Ronald Gagliardi has observed that butterflies have "a truly amazing variety of interpretations and meanings in so many different countries, cultures, civilizations and artistic periods."[6]

And, then there is the snake, a creature of very different and great symbolic significance. In contrast to the elephant and the butterfly, the snake is burdened with largely negative associations, with roots in the inherent fear most people, indeed most primates, have for this legendary creature.

From a strictly physical perspective, the snake is "an elongated, legless, carnivorous [creature] . . . lacking eyelids and external ears." There are some fifteen families and approximately three thousand species of snakes throughout the world, found nearly everywhere with the exception of colder and polar regions and some remote islands. Like all reptiles, snakes are cold-blooded, sunlight largely governing their internal temperature. Lacking limbs, snakes are generally long and cylindrical in shape, and periodically they shed their skin, which is covered by scales. Although possessing limited visual ability, snakes have acute powers of smell and the ability to sense movement. While most snakes are not poisonous to people, some 725 species are venomous. Snakebites are statistically uncommon in most of the world, yet the threat of a bite is one of the reptile's most feared capacities. In India, an estimated 250,000 snakebites have been said to occur in a single year, resulting in some 50,000 deaths.[7]

The snake often signifies something or someone treacherous and sly. Its symbol often elicits the image of an undesirable person or a devil, one possessed by evil. Throughout the ages and in practically all cultures the snake in image and myth has been used to conjure unwanted and fearsome qualities. The snake's power to evoke negative associations originates in our evolution as a terrestrial primate especially vulnerable to these creatures. This inherent aversion to snakes has rendered this animal a potent symbol. The snake powerfully illustrates the human proclivity for using nature to symbolize and to shape communication, as reflected in the observations of E. O. Wilson:

> The snake and the serpent, flesh-and-blood reptile and demonic dream-image, reveal the complexity of our relation to nature and the fascination and beauty inherent in all forms of organisms. Even the deadliest and most repugnant creatures bring an endowment of magic to the human mind. Human beings have an innate fear of snakes or, more precisely, they have an innate propensity to learn such fear quickly and easily. . . . The images they build out of this peculiar mental set are both powerful and ambivalent,

19. There are some three thousand species of snake. The snake's symbolic reputation as dangerous and treacherous has a long history in language, story, myth, and fantasy.

ranging from terror-stricken to the experience of power and male sexuality. As a consequence, the serpent has become an important part of cultures around the world.[8]

Symbolizing nature occurs among all peoples and involves a wide diversity of animals, plants, landscapes, and other natural phenomena. Elephants, butterflies, and snakes are just, so to speak, the "tip of the iceberg"; consider the symbolic associations that come to mind when one thinks of wolves, rats, cranes, frogs, salmon, sharks, bees, leeches, flowers, trees, shrubs, swamps, deserts, meadows, rainbows, tempests, and stars. This list comprises, if you will, but a few grains of sand on the beach of our tendency to symbolize nature. All these features of the natural world are shaped into images and representations that advance our capacity for language, communication, culture, and creation. Whenever humans encounter aspects of nature, they almost always adapt these forms into symbols.

People are especially prone to employ animals for this purpose, particularly species that remind us of ourselves and those with which we have closely evolved. The anthropologist and veterinarian Elizabeth Lawrence, emphasizing the role of animals as symbols, invoked the term *cognitive biophilia* to underscore the importance of symbolic nature in human communication and thought. Cognitive biophilia reflects the critical importance of the natural world as a symbolic resource arguably as fundamental to human fitness as the more material resources of iron and oil. Lawrence elucidates the importance of nature, particularly animals, as symbol, when she observes:

> The human need for metaphorical expression finds its greatest fulfillment through reference to the animal kingdom. No other realm affords such vivid expression of symbolic concepts. . . . Indeed, it is remarkable to contemplate the paucity of other categories for conceptual frames of reference, so preeminent, widespread, and enduring is the habit of symbolizing in terms of animals. . . . Whenever a human being confronts a living creature, whether in actuality or by reflection, the "'real-life" animal is accompanied by an inseparable image of that animal's essence that is made up of, or influenced by, preexisting individual, cultural, or societal conditioning. Thus "nature," as represented by the actual biological and behavioral traits of a particular animal, becomes transformed into a cultural construct that may or may not reflect the empirical reality concerning the animal but generally involves much embellishment. . . . Natural history observations may be a starting point, but they are strongly molded by cultural constructs and by our need to affiliate with the rest of creation through metaphor. Signifying

by means of animals takes place at deep levels of human consciousness, emanating from the same type of psychic experience as myth, poetry, and religion whose language is also symbols.[9]

Nature as symbol originates in our experience of the empirical world, but it is then shaped through imagination and culture into images and metaphors. This is frequently encountered in children's stories, often used to facilitate maturation and development. This tendency occurs across all cultures and throughout history. In our society, it is revealed in such classic tales as "Cinderella," "Little Red Riding Hood," Aesop's fables, the Grimm fairy tales, and a wide variety of legends and myths.[10] It remains a staple of children's stories in the modern era. The interlude that follows, focusing on a modern classic, E. B. White's *Trumpet of the Swan*, illustrates this tendency.

Interlude

The Trumpet of the Swan, by E. B. White, was published in 1970.[11] The story powerfully reflects the symbolic use of nature to advance children's development. More problematically, it also reveals the distortions and anthropomorphizing of the natural world that often occur when nature is transformed from objective reality into image and symbol.

The story involves a young trumpeter swan, Louis, and a boy, Sam, and their special friendship. Louis is mute, a physical affliction usually fatal in swans. He overcomes this handicap by, among other things, learning to write and play music, including the sweetest trumpet one would ever want to hear. Louis has many adventures, performing heroic deeds of epic proportions that climax when he wins the heart of a female swan, rescuing her from a life of captivity.

The story is preposterous in many ways, far removed from the reality of trumpeter swans. Yet symbolically it is a tale for the ages, engaging basic issues of conflict, handicap, coping, courage, tragedy, triumph, love, identity, and other aspects critical to a child's personality and character development. Moreover, the story's effectiveness is enhanced by its fidelity to the real species, despite the exaggerated fantasy of the narrative.

The trumpeter swan is a member of the waterfowl family, which also includes ducks and geese. Waterfowl occur throughout the world, yet comprise fewer than 150 known species. The trumpeter is the biggest bird in North America, with a wingspan of almost seven feet, and weighs as much as twenty-six pounds. The animal is almost entirely white, regal, and magnificent in flight.

Trumpeters typically mate for life, and live on average ten to fifteen years in the wild and as long as thirty-five years in captivity.

The trumpeter swan was among the most endangered bird species in North America. Historically, it was driven nearly to extinction through over-hunting for its meat and feathers and because of the loss of wintering habitat in Idaho and Montana as a consequence of water impoundments and development. The trumpeter today numbers some 24,000 animals, an increase of more than five hundred percent since White wrote his story. This remarkable resurgence during the past half-century is considered a great conservation success. The trumpeter remains vulnerable, however, particularly those birds that winter in the Rocky Mountains, whose seasonal habitat is restricted to a small area of the Snake River in eastern Idaho.[12]

White's book is replete with fantasy, adventure, and romance, and is highly anthropomorphic. Louis learns to write; his father steals a trumpet from a music store to help the young swan compensate for his muteness; Louis becomes so proficient at playing the trumpet that he uses the instrument, along with his ability to write, to communicate with swans and people; he meets Sam, who becomes his best friend, spending time together at Camp Kookooskoos and elsewhere; Louis plays the trumpet in Boston on a swan boat, while spending nights in a bathtub at the ritzy Ritz-Carlton; Louis rescues his true love, whom he had met and fallen in love with in the wilds of Montana, from a life of captivity in a zoo.

The story is quite fantastic, at times bordering on the preposterous. Yet does all this make-believe and anthropomorphism do disservice to the reality of trumpeter swans and the human relationship to nature? Does it represent a perversion of our understanding of the natural world? Does it have any bearing on the challenges of childhood development? My optimistic answer is that the story effectively builds on objective reality, using symbolism and narrative to confer vital lessons relevant to children's growth and maturation. Moreover, the book engenders a greater appreciation and respect for trumpeter swans and their conservation, and the natural world more generally.

White's story inspires and instructs. In addition to confronting issues critical to development, young readers learn something about the natural history and behavior of swans, probably becoming more inclined to support the species' recovery. The bird excels because it appears to be the best and brightest of its kind. Although the book is rife with anthropomorphism, its appeal derives from remaining fundamentally true to the real creature. As the writer John Updike remarked in a review of the book shortly after it first appeared:

If [White] once winked during this accumulation of preposterous particulars, it would all turn flimsy and come tumbling down. But White never forgets that he is telling about serious matters: the overcoming of a handicap, and the joys of music, and the need for creatures to find a mate, and the survival of a beautiful species of swan. . . . White's transparent love of natural detail lifts the prose into felicity.[13]

White does adhere to many aspects of the trumpeter's biology, morphology, and behavior, and this fidelity supports the fantasy and instructional power of the story. The swan is symbolically embellished, but its impact is more convincing because it builds on the natural history of the species. The message of the story is enhanced by extending the empirical into the fantastic and imaginative. On balance, this symbolic embellishment serves well the interests of both humanity and nature.

NATURE AS SYMBOL IN LANGUAGE, DEVELOPMENT, AND DESIGN

E. B. White's story illustrates how the symbolic use of nature can advance human communication, development, and thought. Symbols of nature can be obvious or obscure, buried in the etymological roots of words or designs that, though not actually occurring in nature, are inspired by shapes and processes common to the natural world.

These symbols drawn from nature are all around us. I look about the room where I currently sit and I see swirling leaflike and tree-shaped patterns in the floor coverings, organic forms in the couch and curtain fabrics, flags with eight-pointed stars and a bearlike creature, lighting fixtures and vases that resemble eggs and plants, fishlike mosaics on a countertop. I am also as busy as a bee, longing to spread my wings, to fly away like a bird, at loggerheads with my writing, the metaphors fairly swarming around me.

Nature as symbol is used to facilitate language and speech. In chapter 2, I related the extraordinary information richness and diversity of the natural world to the intellectual processes of labeling, naming, distinguishing, identifying, and classifying, all basic to the development of language and communication. There we saw that the average child, even in the most urban areas, routinely encounters a remarkable variety of plants, animals, landscapes, rocks, water, soils, weather, and other natural phenomena that provide the raw material for speech, language, communication, and thought. This richness and diversity of nature is the stuff of the real and empirical world but, just as important, exists in symbolic form in images, books, stories, fantasies, even on television and computers.[14]

Imagine a young boy living in a typical suburb. He encounters blackbirds in his backyard, different in shape and color from other birds, but like them in having wings, feathers, the ability to fly and lay eggs, and a variety of features that signify this is a bird, not a mammal with fur, a reptile with scales and bony plates, or a fish with gills and fins. Yet the boy also knows that birds are similar to these creatures in having a backbone, quite different from insects, spiders, worms, and others of the invertebrate kingdom. Restricting himself to birds, the boy recognizes that blackbirds are songbirds and vary in basic ways from other birds like hawks, ducks, shorebirds, or seabirds. He uses this and other observations to enhance his capacity to distinguish, identify, and categorize—all skills instrumental in his growing capacity to understand and communicate. He performs analogous acts in responding to other kinds of animals, plants, geology, weather, water, landscapes, and more. All this sorting, differentiating, and naming assists him in learning to speak, in developing the capacity for language, in thinking and communicating with others.

Being a creature of the modern world, this boy spends on average ninety percent of his time indoors, reading books, looking at pictures, and devoting more than fifty hours of a typical week to watching television, using the computer, or playing video games.[15] Even in these pursuits, the imagery of nature remains prominent, and useful in advancing the capacities for language, speech, and communication.

The boy is enchanted by ancient stories and symbols of nature. For example, the blackbird he encounters in his backyard reminds him of one of his favorite nursery rhymes:

Sing a song of sixpence, a pocket full of rye,
Four and twenty blackbirds baked in a pie.
When the pie was opened the birds began to sing,
Oh wasn't that a dainty dish to set before the king?
The king was in his counting house counting out his money,
The queen was in the parlor eating bread and honey
The maid was in the garden hanging out the clothes
When down came a blackbird and pecked off her nose.[16]

Symbols inspired by nature are common in nursery rhymes and books the boy reads, as well as in the programs he sees on television and even his interaction with the computer. He is especially fond of stories like *Winnie the Pooh*,

Curious George, The Cat in the Hat, and *Where the Wild Things Are.*[17] He commonly encounters images of nature in his home, from pretty pictures of fields and mountains on the wall to animal- and plantlike forms in the furnishings and fabrics. His parents' language invokes images of nature, even if he often fails to understand their meaning. For example, he hears them say:

"You know, your friend is a pig."
"He is really a wolf in sheep's clothing."
"She's as gentle as a lamb."
"You're really driving me buggy."
"I think you're making a mountain out of a molehill."
"You're getting bogged down."
"You're stuck in a swamp."
"Honey, sweet pea, please take out the garbage."

Symbols drawn from nature are integral to language and speech. They can be heard in ordinary discourse, as well as in more imaginative and inspirational oratory. Their mundane and at times vulgar expression is often heard in the language of the street and also in much marketing and advertising. It is interesting to note in this regard the seemingly universal tendency to invoke the image of animals, usually domesticated species, to express profanity. For example, in the English language, we encounter the likes of: ass, bitch, bullshit, pig, swine, cock, cur, cunt (from the old English word for bunny or cunny), and pussy, among others.[18]

Savvy marketers are especially adept at using symbols drawn from nature to "hawk" their products. We encounter this in nearly any popular publication. I randomly select by way of illustration a copy of the magazine *Vanity Fair*, said to derive more revenue from advertising copy than any other American publication. Within its covers, I encounter ads that include oaks, maples, palms, grass, forests, flowers, wreaths, pastures, prairies, shorelines, beaches, oceans, lakes, rivers, rain, snow, dogs (repeatedly), cats, horses, giraffes, hippos, elephants, geese, gannets, seals, butterflies, stone walls, and images that are not literally found in nature but are clearly inspired by natural shapes and forms.[19] I turn to a more serious news publication, the *Economist*, and again randomly select an issue. I encounter at the outset a cover that shows a banana on wheels with the caption, "Toyota slips up." Within the magazine's covers, I find advertising that includes windmills on a prairie, a door decorated with garlands, a dog selling pharmaceuticals, a butterfly net capturing butterflies and carbon dioxide, a hotel bedecked in greenery, a smart phone on a rocky outcrop beaten by waves, snowflakes that promote tourism, a starfish marketing software, a satellite picture of the earth suggesting the strength of an insurance company, a foundation whose logo is a stately tree, a bird used to promote a business school.[20]

The symbolic use of nature to market products is also common in electronic media. An article in the *New York Times* business section focuses on the pervasiveness of the use of animals to promote products on the most expensive event in advertising, the Super Bowl football game. Under the headline "Super Bowl Was Animal Lovers' Paradise," the reporter observes:

> The Rams, Bengals, and Eagles were missing from Super Bowl . . . along with the Colts, Jaguars and Cardinals. But in their absence, advertisers unleashed

20. The pig is often portrayed as foul, dirty, stubborn, stupid, and slothful, giving rise to metaphoric labels for human characteristics, such as pigheadedness, living in a pigsty, and pigging out.

an ark's worth of animals upon the game's record estimated audience. . . . The beasts conscripted into pitching products on what is considered the biggest day in advertising included frogs, buzzards, horses and a penguin . . . cattle . . . lions and elephants and zebras . . . wolves . . . a spunky goldfish . . . not to mention the pigs . . . the skeleton of a dinosaur . . . and the animated panther and coyote. . . . Animals in fact accounted for almost a quarter of the 47 spots that ran nationally during the game. . . . These marketers were no doubt strongly influenced by the . . . popularity of animals in popular culture. . . . Clearly, most people love animals, particularly when they are portrayed in an anthropomorphically pleasing manner.[21]

An arguably more elevated use of nature as symbol occurs in poetry and the speech of great orators. Poets frequently invoke the image of nature to convey more vivid impressions and meanings. "Lines Written in Early Spring," by the nineteenth-century English poet William Wordsworth, illustrates this tendency:

I heard a thousand blended notes,
While in a grove I sate reclined,
In that sweet mood when pleasant thoughts
Bring sad thoughts to the mind.

To her fair works did Nature link
The human soul that through me ran;
And much it grieved my heart to think
What man has made of man.

Through primrose tufts, in that green bower,
The periwinkle trailed its wreaths;
And 'tis my faith that every flower
Enjoys the air it breathes.

The birds around me hopped and played,
Their thoughts I cannot measure:—
But the least motion which they made
It seemed a thrill of pleasure.

The budding twigs spread out their fan,
To catch the breezy air;
And I must think, do all I can,
That there was pleasure there.

If this belief from heaven be sent,
If such be Nature's holy plan,
Have I not reason to lament
What man has made of man?[22]

Nature as symbol is also encountered in the speeches of great orators as a way of capturing an audience's attention. Symbolic associations often include metaphors, allusions, and stories intended to enthrall those who listen or read. The oratory of the nineteenth-century American statesman Daniel Webster, sometimes referred to as "the Great Orator," is illustrative. His speeches often include images and symbols originating in nature. For example, in a speech to his fellow legislators before the Civil War, he used natural imagery in his struggle to convey the tragic folly of the nation's dissolution:

> When my eyes shall be turned to behold for the last time the sun in heaven, may I not see him shining on the broken and dishonored fragments of a once glorious Union. . . . Let [the states'] last feeble and lingering glance rather behold the gorgeous ensign of the republic . . . not a stripe erased or polluted, nor a single star obscured . . . but everywhere, spread all over in characters of living light, blazing on all its ample folds, as they float over the sea and over the land, and in every wind under the whole heavens, that other sentiment, dear to every true American heart,—Liberty and Union, now and for ever, one and inseparable![23]

The master of all rhetorical contexts, William Shakespeare combines poetic form with oratorical fervor in the play *Julius Caesar*, giving Cassius speeches that employ natural imagery to captivate and convey meaning to the audience:

> The fault, dear Brutus, is not in our stars,
> But in ourselves, that we are underlings.[24]

In more recent times, the great statesman Winston Churchill often invoked the image of nature to elicit interest and response, often using humorous associations for the purpose. Among his remarks:

> I am fond of pigs. Dogs look up to us. Cats look down on us. Pigs treat us as equals.

> Some people regard private enterprise as a predatory tiger to be shot. Others look on it as a cow they can milk. Not enough people see it as a healthy horse, pulling a sturdy wagon.

It was the nation and the race dwelling all round the globe that had the lion's heart. I had the luck to be called upon to give the roar.[25]

The Trumpet of the Swan is an example of children's literature in which symbolic nature is used to encourage children's character and personality development. Many children's stories, from ancient legends and fairy tales to contemporary fantasies and even dreams, employ imagery of nature to confront basic and often difficult issues of maturation and identity. As we have seen, the issues encountered include conflict, competition, coping, challenge, pain, suffering, sadness, loss, need, desire, authority, power, pleasure, loyalty, and betrayal.[26] Animals are often enlisted in anthropomorphic disguise to render these tales more enticing, enchanting, beguiling, and less threatening, especially when the issues involve conflict with parents and other powerful adults. When animals talk and act like people, and fantastic landscapes vaguely resemble home and human communities, the unsettling issues of authority, autonomy, abandonment, love, hate, sexuality, and death are camouflaged and often muted.

Representations and images of nature are used to address and confront critical issues of childhood development. This occurs in such classic tales as "Cinderella," "Little Red Riding Hood," "The Three Little Pigs," "The Frog Prince," *The Arabian Nights*, "Hansel and Gretel," *The Jungle Book*, and *Alice's Adventures in Wonderland*.[27] A similar tendency can be found in such twentieth-century children's stories as *Peter Rabbit*, *The Lord of the Rings*, *Goodnight Moon*, *Charlotte's Web*, *The Incredible Journey*, *Winnie the Pooh*, *Black Beauty*, *Anne of Green Gables*, *Peter Pan*, *The Wind in the Willows*, *The Secret Garden*, and *The Wizard of Oz*. Whether ancient or contemporary, these stories reveal the universal tendency to use nature as symbol to advance personality and character development, as children everywhere struggle with the basic challenges of safety, security, dependency, selfhood, identity, family, community, authority, obligation, and morality.

The pioneering psychiatrist Harold Searles argued that a child's experience of nature, both real and imagined, remains fundamental to his or her maturation and development. Searles identified four aspects of personality development in which the nonhuman world is especially instrumental in children's growth and identity:

- *Self-realization*: nature used to assist children in forming a secure sense of identity and self, including developing the capacities for discovery, creative expression, and recognizing one's abilities and limitations;

- *Sense of reality*: nature used to engage the world as real, including one's rightful and responsible place in it;
- *Assuaging pain and anxiety*: the natural world invoked to mitigate children's feelings of aloneness, separation, and fear;
- *Appreciating and accepting life*: the experience of nature used to assist in developing children's capacity to value life and accept responsibility for its nurturance and care.[28]

Searles emphasized that these processes of personality development depend on contact with actual nature in the "real" world of the outdoors. Yet he also recognized the importance of symbolic nature experienced in the form of story, myth, fantasy, and dream in confronting, navigating, and resolving issues of personal identity, pain, aloneness, reality, separation, fear, responsibility, love, care, and valuing life.

The social ecologist Paul Shepard also explored the importance of nature as symbol in children's personality development. Like Elizabeth Lawrence, he emphasized the special role of animals in this regard. Shepard identified three important functions in children's maturation addressed by the symbolic use of nature, particularly animals: speech and language development, personal identity and selfhood, and thought and communication.[29] He described the particular impact on identity formation of symbolizing nature and animals:

Personal identity is not so much a matter of disentangling the self or "the human" from nature as it is a farrago of selected correspondences in which aspects of the self are projected into the dense, external world [of nature] where they are discovered among a variety of animals who are both similar [to] and different from us. Aspects of the animal are then reintrojected into our psyches by a wonderful chemistry of imitation. When we observe this unlikely agency at a distance, animals seem like mediators, appearing in music, story, song, narration, dance, and mime as participants in the narrative.[30]

Nature as symbol and representation is also evident in children's outdoor play, where fantastic projection onto the world of reality is an important part of the experience. Children commonly create make-believe worlds of wonder in their backyards, in trees, in parks and open spaces, even in abandoned lots and what has been called "leftover" nature. This play may take place in "real" nature, but it frequently involves fantasy, imagination, and invention. The childhood recollections of the writer and poet Dylan Thomas offer a vivid illustration of this occurrence in a small park in the Irish town where he was raised:

Though it was only a little park, it held within its borders of old tall trees, notched with our names and shabby from our climbing, as many secret places, caverns and forests, prairies and deserts, as a country somewhere at the end of the sea.

And though we would explore it one day, armed and desperate, from end to end, from the robbers' den to the pirates' cabin, the highwayman's inn to the cattle ranch, or the hidden room in the undergrowth, where we held beetle races, and lit the wood fires and roasted potatoes and talked about Africa, and the makes of motor cars, yet still the next day, it remained as unexplored as the Poles. . . .

And that park grew up with me; that small world widened as I learned its secrets and boundaries, as I discovered new refuges and ambushes in its woods and jungles; hidden homes and lairs for the multitudes of imagination.[31]

The use of nature as symbol to advance children's personality and character development occurs across all cultures and throughout the ages. Its cross-cultural expression is described in such seminal works as Joseph Campbell's *The Hero with a Thousand Faces*; Sir James Frazer's *The Golden Bough*; Carl Jung's *Man and His Symbols*; and the anthropological writings of Robert Redfield, Margaret Mead, Claude Lévi-Strauss, and Richard Nelson, among others.[32] The ubiquity of this strategy suggests a biological and evolutionary basis. Elizabeth Lawrence, focusing on animals in a passage applicable to nature more generally, reflects on this universal tendency:

The universality of animal symbolism throughout the world and over eons of time indicates the profound significance of this inherent form of biophilia. Vestiges of the ancient beliefs of our ancestors retain their place in our minds, inextricably interwoven into the human condition because we are evolutionarily and physically, as well as aesthetically, spiritually, psychologically, and emotionally, tied to our animal kin.[33]

The importance of nature as symbol is also revealed in much decoration and design. Representation and images of the natural world commonly occur in fabrics, furnishings, coverings, art, and architectural and landscape design. The symbolic expression of nature in the built environment is something we have called biophilic design, a subject treated in chapter 10.[34]

Symbolizing nature in decorative design is explored in the Victorian architect Owen Jones's seminal work *The Grammar of Ornament*.[35] In this epic study, Jones reveals how often the shapes, forms, and principles of the natural world occur in ornamentation and design. This aspect of ornamentation is found throughout the world irrespective of geography, culture, and history, suggestive of its universal and biological basis. Jones encounters this tendency to symbolize nature in the ornamental designs of preliterate hunter-gatherer peoples, Arabic peoples, Chinese and other Asian societies, India, Turkey, ancient Greece and Rome, Renaissance Italy, and a host of European nations down to the present. The wide variety of cultures yields distinctive designs, each reflecting the particular genius of the peoples and historic influences contributing to it. Yet what is constant is the use of nature in symbolic form to convey basic meanings and understandings.

These designs are also rarely exact copies of nature, but instead often fantastic and surreal, diverging broadly from anything encountered in the natural world. Still, they adhere to authentic principles and processes found in nature. Many of the best designs avoid mimicking nature but maintain their authenticity and achieve their effects through the creation of original forms inspired by nature. Jones describes this critical quality of outstanding design:

> In the best periods of art all ornament was rather based upon an observation of the principles which regulate the arrangement of form in nature, than on an attempt to imitate the absolute forms of those works. . . . True art consists in idealising, and not copying, the forms of nature. . . .
>
> We think it impossible that a student fully impressed with the law of the universal fitness of things in nature, with the wonderful variety of form, yet all arranged around some few fixed laws, the proportionate distribution of areas, the tangential curvatures of lines, and the radiation from a parent stem, whatever type he may borrow from Nature, if he will dismiss from his mind the desire to imitate it, but will only seek to follow still the path which it so plainly shows him, we doubt not that new forms of beauty will more readily arise under his hand, than can ever follow from a continuation in the prevailing fashion of resting only on the works of the past for present inspiration.[36]

In this chapter I have emphasized the importance of symbolizing nature, with a focus on its role in language, communication, human development, decoration, and design. What happens when this symbolic capacity is stunted? Could a decline in the ability to invoke the image and representation of nature invite a corresponding weakening of the human ability to think, communicate, create, and design? Could this be occurring today, when environmental degradation and alienation from nature appear to be spreading afflictions of modern life? Could the arguably diminished quality during the past century of much

21. In *The Grammar of Ornament*, the nineteenth-century architect Owen Jones described the symbolic portrayal of nature in ornamentation and design.

contemporary art, architecture, language, oratory, poetry, communication, and design be symptoms of this growing malaise? Elizabeth Lawrence ponders this possibility:

It is difficult to predict the ways in which our diminishing interactions with the natural world . . . will affect expressions of cognitive biophilia. . . . If we continue our current policy of destructiveness toward nature, does this mean that human language will contain fewer and fewer symbolic references to animals [and the natural world]—with consequent impoverishment of thought and expression?[37]

We hope this is not the case, that the actual and symbolic experience of nature will remain an integral aspect of human thought, communication, and development, and will continue to enrich our imagination, health, culture, and design. Like the poet Walt Whitman, we seek a world where nature remains a vital source of who and what we are, where "the press of my foot to the earth springs a hundred affections."[38] This will necessitate that we maintain a rich and varied real and symbolic connection to the natural world of which we are a part. This relationship may be illustrated by the personal interlude that concludes this chapter, an encounter with a bird, the peregrine falcon, in the city where I live.

Interlude

This experience involved two adult peregrine falcons and the young they reared in a park not far from my home. The peregrine falcon is a bird of prey found across the globe from the tundra to the savannah and even occurring in many cities. Roughly the size of a crow, the bird is renowned for its speed; it is said to be the fastest creature on Earth, reaching almost two hundred miles per hour during its predatory swoop. It typically kills its prey by the concussion of contact after its high-speed dive from great heights—canyon rims, cliffs, and even urban skyscrapers. The peregrine generally feeds on other birds.

Peregrines and people have a long history of close association, starting with the bird's partial domestication some three thousand years ago for the purpose of hunting. The ancient sport of falconry can involve five species choreographed into a deadly dance—the peregrine, a dog to locate and flush prey, sometimes a horse to access remote locations, the prey, and the falconer, using his or her big brain and romantic aspirations to lead and organize this lethal ballet.

In the twentieth century, the peregrine falcon fell victim to the ravages of modern chemistry, mainly the widespread application of powerful pesticides like DDT to control agricultural pests and disease-carrying insects. DDT subverted the peregrines' reproductive processes by thinning the shells of their eggs to the point of collapse. The result was the near extinction of the species in the United States and many other nations. In the eastern United States, the bird was entirely extirpated.[39]

The good news is that the peregrine has largely recovered in the United States following a ban on DDT in the 1970s. This restriction resulted from the heroic efforts of many people and organizations, particularly Rachel Carson and the publication of her seminal book *Silent Spring*.[40] Peregrines are found throughout the United States today, including the northeastern states. They have adapted well even to large cities, where skyscrapers for perching and an abundance of prey, especially pigeons, provide ample food and suitable habitat. For example, in 2011, twenty breeding pairs of peregrine falcons occurred in New York City.

I was personally delighted by the discovery in 2009 of peregrines returning to nest in my hometown, a moderate sized city in Connecticut. In spring 2011 a pair nested on a narrow ledge on a steep cliff in a park not far from my home, where, with the aid of a spotting scope, I observed the birds for much of the breeding season from the comfort of my bedroom window. I enjoyed watching them dive for prey, build their nest, and feed and care for their young.

The peregrines became a symbol for me and others of renewal and rebirth of nature in the modern city. They triumphed not just over poisons but over the presumption that the routine destruction of life, while regrettable, was a practical by-product of the benefits of contemporary life and a morally acceptable outcome. The birds became symbolic of a new covenant of connection with nature and reconciliation for past abuses toward the natural world. They helped us atone for grievous wrongs inflicted, and introduced the possibility of a new relation to the world beyond ourselves. Their return to the city signified a more enlightened humanity aspiring to live in nurturing relation to a universe of creation, even while remaining technologically advanced and residing in a highly constructed, densely populated, and increasingly constructed world.

9

childhood

The importance of contact with nature in children's health and development has been considered in previous chapters. It will be central to this chapter, with a particular focus on the significance of children's experience of the outdoors. Children's need for contact with nature is a reflection of our species' inherent need to affiliate with the natural world as a basis for fitness and productivity. People possess an unusual and perhaps unique capacity for lifelong learning, but as for any species, childhood is the most critical period of maturation and development.

All forms of contact with nature are important to children's health and maturation. As we examined in the previous chapter, symbolic communication can exert a positive and beneficial effect on children's development, especially in our ever more indoor and electronically wired world. Additionally, indirect contact with nature—caring for a pet, working in a garden, tending to a houseplant, maintaining an aquarium, or visiting a zoo or nature center—can provide important experiences for children. Yet there is no sufficient substitute, as a basis for children's learning and development, for the direct experience of nature in the outdoors. Both theory and evidence suggest that the outdoors exert a unique and irreplaceable influence on children's health and maturation. Moreover, this impact tends to be most significant when children have the chance to engage in "free play" in the outdoors, relatively unrestrained by adults. Unfortunately, children's experience of the outdoors, especially in a free-play context, has precipitously declined in modern times, and the result has been a growing threat to their physical and mental health and development.

As an initial insight into the developmental importance of the outdoors for children, imagine an eight-year-old girl fascinated by frogs. Jane's interest in frogs is initiated by seeing pictures and reading books about these odd-looking amphibians, so different, yet familiar to her. She finds frogs fascinating, cute, and amusing. Jane particularly likes the stories of the Frog Prince and Frog and Toad, and watching Kermit the Frog on television. She enjoys picture books of frogs, which she often colors, and she has a number of toys and stuffed animals of frogs. She also has a video about frogs that shows many different kinds of frogs and better reveals what they look like and how they live.

Jane loves these books, pictures, television programs, and films about frogs, but she remains uncertain about how these creatures really live and behave and, in general, what it's like to be a frog. Sensing her frustration, her parents arrange for Jane to visit a local nature center and the city zoo, where she can see live frogs, some that live nearby and others from far away. During these trips, the frogs come to life in so many ways for Jane, revealing themselves as far different and even more interesting than she had previously thought.

At the nature center, Jane has the chance to touch and hold frogs. It makes her queasy at first, but eventually she grows to like the feel of frog skin, and learns how to hold the animals gently and how not to hurt them. At the zoo, Jane also learns many interesting facts about frogs from the signs her father reads to her, and the helpful people who work there. She is amazed by the incredible variety of frogs from around the world, particularly their many differences in shape, size, and color. Yet after a while, she is overwhelmed and even becomes a little bored. Still, Jane loves her visit and has learned more about frogs from her trips to the zoo and the nature center than she knew from her books, television shows, and video.

Jane continues to think and fantasize about frogs, wishing she could visit the nature center and zoo more often. She imagines the lives frogs actually live—how they behave toward other frogs, the places that they inhabit, how they make a home and have families, what happens when frogs run into people and other wild animals who might want to eat or otherwise harm them. Jane yearns to see frogs in places where they actually live, and she becomes determined to do so.

She decides to visit a nearby park and pond not far from her home. She knows she will find frogs there, because just the other day her father told her that the loud noises she heard in the early morning and late afternoon were made by a kind of frog called a spring peeper. Jane is amazed when her father informs her that all that noise comes from little frogs, sounds that seem more like a bird to her than a tiny frog. Her father also identifies another, deeper sound they hear as coming from a different kind of frog; this sound, she agrees, is definitely more froglike.[1]

Jane is afraid to go to the pond alone, as it is surrounded by a muddy and creepy swamp. She decides that for a venture this huge and risky she needs to ask her best friend, Kate, who is always ready for an adventure, to join her. It will be their secret expedition, as she knows that neither Kate's parents nor her own would give them permission to go there on their own.

Kate enthusiastically agrees and they decide to sneak away early Saturday morning just before sunrise, when everyone is still sleeping. All week Jane plans, thinks, and worries about their expedition. By the time Saturday arrives she is a nervous wreck. But she gets up early and goes to meet Kate at their secret hiding place behind a bunch of bushes in her backyard. It is still early spring and cold outside, especially in the early morning. Jane finds Kate and, shivering, they set out for the pond, comforted by the thought that the predawn chill will probably keep most people indoors.

As they approach the swamp, they hear a chorus of cries from the spring peepers. Getting closer, the noise becomes so loud it seems like there must be a million frogs. Excited, they move quickly into the high grass and reeds, but then suddenly everything becomes quiet. They push more forcefully through the reeds, sinking into the muck, finally reaching the pond. But there is no sound or sight of frogs, as if they had imagined all that noise or the frogs had mysteriously vanished into thin air. The girls retreat from the pond, sitting quietly on the wet grass on a slope not far away. But after a while, the sound of the frogs begins again, first only a few cries, then not long after an orchestra of peepers playing their symphony. The high-pitched sounds become shriller and louder, and then almost deafening.

This time Jane and Kate approach the pond slowly and stealthily. Still, it is difficult to be entirely quiet as they have to push through the tall reeds and sink into the horrible muck. Gradually, they get closer, and the frogs continue to call. Trying to quiet the sound of the parting reeds, they crawl on their knees, braving the disgusting mud. The frogs still cry out, though every once in a while they become silent when she and Kate make too much noise. When this occurs, the girls freeze in place, and before long the frogs resume their calls.

Finally, Jane and Kate arrive at the edge of the tall grass and see the standing water. At first, they are disappointed, because they don't see any frogs, though the noise of the peepers continues. Then Kate notices a tiny frog at the base of a tall reed of grass near the pond's edge, and soon they realize that they hadn't seen the frogs before because they are so small; the girls had been looking for much larger animals capable of making such a large noise. Looking carefully now for the tiny frogs, they see many peepers, not more than an inch long, generally along the bottom of the tall grasses. The tiny frogs are different colors, some brown, others gray and tan, a few dark green, each with an unusual X across its back. The girls can tell these frogs are making the loud noises, because a little sac under their chins rises and swells like a balloon, then collapses and inflates again along with the sounds.

After Jane and Kate have stayed beside the pond for a long time, they notice other, larger frogs with bright green-yellow heads and bulging eyes just poking through the surface of the water. These frogs make circles in the pond and cluster about strange-looking masses of egglike blobs.

After a while, the smell of the pond and swamp becomes so strong it stings the girls' eyes. They are also frightened by the sudden and shocking appearance of a green-striped snake, which grabs one of the bigger frogs and pulls it into the grass. In the wake of this incident, all the frogs, including the peepers, disappear, and the place becomes completely quiet. By this time, mosquitoes have begun to bite them. The combination of cold, snake, mosquitoes, and muck, not to mention fear that their parents will by now have discovered their absence, makes them think this a good time to leave.

On their way home, the excited girls talk nonstop about frogs. They speculate about the lives of these critters, their families, who besides snakes eats them, what they eat; Jane recalls reading that spring peepers mainly like beetles, ants, and spiders. They wonder how the different kinds of frogs get along with one another and the other animals of the pond, how they manage to survive the long cold winters, and whether a person who dies can come back as a frog.

When they arrive at her house, Kate's parents are there. The two sets of parents had guessed that the pair had gone off together, but they didn't know where, and they were just about worried enough to call the police when the girls arrive. Their parents are angry at first, and there is a good deal of scolding. After Jane and Kate explain where they went and what they went for, the adults calm down somewhat. Eventually their parents agree it is all right to visit the pond to see, hear, and learn about frogs and the other creatures there, but only after getting permission, and only with an accompanying adult.

She and Kate do make three more expeditions to the pond, each time becoming more familiar with frogs, the swamp, and the plants and animals there. They also learn how to better hide themselves to avoid disturbing the frogs and the other pond critters. One time they even catch frogs and examine them carefully, finding the creatures slimy and unpleasant to touch, but they are careful not to injure the animals, letting them go each time. After touching the frogs, the girls worry that they might contract some disease, and when they get home, they scrub themselves vigorously.

Years afterward, when they are adults with families of their own, they occasionally see each other and reminisce about their great frog adventures as if they had traveled to the wildest place on the planet. They are still proud of their courage as eight-year-olds. They admit that the swamp was spooky and creepy to them, a place where they imagined hidden dangers and unseen and watchful eyes. Yet they also saw the pond and swamp as magical and powerful, a place they had feared but also respected and come to revere. They also recognized that those times instilled in them a lifelong curiosity about and even love of nature that has stayed with them as adults—emotions that they now try to impart to their children.

Our young fictional girl has come to know frogs through stories, pictures, television, video, a zoo, a nature center, a swamp, and a pond. The representational and captive contact she experienced with frogs provided a gratifying wealth of information, but these encounters offered only a restricted kind of knowledge, appreciation, and personal connection with these animals. These sources lacked the information richness and sensory stimulation of her direct encounters with frogs in the swamp and pond. Her vicarious and indirect experiences of frogs were deficient in the vital elements of challenge, adventure, surprise, coping, and even the fear and awe afforded by the outdoors. The pond and the swamp were so much more physically demanding, emotionally salient, and even intellectually rewarding than the indoor and supervised experience of nature.

This story hints at the many reasons why the outdoors remains not only crucial but an irreplaceable source for children's learning and development. Another important aspect of the girls' outdoors experience was its "free play" quality, which allowed them to engage nature in spontaneous and independent ways relatively free from adult control. Free play involves elements of coping and adaptive behavior that rarely occurs through either the representational experience of nature in books and pictures or the managed contact afforded by interactions at an aquarium or a visit to a zoo or nature center.

What are some specific attributes of the outdoor experience that generally make it a more powerful source for children's learning and development than indoor, representational, or managed contacts with nature? Among the most important are its greater degree of variety, challenge, complexity, unpredictability, immediacy, and even danger. These characteristics especially provoke a child's curiosity, imagination, creativity, problem solving, and independence. And the successful resolution of outdoor challenges generally fosters self-confidence and self-esteem.

Consider the extraordinary detail and diversity a child encounters in the outdoors. This variability is revealed in many kinds of plants and animals, geology and soils, changing weather and atmospheric conditions, diversity of landscapes and environmental circumstances, and variations in season and time of day. This versatility provides an endless source of sensory stimulation, detail, and information richness that no book or Web site can match, regardless of sophistication and clever design.

Nature is also in a constant flux; even the most ordinary settings, from a backyard to a corner lot or nearby park, are characterized by shifting conditions and a high degree of uncertainty. These dynamic elements command a child's attention, offering challenge and necessitating adaptive behaviors and coping responses.

The outdoors is also a world of instability and unpredictability, and the inevitable and sometimes intense surprise and even mystery that accompany this volatility. All this instability necessitates coping and problem-solving behaviors on the part of the child. This uncertainty can sometimes be scary for children, but it can also create a sense of adventure, and a chance to build self-confidence and self-worth.

Additionally, the outdoors is multidimensional and complex. Children encounter an abundance of organisms and landscapes, shifting over time and place. Many of these elements are systemically related, providing a practical lesson in ecology for children as they encounter a world of connection, cooperation, and competition. They also experience the reality of community rather than the illusion of a life lived alone and apart.

Perhaps the most compelling feature of the outdoors is that it is the place children engage other life on its own terms and in its own world. Children possess a primal, atavistic attraction to life, especially nonhuman animals. Living creatures can attract and repel, but rarely do they prompt indifference in children. Life's appeal is irresistible to them, and a foundation for learning and maturation. As the conservation biologist Robert Pyle has observed, a child is more likely to be aroused by a direct encounter with a slug or a grasshopper than by the most unusual animals read about in books or even seen on television and experienced at the zoo:

A face-to-face encounter with a banana slug means much more than a Komodo dragon seen on television. Electronic mediation may effectively convey facts and impressions and reinforce interest, but when the world comes edited for maximum impact and bundled into quick bites and bytes, it fails to convey the everyday wonder of the much maligned ordinary. Just as real life does not consist of car chases and exploding buildings, nature is much more about grasshoppers in the pigweed than rhinos mating on a pixilated screen.[2]

22. The outdoor experience exerts a powerful effect on childhood development, especially when parents actively encourage such encounters.

Free play and other spontaneous contact with the outdoors can be an especially potent source of children's learning and development. Free play almost always means challenge, surprise, creativity, and the need for coping and adaptive behavior. Sometimes this degree of independence and separation from adults can produce anxiety, risk, and the prospect of failure and worse. Yet adversity, if not paralyzing, offers unrivaled opportunities for personal growth and the building of self-esteem.

The health and development benefits of playing outdoors were assessed by the physicians Hillary Burdette and Robert Whitaker in a review of the scientific literature. They concluded:

> While playing outdoors a child is likely to encounter opportunities for decision-making that stimulate problem solving and creative thinking because outdoor spaces are more varied and less structured than indoor spaces. In addition, there are usually fewer constraints outdoors on children's gross

motor movement and less restriction on their range of visual and gross motor exploration. Together these factors do not prescribe or limit activity-induced curiosity and the use of imagination. . . . The problem solving that occurs in [outdoor] play may promote executive functioning—a higher-level skill that integrates attention and other cognitive functions such as planning, organizing, sequencing, and decision making.[3]

A backyard or a nearby park can provide children with a wealth of opportunity for examining, exploring, discovering, imagining, fantasizing, coping, and solving problems. The outdoors is generally referred to as the "real world" for good reasons, in contrast to the artificiality and contrivance of the indoors. The real world of the outdoors is dynamic, enriching, and alive, with also the potential for setback and failure that can result in injury, suffering, and even the witnessing of death. Yet these difficult and at times tragic circumstances afford children the chance to become aware of reality's limitations and dangers, and the necessity for struggle and perseverance. The outdoors exposes children to a world where sadness and suffering are as much a part of life as pleasure, satisfaction, and joy. This experience, too, is basic to maturation and development.

As the psychiatrist Harold Searles asserted more than a half-century ago: "The non-human environment, far from being of little or no account to human personality development, constitutes one of the most basically important ingredients of human psychological existence."[4] Unfortunately, little research has occurred since this was written (in 1960) on the role of nature in children's physical and mental health and development. For example, the 2005 *Cambridge Encyclopedia of Childhood Development* lacks a single chapter or even an index citation on the subject of children and nature.[5] Fortunately, there has been a recent surge of study of children's experience of nature and its impacts on their health and development. Reflecting this change, the Children and Nature Network has published five annotated bibliographies on the "Health Benefits to Children from Contact with the Outdoors and Nature."[6]

Figure 23 synthesizes the foregoing discussion by identifying factors critical to how children's experience of nature shapes their physical, emotional, intellectual, and moral development.

The importance of the biophilic values to children's health and development should by now be evident. What follows thus is a summary reprise of these likely developmental impacts:

- *Affection*: Children's emotional attachment and love of nature encourages the development of their capacities to give and receive affection, bond and relate to others, and develop a sense of caring and compassion.

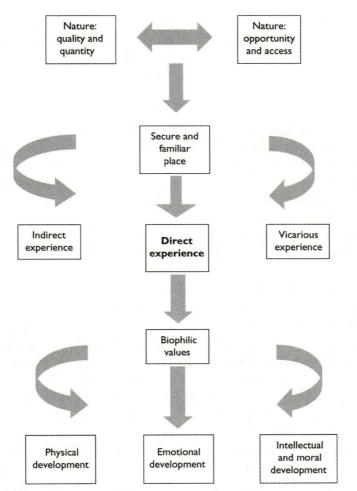

23. The role of nature in children's physical and mental health and development.

- *Attraction*: Nature's aesthetic appeal and beauty assists children in developing their aptitudes for curiosity, creativity, exploration, discovery, imagination, organizing complexity, and discerning balance and harmony.
- *Aversion*: Coping with anxiety and fear in nature facilitates children's handling of challenge and adversity, building self-confidence and self-esteem, and cultivating feelings of respect for the natural world.
- *Exploitation*: The material benefits people derive from the natural world, as well as the ability to exploit nature for this purpose, provide children

with a sense of reality, feelings of competence, physical and mental skills, and independence and autonomy.

- *Reason*: Contact with nature encourages the development of children's cognitive skills, including understanding, analysis, evaluation, and judgment.
- *Dominion*: Children's exercise of control over nature fosters the development of physical and motor skills, problem solving, coping with adversity, courage, and feelings of independence and autonomy.
- *Spirituality*: Connecting with nature ignites children's sense of relationship to a world beyond themselves that seems meaningful, valuable, and purposeful to them.
- *Symbolism*: Children's representational experience of nature promotes language and verbal skills, the ability to communicate, and personality and character development.

A secure and familiar relation to place is also critical to children's health and maturation. Children need to feel safe and acquainted with nature to be motivated to experience it in satisfying and beneficial ways. The average child is wary, cautious, and not unusually threatened by the outdoors when the experience occurs in strange and unfamiliar places. People are largely territorial creatures inclined to attach themselves to a particular setting, because over the long course of human evolution, familiarity and understanding of certain localities greatly enhanced safety, security, access to resources, and the ability to move across and make sense of one's environment. This territorial need is especially strong in children as a consequence of their relative helplessness and much greater dependence on others. When children feel familiar and secure in the places they encounter, they are far more likely to access, engage, and experience nature than if these places seem strange and unknown. Dropping a child into the wild, even in settings rich in resources and beauty, is far less likely to elicit interest and involvement than places they know and understand well.[7]

Despite theory and growing evidence that nature plays a critical role in children's health and development, we have witnessed in the modern age a precipitous decline in children's contact with the outdoors. This decrease prompted the journalist Richard Louv to coin the term *nature-deficit disorder*, to bring attention to the growing disconnect between children and nature in the modern world and its potentially adverse effects on their health and maturation. "Within the space of decades," Louv writes, "the ways children understand and experience nature has changed radically. For a new generation, nature is more abstraction than reality. Increasingly, nature is something to watch, to consume, to wear—to ignore. . . . Our society is teaching young people to avoid direct experience in nature."[8]

The biologist Robert Pyle has also decried children's diminishing contact with nature, referring to it as an "extinction of experience." Pyle is especially disturbed by a dramatic decline in outdoor free play among youth today. As a result, he writes, "We lack a sense of intimacy with the living world. The extinction of experience implies a cycle of disaffection. The extinction of experience sucks the life from the land, the intimacy from the connections. As cities and metastasizing suburbs forsake their natural diversity, their citizens grow removed from personal contact with nature, awareness and appreciation retreat."[9]

Although nature-deficit disorder does not exist as a clinically diagnosed condition, and it is an exaggeration to refer to an extinction of experience, Louv and Pyle draw our attention to a drastic decrease in children's direct contact with nature, and the potentially dire effects of that decline on their physical and mental health and development. Empirical evidence is still fragmentary, but its cumulative weight is consistent and convincing, and warns of the dramatic decrease in children's contact with nature:

- The typical child today spends less than forty minutes of an average week outdoors, compared with more than four hours twenty years ago.
- Ninety-six percent of adults report the outdoors was their most important environment during childhood, while forty-six percent of children today acknowledge this importance.
- Thirty-one percent of children regularly play outside, compared with more than seventy percent of their mothers when they were children.
- In 2010, children spent fifty-two hours of an average week engaged with the electronic media of television, computers, and video games. In 2005 this already high figure was forty-six hours per week.
- The average eight-year-old child's "home range" (the area where the child plays outside on his or her own) has decreased by ninety percent during the past half-century.
- The average child today spends ninety percent of his or her time indoors.[10]

Collectively, these statistics point to a profound decline in children's contact with nature and the outdoors. What are factors contributing to this decline in contact with the natural world? In summary form, the following appear important:

- The diminishing quality of the natural environment has resulted in fewer opportunities for children to experience rich and diverse natural systems, especially local species and habitats.
- Adults increasingly restrict children's free play outdoors, tending to replace this time with structured activities like organized sports.
- Children and adults are often less familiar with local outdoor environments than in the past.
- There is increasing emphasis on children learning through primarily formal education in indoor settings.
- The dramatic expansion in electronic media, particularly the television and computer, have encouraged children to substitute indoor and vicarious experience for the outdoors and direct contact with nature.

24. Mounting evidence suggests a precipitous decline in children's contact with the outdoors. The typical child today spends less than forty minutes playing outdoors each week, and more than fifty-two hours in an average week engaged with electronic media.

- The growth of the human-built environment and increasing reliance on vehicular transportation have contributed to a growing separation of children from nature.
- Households in which both parents work and the decline of the extended family have resulted in less time outdoors and fewer adults serving as outdoor role models for children.[11]

Together, these factors have conspired to create a host of impediments to children's contact with the outdoors. Growing awareness and concern regarding these trends, and their potentially adverse impacts on children's health and development, have spawned a movement aimed at reconnecting children with the outdoors. In the United States, noteworthy efforts especially include the pioneering work of the Children and Nature Network and the No Child Left Inside movement.[12]

I am also encouraged by children's intuitive realization of the importance of nature in their lives. Reflecting this recognition and even unconscious awareness, the chapter concludes with three interludes—two fictional stories and three poems—that reflect children's continuing contact with the natural world.

Interlude

Of Forests and the Sea

I remember it as a mostly tumbledown world, geographic precision being of little concern at age six, when physics is more feeling than substance. All I knew was that my world had this peculiar pitch gradually leading down through outdoor furniture and then winding through paths and thickets eventually to the road. The path across the road passed through beach roses and poison ivy before entering spiky grass, where thousands of ticks lurked, waiting to pounce. You were almost at the beach here, although you still had many stones to cross. A few prickly plants grew in this world of high sand beyond the tides and waves; in the spring, they formed a carpet of yellow, pink, and blue flowers. Beyond the rocks and plants lay the beach, exquisite, soft, stretching on endlessly, a place where time passed so slowly it almost seemed to stop and bend backward.

A trip to the beach often included Mom, older siblings, occasional cousins, friends and their parents, and sometimes neighbors. It wasn't unusual to meet someone on the beach you didn't know but who became a new friend. Even when by yourself, you never felt alone because there were so many things to do, and so many creatures in the sand, below the sand, in the water, in the air, just about everywhere. The place teemed with crabs, beetles, terns, fish, cormorants, and fishermen. Though I rarely brought much with me, I was never bored. The beach provided endless adventure and exploration with few specific objectives or destinations.

It was just a big pile of sand, unending monotonous color stretching unchanged to the horizon and complementing a gray sea. Yet it always enthralled us. We passed hours like minutes, punctuated by forays into the cool waters to shed the irritating heat or, sometimes, excess energy. We built forts, castles, channels, and moats, chased after crabs, engaged in small but never unimportant acts. Why did this pile of sand so enchant us? Perhaps because we felt intensely alive. We molded wonders from raw creation, modifying the world around us but never fundamentally changing or diminishing it. We simply reorganized its "beachness," enlarging its properties and boundaries.

The beach was a special part of our neighborhood. Ours was a small village by the sea in the mid-1950s. I have learned since then that people in the cities can be as numerous as flies living close to one another but still be mostly alone and apart. In our neighborhood, though, people always seemed aware of one another as if the place were alive. Don't get me wrong—not everyone liked everyone else, and we were certainly not some saintly group. We had plenty of rivalries, jealousies, petty quarrels, and worse. Yet most of us operated in a kind of shared mutuality, a respectful alliance and feeling of responsibility for the whole, especially for the young. Whether we liked it or not, everybody knew just about everybody else.

We were also aware, especially the kids, of our physical world, taking pride, and even a measure of identity, in our special blending of the human with the natural. The houses were covered in rarely painted cedar shingles, the gray textures seemingly merging with the land and the muted colors of the sea. For unknown reasons, most homeowners left the surrounding pine-oak forest and understory of bayberry and blueberry largely untouched rather than converting them to grass and ornamental shrubs. Still, nearly everyone had a lawn bordered by flowers and gardens that thrived in the humid air. These were mostly modest additions that soon blended back into the forest. The forest itself was simple, consisting mostly of two kinds of trees, pitch pine and scrub oak. The area was known historically as the pine barrens, because few trees and plants survived in its mostly sandy, impoverished soil. Yet people seemed to like that simple pine-oak forest as if it defined what was normal and expected about our neighborhood. People were reluctant to get rid of the trees, perhaps captivated by the sounds of the prairie warblers and bobwhites in spring and of the screech owls and cicadas in summer, or by the cushion the trees provided against the biting winds and northeasters of fall and winter. I suspect the adults also responded to the wonder shown by the kids in response to the forest and sea—and perhaps by the kids they still carried around in themselves.

For us children, the forest and sea were our neighborhood, our place of unending exploration, adventure, and discovery, perhaps even the birthplace of our sense of beauty and respect for creation. We constructed places of wonder in its bushes and brambles, bush houses and games of challenge and competition at the frontiers of curiosity and creation. We also relished being apart from the adults, though always close by, wild but within striking distance of security, engaging in various risks but not too removed from the comfort and shelter of our homes and backyards. The hazards were real to us—skunks, poison ivy, ticks, climbing too high or falling too far, venturing away and perhaps getting lost, coming too close to the choppy waters and being swept away. Like all children, we tested the boundaries of our world, probing and indulging our curiosities and inventiveness. Most of the adults accepted this craving for adventure but rarely endorsed it aloud, usually warning us instead of the dangers of disregarding our fears.

Still, this world of intimacy had its share of somber moments, even terrible ones, which I recall today with an almost paralyzing sadness. Above all else, I remember the death of my father and, soon after, nearly losing my own life as well. I don't wish to indulge my particular pathos, recognizing how often boys and girls lose their parents to premature death, whether by accident, illness, or more deliberate design, and yet learn to get on with the business of living. Still, his death when I was six years old lodged a sense of inexplicable loss in my gut like some deep black hole I continue to carry around inside of me as if it were a disaster waiting to happen.

I knew Dad was ill, but his illness hardly registered in my young brain as something that could end a life so central to my existence. No one explained to me how sick he was, probably assuming, as adults often do, that young people need to be shielded from the realities of pain and irreversible loss. So one night when Dad, stricken once more, was rushed to the hospital, it didn't occur to me that I would never see him again. When it finally became clear, the intensity of the news was bewildering and I denied it, looking for some different, more plausible explanation.

Looking back, I believe the only thing that kept me from becoming entirely swallowed up by my sadness was the forest—most particularly the company of a wren. I had by then retreated to the woods, because it was a good place to be alone. I also secretly hoped that I could wander about and perhaps find Dad again. One time while sitting in the woods, I retreated into a strange fantasy, imagining myself far off in some backcountry, a place of deep craters and broken ground and a peculiar dark purple and blue sky above. I followed a tortuous route, being called back only after a long while by a distant, distracting sound. The sound became louder and more insistent and, finally, impossible to ignore.

As my fantasy dissolved, out of the haze emerged a small wren. The tiny bird perched on a low branch no more than a foot from my nose above a thick, dwarfish tree. Its shiny eyes stared at me intently, its small head crowned by a lighter curved stripe, speckled white spots on its brown body, the creature's smallness at odds with the intensity of its call and its seemingly angry eyes. The bird's song as much as its presence commanded my attention, forcing me to retreat from my sorrow. Its song rose in a loud, aggressive melody, hypnotic and forceful, an ebullient cry from a creature so small it would have fit in the palm of my hand.

Only the most optimistic would think that the wren had actually been singing to me, imparting some brand of solace. But to my six-year-old brain—and, truthfully, to part of me today—I was convinced that it was. At the time, I did not doubt that the bird was communicating with me and, in fact, recognized me. Wrens were very much a part of our lives back then, thriving in the pine-oak forest at the margins of the wild and tame, each morning loudly advertising their presence, sounding at first light with their long lyrical cries, taking possession of the woods as if they owned it, the sound always shocking when you spied its tiny origin.

More important, wrens had occupied a special place in our family, and not long before, one had actually become an unofficial part of the household. This event had occurred the previous spring, while we were on vacation. A female wren had flown through the laundry room window mistakenly left ajar and proceeded to build a nest atop folded laundry at the bottom of a wicker basket. There she sat on her unhatched eggs upon our return. Most birds confronted by people under such circumstances would have panicked and abandoned their nest. But wrens, bold and nearly fearless, are not so easily intimidated. Then too, most people encountering a wild animal in their home would chase it away or worse. But my mother just accepted the bird's presence.

So although the bird was at first agitated by the sight of my mother, it soon settled down, and Mom acted as if a nesting wren in the laundry basket was really not so unusual. The two of them—and then all of us, staring in disbelief and awe—settled into an accommodation, the wren allowing Mom to go about her laundry business while it continued to warm her eggs—and then hatch them and, along with her mate, feed the incessantly demanding chicks. The adult wrens would fly in and out of the window, bringing insects and other fare, and before long the chicks were jumping onto the windowsill and flying out. Soon enough, they disappeared back into the forest.

As I leaned against the tree that lonely, disturbing day staring in utter still-ness at the wren, mesmerized by its melodious song and fierce countenance, I wondered whether this bird might be one of the chicks raised in the laundry basket, perhaps returning to help one of those humans who had opted for its life rather than its death. I also remember wondering whether pity could be a solely human possession. What was undeniably real to me was the bird's insis-tence on my full attention as it sang for the longest time. I sat staring back, the creature inches from my face, its flutelike warble rising louder but never shrill, reaching a crescendo then tumbling back, one note falling on top of another before reaching bottom and rising again.

The song became unbearable, and I spoke to the bird. Rather than fleeing, the wren became tensely silent as it continued to pay me full and mindful at-tention. So I poured my heart out—perhaps more inside my head than aloud—telling the bird of my sufferings and seeking some explanation and validation but, of course, receiving none. Yet I felt oddly relieved, more accepting of the tenuous relation between life and death, of connections that might dissolve my terrible loneliness, comforted by a broader encompassing world that included Dad and myself. This six-year-old even wondered whether the branch, the tree, the soil, the clouds on high, a single species of bird, and a little boy could be bound by some string of substance and time.

As I stayed there, I felt myself become another speck in the woods, attuned to its many details and happenings. An ever-widening circle of awareness and connection radiated out, starting with the wren. A vole entered and exited, then a catbird, soon a honeybee, a dragonfly, beetles and ants, scrub oaks and poison ivy, the wind and the sky—all alive and a part of me. Boundaries be-tween life and nonlife dissolved. A garter snake appeared, and I felt fear and an impulse to flee. The wren spied the serpent and flew off, making me feel more alone and afraid. But I remained, and after a while, the snake basking in the warm sun became just another part of it all. For the first time since Dad's death, I felt alert and alive, preferring the company of even a snake to the loneliness of the black hole inside me.

I realized then how much I wanted to be with my family. Yet even after returning to the land of humanity, I still visited that special spot in the woods where I had encountered my peculiar communion with the wren. The place became a halfway house for me between human creation and a broader one.

I saw in the wren a parallel universe, autonomous yet familiar, a place where kinship could occur despite immense differences.

I have no desire to continue dwelling on my loss, although I must conclude with what happened next—my particular brush with mortality, an incident of terror that still makes me shudder to this day. Ironically, what occurred stemmed from the generous intentions of those helping me at the time. Walking with me during the full moon following Dad's death, my uncle pointed out a vague face in the moon that I had never noticed before. He said Dad was looking down on me. The revelation never left me, and the next day I impatiently waited for darkness to see my father's face again in the moon and perhaps get closer to him.

I went to bed early, much to everybody's surprise. When it was completely dark, I climbed down the tree outside my window. I made my way to the beach as the full moon was just above the horizon, orange and magnified by the heat rising from the ground. I stared for a long time before proceeding and then sought the rowboat beneath the pier, used to rescue people foolish enough to venture into the dangerous riptide just offshore. I reasoned with the unassailable logic of a six-year-old boy that if I could get close enough I could even talk to Dad. But we lived where two sounds joined, a place known as the chop because of its almost continuously choppy waters. Indeed, if the tide and currents were just right, as often occurred during a full moon, the waves would become a breaking surf, and even small skiffs would stay away.

My little boat soon encountered the chop and gathered speed, unavoidably turning to the northeast despite my best efforts. The water passed quickly underneath the thin hull separating me from the sea. The boat soon slipped out of my control, and I was swept out to the open water, helpless and afraid. In the distance, I could see and hear the bell of the green channel buoy, its eerie light blinking like some horrible eye. The wooden boat started to fill as seawater splashed over the sides. The boat swayed and bounced in the virulent surf, sending an awful terror through me. The boat slowly filled with water, becoming unbalanced, its rotation increasing with the swell as I paddled furiously to escape the vortex.

The boat twisted more and then suddenly flipped over. I was in the water, helplessly swept by the current, strangely wondering whether, if I drowned, I would join Dad in the sky. Despite my gathering panic, I remember thinking how warm the waters felt. I cried for help but no one heard, and even in my youth I sensed the hopelessness of it all. A peculiar calm replaced my terror as furious waves passed over me. It had been only seconds, but it felt like forever.

I then saw the blinking light of the buoy as I was carried rapidly toward it. I tried angling myself into its sweeping tide, hoping to intercept the great metal float. Some internal compass worked, and after much thrashing it appeared that I just might reach it. The buoy suddenly loomed much closer and larger than I had imagined. Hard and metallic, emerging out of the darkness, it had metal ladders joining a circular rail and walkway that encircled the structure. Sooner than expected, I was thrown against the hard metal surface, the air knocked out of me as I painfully crashed into its side. In blind panic, I somehow managed to grab onto a metal rung. Desperately holding fast, I clung to its side, rushing waters swirling past me, my life hanging by a thread of ebbing strength. Slowly, using all the power left in me, I pulled myself closer to the buoy. I felt a gentle eddy as the tumultuous waters swept past me on both sides. Exhausted, I lingered in relief before gathering some reserve and then slowly, painfully climbing one rung after another until I reached the circular shelf, where I collapsed.

I lay there drained and thankful, eventually dropping into a consuming stupor and then sleep. I was soon awakened by the noise of a helicopter and not long after by a flotilla of boats. Mother, discovering my disappearance, had started a search that soon revealed the missing rowboat.

The rest was my particular fifteen minutes of fame, followed by the more mundane business of growing up. Dad's death and my close call left some lingering wounds as well as much wisdom. If nothing else, I felt a deeper appreciation of the varied creation that surrounded me and of my rightful place within it. Even for a little boy, it bordered on a kind of serenity.

Interlude
Three Poems

OWL
Hope flies on silent wings.
Standing on that moonlight beam.
Big, but hopeful if it's seen.
Crouching down eyeing its prey.
Weaving its way through the trees
Under the moon
And that's how hope flies on silent wings.
                    Ellanora R. Lerner, age seven
SPRING
Where the wind comes
It might never come back.

Every wind has its own path.
As the red and blue come
There are flowers.
Stay . . . the sunlight comes every way
The people don't watch
The flowers bloom.
Magic comes with the little flowers that bloom.
FLOWERS—SUN—RAIN all have a different path.
SPRING.

Olivia Shaffer, age eight

DREAM
I dreamed I was in an elephant.
I dreamed I was stepped on by a giant chicken.
I dreamed I was dreaming.
I dreamed I had no brain.
I dreamed that my ears were bigger than me.
I dreamed that I had static hair forever.
I dreamed that I ate too much food.
I dreamed that when I sneezed it was a tornado.
I dreamed when I spit it was a great flood.
I dreamed that I flew to a different galaxy.
I dreamed that I was a brownie and I ate myself.
I dreamed I turned into a hockey puck and got a lot of concussions.
I dreamed I had to be cross-eyed forever.
I dreamed I finished my poem.

Peter Weinberg, age seven

Interlude

From Apple Orchards to Shopping Malls

My world had become anonymous after having lived where every bird, bush, neighbor, and school chum felt like one extended family. Mom had not wanted to move after Dad's death, but eventually she could no longer deny the difficulty of a single woman in the late 1960s finding a job in a rural area that could support three kids and pay tuition for one about to go to college. And our house by the shore had become valuable. So—sacrifice being her second nature—Mom sold it. Shortly after, we moved to the suburbs of the medium-size city where Mom and Dad had lived during college, when she had studied nursing, and Dad law.

I was sad to leave our village, but teenage boys are resilient and moving to the city seemed pretty exciting. Initially, I had no quarrel with our new town, although our neighborhood—despite its many houses—was distinguished mostly by a lack of distinction, every house looking just about like the others and the parallel streets forming a maze to challenge the savviest rodent. Still, the development had its charms, not the least being the large number of children my age and the many activities that ruled most of our days. I was also delighted that some wild places could be found not far away, though getting there required passing through a jungle of look-alike houses squarely pegged on tiny lots and surrounded by a sea of grass.

Arriving at the nearby river was more than worth the effort. At first little more than a ten-foot-wide creek and shallow enough to wade across, the river also had some deep holes where you could swim and where trout and ducks occasionally congregated. Partly because of its constant motion and many changing moods as it moved through new banks and vegetation, amid a community of critters, to us kids the river had a personality like some living thing that adapted but somehow always remained the same. One moment the river was black; the next, blinding sparkles reflected off its surface. Sometimes it was barely audible as it slid over some smooth bottom; other times, it cascaded loudly over some ledge or forgotten dam, where people had once struggled mightily to harness its fickle power.

Apart from us, though, the neighborhood seemed barely aware of the river, although I suppose most recognized its presence in less obvious ways. It certainly lent our ordinary housing development a special quality that most recognized with pride, and the homes closest to the river always sold the quickest and for the highest price. Once when a major road was proposed that would have covered a stretch of the river, the neighborhood rose like a mighty storm, howling and protesting, until the project was killed.

The world of people that surrounded this little island of wildness included our housing development, some big roads, and a nearby shopping strip astride one of the larger thoroughfares. This road was our great ribbon of commerce, the site of countless convenience stores, minimalls, fast-food restaurants, gas stations, auto dealers, and more. You could buy just about anything there— even if you could never find exactly what you wanted—and the employees never seemed to recognize you. Just beyond the main drag, a new interstate had been completed the year before, a road so large that it cut the landscape like a knife, indifferent to most natural obstacles and more than willing to transform a hill or swamp into four lanes of asphalt. Few developments had yet been built along the interstate, but rumors flew fast about the greatest of shopping malls slated to be built next to the town's last-remaining farm and one of its largest forests. The interstate and the farm were both near the high school I attended.

At the time, the high school consumed most of my thoughts, if for no other reason than that I felt like a misfit and prisoner there. Its hugeness overwhelmed me. The red brick façade, large white columns, and huge clock tower made it seem like a temple from the ancient world, a seat of power that dwarfed the lowly adolescents who occupied it. Yet paradoxically, the building's interior was drab, with dreary halls and rooms lacking color, light, or anything resembling the magnificent exterior. The teachers were largely well meaning, a few instructing with insight and eloquence, but like the students, they seemed numbed by the size and sameness of the school, its lack of stimulation dominating not only the architecture but also the pedagogy. Confronted by the raging hormones of two thousand teenagers, the administration imposed various rules and a prevailing rigidity to cap this volatile stew.

One particular day, boiling with anger out of proportion to the provocation that had stirred it, I actually bolted from the school. This would be hardly worth mentioning except that it set into motion a sequence of events that just possibly altered the rest of my life. Fleeing from school, I ran northward, away from my normal route home into a woodland, where I hoped to escape discovery and punishment. I wandered the forest, eventually becoming hopelessly lost despite my best efforts at following a deer trail, which I hoped might intersect some road.

I was completely unprepared to encounter another person, especially a scowling old man with a dog. I had become so anxious by then and preoccupied with not shifting my direction yet again that I did not notice them at first. Then, looking up, I was shocked by the sight of the baleful pair not a hundred feet ahead. I can still see the old man's stern look, the border collie beside him motionless, but its upper lip curling back over canines with a predatory gleam. Their body language clearly communicated that my presence was neither welcome nor legitimate. After watching me squirm for a while, the old man announced that I was trespassing and demanded to know why I was there. I offered clumsy, unconvincing excuses replete with promises that I would never return and pleas that he not turn me in. A heavy silence followed. Finally, he scolded me, remarking that if he had been hunting, I might have been shot, then adding various other complaints about the state of youth in a world gone awry. But having settled all territorial and social issues, the old farmer congratulated me on fleeing the sterile halls of academia and heading into the real world of fields and forests. Most shocking of all, he invited me to join him and his dog on their walk.

Gratefully accepting, I felt like a man saved from the gallows who now was, miraculously, privileged to do what he wanted to do most. We walked for a long time, the old man's angry scowl soon replaced by an animated, nonstop recitation about the land and its animals, plants, soils, and history. His knowledge was extraordinary, his intimacy with the land undeniable. His name was Mortimer Richmond, although for me, no matter how close we became, he would always be Mr. Richmond or, as he was more generally known, Farmer Richmond. He was seventy-five years old, born and raised on his farm, the sixth generation since his ancestors had settled there in the early nineteenth century. His arthritis caused him to sway, but I soon learned that he possessed more stamina than the sixteen-year-old at his side. By the time we arrived at his farmhouse, I was exhausted, yet he showed little sign of fatigue.

To say that Farmer Richmond loved the land obscured a deeper, more complicated relationship. It was more like he was a part of it, an intimate participant in its many rhythms and processes. While he obviously felt affection for the land, he embraced it with a wider breadth of emotions, including an occasional adversarial stance. His knowledge of the farm was encyclopedic, extending far beyond matters of mere utility. He delighted in the land's beauty, its secrets, the opportunities it presented for mystery and challenge, and he deeply respected and feared its power. He never grew tired of deciphering the many complexities of its creatures, both great and small. He took pride in feeling in charge, but more as steward than as a conqueror. He was a participant who collaborated rather than took and who sought to add richness to what he saw as his extended family. Farmer Richmond regarded himself as chief trafficker in the flow of materials and nutrients that passed through the land like a fountain of living energy. He took possession of the land, but always with a sense of duty and a gentleness and respect for its independent birthright.

Perhaps I make Mortimer Richmond sound like some modern druid, a kind of pagan exercising an indiscriminate love for the natural and nonhuman. That would be misleading. In fact, he reveled in manipulating the land and rarely hesitated, for example, to slaughter some animal, wild or domestic, although I never saw him do so wantonly or cruelly. He absolutely delighted in hunting, over the years having harvested just about anything legal and edible, including several creatures no longer on the list of game animals. I was initially appalled by this killing, but over time I recognized that it represented for him another way of being an active, intimate participant with the land rather than an outsider. He never killed unless he consumed his prey, consciously making the creature part of himself and, paradoxically, never hunting unless he had a reasonable chance of failing. The hunt was always serious and conducted with skill, was never seen as amusement or sport, and was practiced with restraint and never wastefully. I truly believe that for Mortimer Richmond, hunting was sacramental, another way he irrevocably tied himself to the land and its creatures.

This mentality revealed itself in his relationship not only with deer and ducks but also with domesticated animals, plants, and even the inert soils and waters. He rarely hesitated to use, manage, or consume creatures and resources, and he worked at manipulating the land to increase its productivity. But beyond the objectives of security and abundance, he sought a shared, caring relationship with the land and all its life. He saw himself as a colleague more than a controller and sought full membership in the grace of what he called the "land community." Most of all, he sought to impart a more lush, diverse, and resilient world than the one he had inherited.

I owe to Mortimer Richmond much of my abiding interest, knowledge, and emotional attachment to the natural world. At the time, I was not above exploiting his knowledge for my own purposes with surprising effect. My natural history skills increased, particularly the ability to use my ears and other senses rather than just my eyes to see and identify all that surrounded me. Farmer Richmond taught me to discern the slightest anomaly in the landscape, to locate my visual prey by recognizing the variation in the setting; in doing so, he helped me to experience so much more of interest and quality than I would otherwise have encountered. I drank deeply from this stimulation and understanding and emerged ravenous for previously unknown treasures, determined to experience as much as possible before it disappeared in a tenuous world. Given my adolescent shallowness and his gruff ways, I sometimes wonder why we became such steadfast friends, and why he took me under his wing at a particularly difficult time in his as well as my own life. Possibly he discerned a kindred spirit in this teenage boy's affinity for nature that perhaps reminded him of an earlier version of himself, albeit one needing cultivation and refinement.

He probably enjoyed my unabashed admiration, so at odds with the increasing hostility he encountered from his two children, a thirty-two-year-old son and a thirty-year-old daughter. The children had fallen under the spell of an economic fortune being dangled before this historically poor family by a major shopping center developer who wanted to purchase the farm. Farmer Richmond had already rejected three progressively higher offers for the property So while he seemed the epicenter of knowledge and wisdom to me, Mortimer Richmond's children considered him a stubborn old man who was standing in the way of wealth and status none of them had ever known or thought possible and now desperately wanted.

The farm had originally been 350 acres, but when I met Farmer Richmond, it had been reduced to about 200. He had sold lots to people who had thought they wanted a rural setting but who, once they moved there, typically objected to the pungent smell of cow manure in summer, brush burning in spring, and gunfire in the fall. Selling the lots helped financially, but the farm continued to struggle, bringing in little more than a subsistence income. Farmer Richmond raised dairy cows, but regulations, huge new industrial farms, and a growing distrust of local agriculture had marginalized his cattle operation. He had shifted to more profitable crops such as apples and established a roadside stand, but sales were seasonal and the apple business also succumbed to factory farming and the consumers' inclination for bright red, perfectly formed apples. The growing relationship between the agribusiness operators and big commercial shopping chains further undercut his efforts. Probably his worst mistake economically was refusing to bathe his soil in and subject his animals to a vast array of chemicals, pesticides, growth hormones, antibiotics, and the like. He rejected the logic of the new ways of farming trumpeted as the triumph of science and technology over nature. He denied both the rhetoric and the supposed evidence, thereby confirming for all, particularly his children, that he was an ornery primitive out of step with progress and the modern world.

Mortimer Richmond was thus perceived as an impediment to prosperity and the chance his children craved to escape the pejorative label "swamp Yankee." I am sure they loved and admired their father, having known a lifetime of his keen insight and intelligence, but they resented his stubborn desire to remain a dirt farmer. Their mother had been the family's glue; their father had been larger than life, and usually away in the fields and forests. After their mother's death, the family had grown apart, his children going to college and then moving to the city, the first generation in the family to have college educations and live apart from the land. They had become urban professionals—the son an accountant and the daughter a medical technician. They were proud of their education and that they no longer worked with their hands, smug in knowing they now earned more than their father ever had as a farmer. They occasionally visited the farm but did not find its long, hard labors and economic uncertainty appealing. To them, the farm represented backwardness and oppression—and, now, an obstacle to unimaginable wealth and security.

This all became clear to me one early Saturday morning when I arrived at the farmhouse. Mr. Richmond had told me to come early so he could show me the rattlesnake den that had miraculously survived in the forest despite the area's extensive development and influx of humanity. He had never told anyone about it before and swore me to secrecy, fearing that if it were found out, there would be a chorus of demands for the snakes' annihilation.

As I approached the house, I heard angry voices inside. Letting my curiosity get the better of me, I waited silently at the foot of the stairs. Farmer Richmond's son was berating him, arguing that the farm was worth more money than he might earn in many lifetimes and that besides, his father could use a portion of the sale to buy a bigger, better farm elsewhere. His daughter scolded their father for unfairly denying them prosperity just so he could indulge his romantic fantasy of an obsolete way of life. She claimed that the world had changed and that it was now time for them to move on and enjoy a wealth none of their family had ever known before. Farmer Richmond responded angrily and, after some heated arguing, told his children to leave and never return until they accepted his right to determine the future of the land. Looking back, I wonder whether that particularly painful moment had not provoked his children to justify their subsequent legal actions in collusion with the developer and town officials, which finally settled the issue. I later learned that the children actually owned the farm, their parents having transferred the title years before, ironically to avoid taxes that would have forced them to sell the farm.

All these Byzantine family and financial matters were irrelevant to me at the time. All I wanted was to romp in the woods with Farmer Richmond and help out on the farm. So, following his children's departure, I was delighted to set out with him in search of the incredible rattlesnake den. As always, he knew every hill, valley, stream, and wetland, never using a map or compass. He instead invoked memories of particular trees, stonewalls, creeks, and other cues that eventually led him to a nondescript spot in the woods that marked the serpents' den. I was both excited and scared by the prospect of confronting this creature that no one else knew remained in our suburban town. Also, I felt anxious around snakes despite my fascination for all wild things.

The entry to the den was at the base of a great rock tucked into a hollow almost out of sight. The hole was extremely small as we forced our way through to what Farmer Richmond promised would be a much larger cave. I was nearly paralyzed with fear as I peered into that dark hole. I probably would have fled if not for Farmer Richmond telling me he had also been terrified when he first discovered the den many years before until he had finally screwed up the courage to enter.

The cave did indeed get much larger once we entered. We then made our way to a narrow ledge where we could spy the creatures below. In the restricted light, we at first could see the coiling mass only vaguely. Because it was early spring, the cold-blooded creatures hardly moved. Still, as my eyes adjusted, I began to make out the snakes. I counted at least ten. They were oblivious to our presence at first, but soon our movement alerted them. I suppose the heat of our bodies, as much as our sound, aroused their attention; I had read that a rattlesnake's ability to sense temperature allowed it to find a mouse six feet away even if blindfolded and deprived of its sense of smell.

We squeezed into the corner of the overhanging ledge, peering down into the now-alerted colony. As minutes passed, it became apparent how little actual danger these creatures posed. A mounting confidence and false bravado took hold of me as we continued to observe the snakes in utter fascination. Looking back decades later, I recognize the moment as among the most intense of my life, totally absorbing and incredibly intimate. For that instant, the world stood utterly still and I was suspended in time and place. Many years later, I still vividly recall the sight and even the smell of the place, its shapes, the quality of the light and air, the memory of it all permanently seared into my mind. Few experiences have since offered the clarity, even peace and reverence, which I felt that day in the company of the snakes and Farmer Richmond.

For the rest of the year, I continued to roam the woods and leftover margins of our rapidly developing suburb. I had found a new sense of balance, and I carried it around inside me like some treasure. Somehow the experience seemed to have reconciled for me the solitary and the social, the civilized and the primitive, the wild and the tame. I had found my place in my town, and part of me now identified with it.

But this newly discovered calm soon disappeared before a mighty storm that descended. Following relentless, behind-the-scenes economic and political machinations, the powerful forces arrayed against Mortimer Richmond finally succeeded. Aided by a team of lawyers and officials, his children had managed to sell the property to the developers. When I first heard about it, I ran from school to the farmhouse, bursting in on Farmer Richmond and demanding to know if it was true. He confirmed the sale but, strangely, seemed less angry than tired, and determined to move on. His children had given him a golden parachute with a substantial share of the sale price. He announced to my shock that he would be moving and purchasing a new farm in upstate New York, where a modest agricultural economy still persisted and farms were available at reasonable prices. In a bewildering few months, Mortimer Richmond departed the town of his ancestors, physically and spiritually uprooted and feeling a profound loss, but relatively cheerful at the prospect of his new home and life. His children's betrayal, however, was unforgivable to him, and father and children never spoke again.

What crushed Farmer Richmond most was the developers' actions just two days following the sale. They descended on the farm with an army of bulldozers and proceeded to level more than fifty acres of forests, fields, and orchards. Soon after, the devastated landscape was transformed into a series of indistinguishable boxes and temples of merchandise decorated by an occasional prisoner shrub or tree. What had been a mosaic of apple blossoms in spring, golden grass in summer, bright leaves in fall, and lingering lavender in winter had become oppressive geometric edifices surrounded by asphalt, concrete, and an altogether suffocating homogeneity. The access road to the mall had also destroyed the rattlesnake den. I never saw or heard of one again, although perhaps a few clung to survival in some remote hollow on the water company's land.

After graduating from high school, I soon left town for college on the West Coast. The destruction of the farm had become my defining moment, closing the door on my particular childhood and home. Nonetheless, I had excelled in school, and—aided by some athletic success—I had been admitted to a prestigious university. My passion now was to become financially successful and independent. Without realizing it, I had embarked on a path that someday would transform me into those I had come to loathe. Yet despite many dead ends over the ensuing years, I would eventually return to the wisdom and spirit of Farmer Richmond and the beauty of the land. But that is another story for another time.

10

design

We now spend on average ninety percent of our time indoors in essentially an artificial, human-designed and -created world. Moreover, some four-fifths of the people living in the most developed nations, and for the first time in human history a majority of the world's population, now reside in a city or suburb, generally the most environmentally transformed and degraded of all human environments, where separation from nature has become normal.[1] Our species may have evolved in the natural world, but the "natural habitat" of people today has increasingly become the human-designed and -developed environment. This contemporary reality does not diminish people's inherent need to affiliate with nature as a necessary basis for health, productivity, and well-being. It does, however, make that goal far more challenging and difficult to achieve. Only a deliberate and knowing process of design and development, especially of our urban areas, can restore a world that nurtures and enriches the human body, mind, and spirit through its beneficial association with the natural world.

When nature and humanity exist in a complementary relationship, each prospers from the association. People inevitably transform the natural world through their development activities, especially in modern society, where we tend to rely on large-scale and rapidly implemented change. But if the relationship between people and nature is based on affection, knowledge, and respect, the outcome can be a richer and more fulfilled humanity, and a more resilient and productive nature. If this human-nature relationship is dominated instead by antagonism and disconnection, the result will be not only environmental degradation but also a more isolated and impoverished humanity. Among the greatest challenges of our time is to create good habitat for people in our cities and other designed environments that satisfies our inherent need for beneficial contact with the natural world.

Can we imagine such a possibility? Its promise and potential are reflected in the strategy of "biophilic design," in which buildings and other human constructions are designed in ways that foster people's physical and mental health through providing positive connections to nature in a context of ecological and cultural meaning. This design paradigm is innovative, but in many respects harks back to ancient practices and principles. Before addressing the specifics of biophilic design, we begin this chapter with an illustration, a personal interlude involving a park close to the urban neighborhood where I live.

Interlude

I am fond of the large and relatively undeveloped park near my home where I often walk my dogs. It has a paradoxical quality like most modern urban parks, a creature of human invention, yet retaining a wildness that surprisingly reveals an abundance and diversity of nonhuman life that continues to call it home. The park also possesses a nostalgic feeling, a place where people once labored mightily in factories or quarried its stone. Today, these are remnants of the past and the source for imaginings of a time when people largely worked the land and extracted its resources.

It's early spring when I visit the park, and one of the first things I notice is the ground cover of blooming Dutchman's breeches, among the first flowers of the year. I also see out of the corner of my eye quick and elusive movements of birds in the high branches that signal the return of migrating warblers. I walk alongside the river, and I am delighted by the sight of wood ducks, one of the most beautiful birds that nest within trees in the floodplain. I also spy a brilliant white egret at the water's edge, and on the river, mallards and geese.

The river is in full flood from recent rains and large quantities of water released by the thawing ground. Cascading water rushes over the high stone dam just upstream of the covered bridge, its volume thrilling yet unsettling. Although constructed more than two hundred years ago, the still maintained dam impounds water in an upstream lake that contributes to the area's water supply. The river rushes past the dogs and me, sunlight reflecting brightly off its swollen waters. Despite all the movement, I feel calm and content, the burden of accumulated tension seeping from me like sap from the reviving trees. Both the maples and I appear to be awakening from the long winter doldrums, sharing the rebirth of this time of year.

This park is far from pristine, and is a creature of largely human artifice and design. The old wooden covered bridge at its entrance, lovingly restored, signifies the start of the old stagecoach road leading to the state's capital thirty-two miles away. The dam beside the river marks the site where one of the new nation's first factories was constructed, a manufacturer of guns from interchangeable parts that helped launch an industrial revolution that ironically contributed to the degradation of the watercourse that I enjoy today. All that remains of the factory is a small industrial museum and widely scattered stones of buildings that once employed thousands—plus, of course, the high stone dam that provided power for the factory's pioneering mass-production techniques. The craftsmanship of the covered bridge, the masonry of the waterfalls, the remains of the old factory are impressive and beautiful in their way.

The dogs and I continue our walk along the path, taking in the meandering river, the swollen floodplain, the resuscitating forest. I hear the plaintive cries of white-throated sparrows, the raspy sounds of recently returned redwinged blackbirds, the resilient calls of blue jays, cardinals, and chickadees that lingered through the long winter, the insectlike buzz of newly arrived warblers. I cast a look at the river and can just make out the passing shadows of alewife and herring, fish returning from the ocean to spawn in the substrate of gravel at the base of the falls. I also spy a black-crowned night heron in a willow tree, and circling overhead, an osprey. Flying across my path is a mourning cloak butterfly, a colorful insect emerging from this reawakening oasis of an environmentally transformed city. I am thrilled by the sight of muskrats swimming along the distant riverbank. They remind me of once having seen river otters here, an animal far less tolerant of human proximity, and I wonder whether I will ever see them again. This in turn calls to mind the image of white-tailed deer that recently recolonized the park despite a sea of encircling people, vehicles, and development.

I have nearly completed my circuit and come again to the blossoming Dutchman's breeches, along with yellow trout lilies, blue iris, daylilies beginning to bud, and I start to anticipate spring colors to come. I am enthralled by the intense pubescent green of barely emergent leaves on the willows, oaks, birches, and beeches, the soft red buds of maples, the showy white flowers of American hornbeams. I recall that just a few short weeks before, tough skunk cabbage first appeared, this early hint of spring managing to push up through a frozen crust of snow-covered ground, heralding the elusive return of life, warm stalks resisting the cold air.

I am nurtured by this feast of sensations from these multiple signs of renewal. The neighborhood and the city remain sites of intense human activity, environmental transformation, and dominance over nature. It is a world of human creation and construction that encroaches upon this natural oasis. Yet the park remains intact, environmentally productive, distinguished by its beauty, and rich in physical, psychological, and spiritual reward for its human community. It continues to be a place where nature and humanity fruitfully interact with and enrich each other.

The cool spring morning brings the usual surfeit of joggers, dog walkers, the first birders of the year, resplendent in their gear, like the returning birds they seek. Later in the day, there will be families walking together, a few picnicking, students and teachers visiting the industrial museum and water education center, some early anglers working the spillway and bridge. The water supply provided by the impounded river relies on a newly installed primary, secondary, and tertiary treatment plant that replaced the obsolete one hundred year–old system that once pioneered an innovative sand filtration process. And there are the ghosts of the old armory, the great dam, the wooden covered bridge that marked the start of the ancient highway.

The park retains a health and vitality that benefits the human community, despite historic scars and continuing insults. This contribution inspires affection, appreciation, and, among some who engage it, respect and stewardship. There persists a mutually beneficial relationship between people and the natural world. People relish this place for the relaxation, understanding, and beauty it brings. It retains qualities of symmetry, even a hint of harmony, which add currents to the warming air that contribute to the reviving spring.

NATURE AND THE HUMAN-BUILT ENVIRONMENT

The interlude of the park reflects a multiplicity of values people extract from largely intact and productive natural systems even in a modern city. Yet like most urban parks, this is a restricted and limited exposure of people to nature, an exceptional, not routine, part of their lives. By contrast, the dominant reality of contemporary life, especially in the modern city, is one of development marked by environmental degradation and disconnection from nature. Indeed, no other human-engineered activity seems more committed to the belief that human progress relies on the transformation of the natural world and the dream of people transcending their natural origins and biological roots.

If measured by environmental impact, construction and development in the United States has had a profound impact. It accounts today for one-fifth of the nation's pollutants, one-quarter of its wastes, one-third of its greenhouse gas emissions, and nearly forty percent of the country's consumption of fossil fuel and water resources. Moreover, most of our structures are designed as if people, like some machine or artificial technology, no longer require contact with the natural environment.[2] The average office worker in the United States today, for example, toils in a windowless setting, breathing processed air, surrounded by artificial chemicals and materials, enclosed within small cubicles, generally cut off from natural features or processes. These office settings are so sterile that they remind us of the barren cages of the old-style zoo, now ironically banned as "inhumane" to nonhuman animals. Yet modern office workers are expected to be alert, motivated, and productive in these featureless and sensory-deprived environments. Many are instead plagued by fatigue, poor morale, and a panoply of physically and mentally debilitating symptoms. Researchers are now learning that introducing into these barren settings plants, pictures of nature, and views to the outside can enhance worker comfort, satisfaction, and productivity.

Yet the lamentable reality is that the great majority of our office buildings, as well as our shopping malls, manufacturing facilities, educational institutions, housing developments, and other standard constructions are characterized by widespread environmental damage and separation from nature. The everyday experience of these structures is one of sensory deprivation, where monotony, artificiality, and the widespread dulling of the human senses are the norm rather than the exception. This failure of our typical designs and developments prompted the political scientist David Orr to remark:

> Most modern buildings and landscapes reflect no understanding of ecology or ecological processes. Most tell [their] users that knowing where they are is unimportant. Most tell [their] users that energy is cheap and abundant and can be squandered. Most are provisioned with materials and water and dispose of their wastes in ways that tell [their] occupants they are not part of the larger web of life. Most resonate with no part of [our] ecology, evolutionary experience, or aesthetic sensibilities.[3]

Recent progress in what has been called "sustainable design and development" has certainly improved this situation. Yet this change has mostly focused on reducing environmental damage caused by modern construction and development. This "low-environmental-impact approach" largely emphasizes avoiding pollution, eliminating chemical toxins, minimizing waste, increasing energy efficiency, decreasing water and other resource use, mitigating adverse ecological impacts, and reducing carbon emissions. This focus on minimizing and avoiding environmental damage caused by building and construction practices is reflected in the most widely adopted guide to sustainable design in the United States, the US Green Building Council's LEED (Leadership in Energy and Environmental Design) system.[4]

These low-environmental-impact strategies aimed at reducing environmental damage are without question necessary and laudable. By itself, however, minimizing environmental harm is an insufficient basis for achieving true and lasting sustainability, and will not ameliorate the prevailing malaise of people increasingly cut off from their need to affiliate with nature. Low-impact designs do not enhance human physical and mental well-being because they fail to focus on the beneficial experience of nature. By ignoring the human need to connect with nature, these constructions are often experientially and aesthetically impoverished.

Ultimately, low-impact design fails to achieve its goal of sustainability, because it falls short of nurturing the physical and mental benefits that create the emotional and intellectual attachment that motivates people to be good stewards of their constructions and to retain them over the long term. Technology inevitably becomes obsolete, and even the most energy-efficient or low-toxicity innovation will not preserve a building whose occupants lack commitment to these creations and are inclined to abandon these structures once they have lost their technological edge. Sustainability remains an elusive goal if it requires people to build something new to achieve its objectives. As the architect James Wines suggested: "People will never want to keep an aesthetically inferior building around, no matter how well stocked with cutting edge thermal glass, photovoltaic cells, recycled materials, and zero emissions carpeting. The mission is also to recover [our] . . . connectedness with nature."[5]

Low-environmental-impact design has largely failed to address the need to restore and reconnect people with nature in our constructed environments. This is the fundamental lesson of biophilia, whose accomplishment in the built environment necessitates biophilic design, the missing link in most sustainable design. Development that incorporates both biophilic and low-environmental-impact design can achieve true and lasting sustainability, what we call restorative environmental design. Environmental degradation and alienation from nature are not inevitable consequences of modern life but rather failures in how we have deliberately chosen to design and develop our world. We have designed ourselves into this predicament, and we can design ourselves out of it.

But, what specifically is meant by biophilic design, and how can it be achieved? As I have suggested, biophilic design reflects an ancient understanding, and its principles are revealed in structures throughout human history. Indeed, some of the world's most admired buildings and designs possess powerful affinities for the natural world. As the psychologist Judith Heerwagen has remarked: "Many of the world's most revered buildings contain biophilic features. That is, they contain the essence of natural objects without being exact copies. They draw on design principles of natural forms."[6]

But what specifically are the elements of biophilic design? We might start with two historic examples—the great cathedral in Chartres, France, and the more contemporary residential design Fallingwater in rural Pennsylvania, designed by the architect Frank Lloyd Wright. These are extraordinary constructions, yet they highlight certain prominent characteristics of biophilic design.

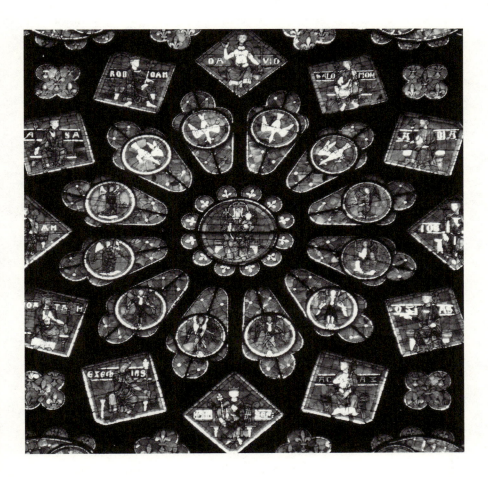

25. Like much sacred architecture, Chartres cathedral reflects the inspiration of nature in its materials, shapes, and forms, including the aptly named rose windows.

Chartres cathedral, like most sacred architecture, is inspired by an inherent affinity for nature reflected in its materials, shapes, forms, principles, and processes.[7] For example, its exterior is largely stone and wood, its towers and spires are reminiscent of trees, its exterior doors and façade bear carvings that evoke features of the natural world, its arches and supports reflect organic forms. Within the building's interior, great vaulted spaces mimic the loftiness of the outdoors, pools of sculpted natural light stream through many colored stained-glass windows, great treelike columns rise and lift the structure like a forest canopy. Nature is redolent throughout and seen in the many simulations of foliated leaflike ornaments and vine-, shell-, egg-, and fernlike forms. Natural materials predominate. Above all, its 176 stained-glass windows, particularly the great rose windows, allow hues of colored natural light to stream into the building interior. The organic forms and tracery of the windows in turn lift the gravity-bound ground dweller up and out of the building, back into nature.

Fallingwater, by contrast, is a contemporary construction designed for private rather than public use. Yet like Chartres, it owes its extraordinary appeal, which attracts hundreds of thousands of visitors annually to its remote location, to its profound affinity for the natural world.[8]

The building captivates the visitor by a palpable sense of connection to the landscape. It sits astride a waterfall, which appears to flow out of the structure, conveying the feeling of being a participant in rather than a spectator of the natural world. The building's long horizontal plane and stone façade blend into the surrounding ledges and forest, making the structure seem a part of the landscape rather than simply a product of human engineering.

Within the building's interior, extensive natural lighting, the widespread use of natural materials, and vistas to the outside reinforce the sense of connection to nature. Large overhanging eaves and great cantilever terraces further join the building to its landscape, yet in ways that thrill by the precipitous perch high above the cataract and waterfalls. As at Chartres, decorative glass brings sculpted natural light into the structure. Deep interior living spaces provide a sense of refuge, while vistas and prospects from these interior spaces to the outside enhance the feeling of connection to the distant landscape. The rooms are visually linked, and that, along with the widespread presence of stone and other natural materials and fireplaces, results in a paradoxical sense of security and spaciousness.

Both Chartres cathedral and Fallingwater reflect powerful affinities for nature and fundamental attributes of biophilic design. The architect David Pearson describes these qualities of biophilic design as "rooted in a passion for life, nature, and natural forms . . . full of the vitality of the natural world with its biological forms and processes."[9] Both buildings contrast sharply with much contemporary design characterized by the extensive presence of artificial materials, sensory-deprived and featureless environments, windowless settings, processed air, aesthetic impoverishment, and ecological and cultural separation from place.

Chartres cathedral and Fallingwater also provide clues to basic elements and attributes of biophilic design. For example, both structures widely employ natural materials, natural lighting, shapes and forms inspired by nature, connections between interior and outside spaces, place-based relationships, and other design features that reflect an affinity for the natural world. Can we be more precise, however, regarding the features of biophilic design? We need to go beyond illustrative examples and subjective impressions to a more precise specification of the elements and attributes of biophilic design because the

26. Much of the appeal of Frank Lloyd Wright's residential design Fallingwater derives from its seeming emergence from the landscape, particularly the waterfall on which it sits.

rapid pace and large-scale tendencies of modern development often exert enormous and irreversible impacts.

With this goal in mind, six elements and more than seventy attributes of biophilic design have been specified. These biophilic design features encompass a variety of direct, indirect, and more subtle ways people can experience nature in modern buildings and constructions. These elements involve more than the direct experience of nature—contact with actual plants, animals, water, landscapes, or the outside environment, for example. People often limit the experience of nature in buildings to actual contact with natural features. They assume that biophilic design only means bringing plants into a building, relying on natural lighting, constructing a water feature, improving views to the outside, or adding naturalistic landscaping. These are all important expressions of biophilic design. But just as important is to encourage the indirect and representational experience of nature in constructions and other human designs: strategies that mimic forms found in nature, simulate organic shapes and patterns, stimulate a diversity of senses, and a variety of other means.

These direct, indirect, and subtle expressions of biophilic design are described below; a fuller description can be found in other publications and a video.[10] The six design elements include:

1. *Environmental features*—Characteristic features of the natural environment such as sunlight, fresh air, plants, animals, water, soils, landscapes, natural colors, or natural materials such as wood and stone.
2. *Natural shapes and forms*—The simulation and mimicking of shapes and forms found in nature. These include botanical and animal forms such as leaves, shells, trees, foliage, ferns, honeycombs, insects, other animal species, and body parts. Examples include treelike columns rising in a building interior to support a roof that projects the feeling of a forest canopy; building shapes that simulate the appearance of bird wings; ornamentation that intimates a natural shape like a crystal or geological feature.
3. *Natural patterns and processes*—Functions and principles of the natural world, especially those that have been instrumental in human evolution and development. For example, designs that stimulate a variety of senses, simulate the qualities of organic growth, or reflect the processes of aging and the passage of time.
4. *Light and space*—Spatial and lighting features that evoke the feeling of being in a natural setting. These include natural lighting, a sense of spaciousness, and more subtle and indirect expressions such as sculp-

tural qualities of light and space, and the integration of light, space, and mass.

5. *Place-based relationships*—Connections between buildings and the distinctive geographic, ecological, and cultural context of particular places. This may be achieved by the incorporation of geological and landscape features, the use of local and indigenous materials, and the occurrence of particular historical and cultural traditions.

6. *Evolved human relationships to nature*—Basic inclinations to affiliate with nature, such as the feeling of being in a coherent and legible environment, the sense of refuge and prospect, the simulation of living growth and development, or the evocation of various biophilic values.

These elements of biophilic design are in turn revealed through more than seventy attributes. Each attribute offers a pathway for eliciting people's affinity for nature, even though these connections may sometimes be quite indirect and obscure. A detailed delineation of the attributes of biophilic design can be found in the book *Biophilic Design: The Theory, Science, and Practice of Bringing Buildings to Life*, and a sixty-minute video, *Biophilic Design: The Architecture of Life*.[11] What follows is a brief listing, with some illustrative examples of how positive connections between people and nature can be achieved through design and development.

The biophilic design element of environmental features includes the following attributes: air, light, water, plants, animals, geology, landscape, natural habitats, ecosystems, fire, natural materials, natural views, and natural colors. The attribute of color, for example, figures prominently in human evolution. As a largely daytime species with a strong visual orientation, people have historically used color to identify food sources and safe and secure settings, spy danger, locate potable water, or organize and navigate complex landscapes. This affinity for color is reflected in the universal appeal of flowers, sunsets, rainbows, colorful foliage, and certain plants and animals, and is often revealed in building and ornamental design. Another important environmental feature is water. Some of the most consistently appealing designs simulate shapes and patterns reminiscent of flowing water, or incorporate water into such building features as fountains and pools. People also possess an inherent attraction to natural materials like wood, stone, and clay, which have played significant roles in human evolution and development.

Natural shapes and forms are revealed in the following biophilic design attributes: plant and animal forms; the shapes of shells, spirals, eggs, and ovals; geological patterns; rounded and curved forms; simulating natural features;

27. Many biophilic designs suggest rather than directly mimic organic forms. The Sydney Opera House, for example, reminds some viewers of bird wings, others of a bird of paradise plant.

and the mimicking of organic forms. For example, a considerable amount of ornamentation and architectural design is reminiscent of leaves, foliage, ferns, cones, shells, insects, and a variety of plants, animals, and natural features. Often, these resemblances are not exact copies of what we find in the natural world. A powerful illustration is the famous Sydney Opera House, which reminds us of bird wings or a bird of paradise plant, or the TWA Terminal at New York's John F. Kennedy International Airport, which also resembles a bird in flight. Nonetheless, neither structure is anything like an actual bird, plant, or feature found in nature.

Natural patterns and processes are even more subtle expressions of the human affinity for nature. Design attributes include the stimulation of diverse senses, information richness, organic growth and development, the sense of aging and the passage of time, patterned images and bounded spaces, similar forms at different scales (fractals), hierarchically organized relationships, the relation of parts to wholes, linked series and chains, central focal points, and dynamic balance. Each of these attributes reflects the human response to patterns and processes in nature that over time have contributed to human fitness and survival. For example, some of the most successful building and ornamental designs stimulate our senses and elicit our response to detail, variability, and information richness such as we might encounter in nature. These qualities arouse our awareness, attention, and engagement, and often imaginative and creative response. By contrast, featureless designs devoid of sensory stimulation strike us as monotonous and dull, provoking boredom and fatigue, no matter how efficient they may be. On the other hand, if the detail and variability we encounter is not coherent and organized, then we face the opposite problem of feeling overwhelmed by what seems chaotic and confusing. Some of our most effective designs possess variability that is patterned and structured, conditions often facilitated by such biophilic design attributes as parts connected to wholes, linked spaces, central focal points, or fractal geometry.

Light and space include the following attributes: natural light, filtered and diffused light, light and shadow, reflected light, pools of light, warm light, light as shape and form, spaciousness, spatial variability, space as shape and form, spatial harmony, the integration of light, space and mass, connections between inside and outside spaces, and transitional spaces linking interior and exterior environments. For example, people have an affinity for natural light, which studies have found enhances attentiveness, motivation, and productivity. Moreover, varying the motion and shape of light and space can create more stimulating and satisfying experiences and more informative environments.

Place-based relationships reflect the human desire for settings that feel familiar, safe, secure, intelligible, and accessible. Design attributes include connections to the geology and ecology of particular places, a feeling of relationship to the culture and history of these locations, the integration of culture and ecology, the use of local and native (indigenous) materials, landscape features that help define building forms, what have been called a "sense or spirit of place," and avoiding its opposite, a sense of "placelessness." Some of our most effective architectural and decorative designs evoke strong affinities for the ecology, natural history, and culture of certain localities, often referred to as "vernacular design." By contrast, much dissatisfaction with contemporary design and the so-called international style characteristic of many modern structures is a pervasive feeling of disconnect from the geographical and historical context. The geographer Edward Relph describes this feeling of "placelessness":

> If places are indeed a fundamental aspect of . . . security and identity . . .
> then it is important that the means of experiencing, creating, and maintaining significant places are not lost. There are signs that these very means are disappearing and that "placelessness"—the weakening of distinct and

28. Dissatisfaction with much contemporary design reflects a feeling of "placeless-ness," the disconnection from local culture, history, and geography.

diverse experiences and identities of places—is now a dominant force. Such a trend marks a major shift in the geographical bases of existence from a deep association with places to rootlessness.[12]

Finally, "evolved human relationships to nature" is something of a mis-nomer, as all the biophilic design attributes reflect some element of evolved human adaptation to the natural world. What makes this last design element distinctive is its emphasis on fundamental aspects of the human evolutionary affinity for nature. In this regard, attributes include designs that elicit any of the basic values of biophilia, such as affection, attraction, aversion, exploitation, reason, dominion, spirituality, and symbolism. Other basic aspects of our in-herent response to the natural world include the desire for prospect and refuge, change and metamorphosis, and order and complexity. For example, some of our most satisfying architectural and decorative designs possess opportunities for both prospect and refuge, where we feel safe in secure settings, but are none-theless stimulated and informed by seeing long distances and having broad views. Likewise, we often find appealing designs that capture the dynamic qual-ities of change and metamorphosis characteristic of life and the natural world.

A summary of the six biophilic design elements and more than seventy at-tributes is found in Tables 2 and 3.

Do these various biophilic design elements and attributes exert a significant beneficial impact on people's lives, given that our world is increasingly artifi-cial, fabricated, and urban? Although the data remains sparse and fragmentary,

TABLE 2. ATTRIBUTES OF BIOPHILIC DESIGN

ENVIRONMENTAL FEATURES	NATURAL SHAPES AND FORMS	NATURAL PATTERNS AND PROCESSES
Natural materials	Botanical motifs	Sensory variability
Natural colors	Animal motifs	Information richness
Water	Shell and spiral forms	Age, change, patina of time
Air	Egg, ovular, tubular forms	Growth and efflorescence
Sunlight	Arches, vaults, domes	Central focal point
Plants	Tree and columnar supports	Patterned whole
Animals	Shapes lacking right angles	Bounded spaces
Natural views and vistas	Simulation of natural features	Transitional spaces
Façade greening	Resemblance to natural features	Linked series and chains
Geology and landscape	Geomorphology	Integration of parts to wholes
Habitats and ecosystems	Mimicking organic function—"biomimicry"	Similar forms at different sales—"fractals"
Fire		Dynamic balance and tension
		Complementary contrasts
		Hierarchically organized scales

TABLE 3. ELEMENTS AND ATTRIBUTES OF BIOPHILIC DESIGN

LIGHT AND SPACE	PLACE CONNECTIONS	EVOLVED RELATIONS TO NATURE
Natural light	Geographical connection to place	Prospect and refuge
Filtered and diffused light	Historical connection to place	Order and complexity
Light and shadow	Cultural connection to place	Enticement and curiosity
Reflected light	Ecological connection to place	Change and metamorphosis
Light pools	Indigenous materials	Affection and attachment
Warm light	Landscape orientation	Attraction and beauty
Light as shape and form	Landscape ecology	Exploration and discovery
Spaciousness	Integrating culture and ecology	Fear and awe
Spatial variability	Sense or spirit of place	Information and understanding
Space as shape and form	Avoided placelessness	Mastery and control
Spatial integration of light, mass, and scale	Landscape features that define building form	Security and protection
Inside-outside spaces		Reverence and spirituality

increasing evidence suggests that biophilic design can enhance people's physical and mental health, productivity, and well-being. For example, research in office and manufacturing facilities has revealed that improved natural lighting and natural ventilation, the use of natural materials, the presence of vegetation, and pictures of nature can enhance worker satisfaction, morale, motivation, and attentiveness, while reducing stress, absenteeism, and illness-related symptoms.[13]

An especially informative study was conducted by the psychologist Judith Heerwagen and colleagues, who examined the effects of a new office and manufacturing complex constructed for an office furniture company in Michigan. The new facilities included such biophilic design features as greater natural lighting and natural ventilation, extensive interior vegetation, widespread use of natural materials, restored wetlands and prairie habitats, outdoor sitting and picnic areas, and walking trails. The study examined workers before construction, immediately following its completion, and nine months after employees had occupied the new manufacturing complex. Nine months following the move to the new facility, the researchers reported a twenty-two percent increase in worker productivity, significant improvements in job satisfaction, better health, reductions in stress, increased morale, and a twenty percent increase in employees' sense of well-being.[14]

Educational studies of high school and grade school students also found that significant improvements in natural lighting, natural ventilation, and access to the outdoors, along with a decrease in the use of artificial materials, resulted in improved standardized test scores, less sickness and absenteeism, reduced health problems, and improved attentiveness. Teachers in these schools also reported improved morale, fewer health problems, and a decreased inclination to seek employment elsewhere.[15]

Healthcare studies have also found that increased patient exposure to vegetation, outside views, and pictures of nature results in improved rates of healing, faster recovery from illness and surgery, diminished need for medication, and, among psychiatric patients, fewer restraints and behavioral problems. Previously cited studies by Roger Ulrich of patients recovering from gall bladder surgery, and by Aaron Katcher and colleagues of patients recovering from heart surgery, found that increased contact with nature resulted in improved healing, recovery, and reductions in the use of painkillers and other sedatives.[16]

Ulrich also studied patients and visitors to a hospital emergency room before and after its redesign. The original emergency room was a featureless, windowless space that included plain white walls and extensive artificial materials and furnishings. This emergency room was notorious for its high levels of stress, hostility among users, and aggressive behavior toward hospital staff. The redesign of the emergency room included an aesthetically attractive mural of plants and animals in a colorful landscape, natural fiber chairs and carpeting, various organic shapes and forms introduced into the space, and some vegetation. It is notable that this redesign mainly included symbolic and representational

29. Dr. Roger Ulrich examined a hospital emergency room before and after its re-design. The original emergency room was a featureless and windowless space of white walls and artificial materials. The redesign included an aesthetically attractive mural of plants and animals in a colorful landscape, naturalistic fabric designs and colors, plants, and organic materials. Researchers found significant reductions in stress, hostility, and aggressive behavior among people using the redesigned facility.

expressions of nature rather than any significant increase in contact with actual elements of the natural world. Moreover, the room remained the same windowless space. Still, the researchers reported significant reductions in stress, hostility, and aggressive behavior among people using the facility following its redesign.[17]

Similar indications of the benefits of biophilic design have been found at the scale of a neighborhood or community. For example, colleagues and I conducted an ambitious study of an entire watershed in south central Connecticut, home to some 500,000 people in a roughly two hundred–square mile area. The watershed encompasses the drainage of three rivers that converge at Long Island Sound in the city of New Haven, with a population of roughly 130,000. Land use in the watershed is thirteen percent urban, twenty-four percent suburban, eleven percent rural, eleven percent agriculture, and forty-one percent open space under mostly forest cover.[18]

This study examined the relationship between the quality of the natural environment and people's physical and mental well-being in eighteen urban, rural, and suburban communities. Many indicators were used to assess environmental quality, including water quality, pollution levels, biodiversity, rates of nutrient cycling, invasive species, and other measures. Human quality of life was assessed by such diverse indicators as property values, household and neighborhood quality, crime rates, employment, transportation, roads, recreational opportunities, open space, and more qualitative measures such as attachment to place, optimism, and perceived safety and security.

The study found a significant correlation between environmental quality and the quality of people's physical and mental lives. Conversely, it revealed that the more degraded and damaged the natural environment, the more likely residents were to report a lower quality of life and less positive values of nature. These results occurred in urban as well rural and suburban neighborhoods, and among all education and income groups. The study also found that the relationship between environmental quality and human quality of life was highly influenced by prominent landscape features of special significance to people. These included large and stately trees, attractive streams and water bodies, prominent geological features, and parks and open space. For most people, the study's measures of environmental quality—vegetative cover, nutrient cycling, hydrologic regulation, biomass, dissolved oxygen, invasive species, and other biophysical indicators—are either unimportant or largely unknown. What most people do recognize and appreciate, however, are landscape features and land uses that reflect these underlying conditions, such as aesthetically appealing landscapes, fast-flowing and clean streams, pleasant and uncongested roadways, noneroded and fertile soils.

In other words, relatively healthy natural systems give rise to landscape features that people value and appreciate. These features in turn encourage them to design and maintain structures and communities that reflect their perception of a high quality of life and a good place to live. When these connections between environmental and human quality of life occur, people tend to be far more motivated to take responsibility and be good stewards of their communities and places. Few people who lived in these communities depended on the land to make a living, with many commuting long distances to jobs increasingly tied to a global economy. Still, in subtle ways, their sense of a worthy life remained tied to their experience of nature and design features that fostered a healthy and attractive natural environment.

Even in places where the natural and human-constructed environments are impoverished and people are poor and have limited economic and social opportunities, the experience of nature has been found to yield significant benefits. This was the important finding of a study of a Chicago public housing project whose residents were largely poor African-Americans.[19] This 2001 investigation focused on publicly owned sixteen-story apartment buildings. Residents were randomly assigned to the buildings, and the structures were architecturally identical and generally regarded as aesthetically unappealing. The only major difference between the buildings was the landscape, with some units having grass and a scattering of trees, while others were surrounded by concrete and asphalt. All the buildings had previously been surrounded by vegetation, but many of these landscapes had been replaced by artificial surface, presumably for safety and ease of maintenance reasons.

The researchers examined the health and quality of life of residents of all the buildings, controlling for a wide range of potentially confounding factors such as age, sex, income, education, and others. They reported that residents of the buildings surrounded by natural landscaping had lower rates of crime and drug use, were healthier and better able to cope with stress, had more effective social ties, were more optimistic about the future, were more positively attached to the buildings where they lived, and showed better "cognitive functioning." These findings emerged even though the natural landscape of the buildings consisted of poorly maintained grass and a small number of trees. As the Chicago researchers concluded:

Attentional performance [was] systematically higher in individuals living in greener surroundings; and management of [social and psychological] issues [was] systematically more effective for individuals . . . living in greener surroundings. It is striking that the presence of a few trees and some grass outside a 16-story apartment building could have [such a] measurable effect on its inhabitants' functioning.[20]

As noted, we also found in our New Haven study a positive relationship between environmental quality and human quality of life independent of income and education level. Both this finding and the Chicago public housing results counter the conventional wisdom that the experience of nature is a luxury, of relevance only to those who have the time and resources to afford it, and largely irrelevant to the lives of poor people. On the contrary, these results suggest that all people derive basic satisfactions and benefits from contact with nature, even in the most limited circumstances.

A less scientific study of the effects of biophilic design at the community level is provided by data from a thirty-year-old residential project in Davis, California, called Village Homes. This residential development includes 220 modest-sized homes (averaging 2,200 square feet), a small office building, and a community center on a sixty-acre tract. Despite the high building density, the development devoted nearly one-quarter of its area to open space, shared agricultural and recreational land, pedestrian paths, and a greenbelt. Houses were situated on relatively small lots separated by narrow, winding paths lined with shrubs and trees. Vehicular roads were positioned at the periphery of the project, along with the parking areas. The streets were narrower than typical for residential developments, and in place of underground pipes to control storm water, aboveground swales with vegetation followed the landscape's natural contours.

The high quality of life at Village Homes is reflected in residents' knowing, on average, "forty neighbors, compared with seventeen in the standard development, [with] three or four close friends in the neighborhood compared with one in the control group."[21] Additionally, Village Homes properties typically sell for significantly higher prices and come up for sale less often than homes in comparable developments. Reflecting these differences, the developer of Village Homes reported:

> In the beginning, housing prices in Village Homes were comparable to prices elsewhere in Davis. However, . . . calculated in square footage, Village Homes is the most expensive place in Davis. . . . This is due less to the houses themselves—they were built at the modest end of the housing scale—and more to the neighborhood, which is seen as a very desirable place to live. The homes come on the market less frequently . . . and they sell twice as quickly.[22]

The moving recollections of a former resident of Village Homes of his boyhood there offers another kind of insight regarding the perceived benefits of greater contact with nature during childhood:

> Growing up in Village Homes gave me a sense of freedom and safety that would be difficult to find in the usual urban neighborhood. The orchards . . . gardens, and greenbelts within Village Homes offered many stimulating, exciting, joyful places for me to play with friends. We could walk out our back doors into greenbelts full of all kinds of trees to climb with fruit to eat and gardens with vegetables to nibble on. Even though we were young, the network of green belts allowed my friends and I to go anywhere in the community without facing the danger of crossing a street. Now that I am no longer living in Village Homes, I feel locked in by the

30. Village Homes in Davis, California, is a development comprising 220 modest-sized homes, a small office building, and a community center on a sixty-acre tract. Despite the high building density, the development devoted nearly one-quarter of its area to open space.

fence in my backyard and the street in front of my house. I feel a loss of the freedom I had as a child.[23]

The original low-environmental-impact design features of Village Homes have become largely obsolete. Yet the development's biophilic design attributes continue to exert substantial positive effects that contribute to the development's superior quality of life, reputation, and significantly higher property values.

The chapter concludes with an interlude in which I imagine the revival of an environmentally and economically depressed community through the integration of biophilic and low-environmental-impact design features that contributed to its physical, psychological, and spiritual health and renewal.

Interlude

I had come to recognize that my life had not turned out the way I had dreamed. I didn't necessarily feel like a failure, having understood that most of my fantasies of success were unrealistic to begin with. I had accommodated myself and emerged largely content with the life I had achieved, despite its limitations and disappointments. Twenty years previously, I had abandoned a promising career in international finance, which I suppose would have made me a rich man. Instead, I had made the deliberate choice to embark on a risky venture that eventually flamed out. I actually believed until then that I had been living a kind of charmed life predestined for success. My eventual failure was at first a harsh lesson in reality.

After returning to the States from Japan, I joined with my business partner, Nicole, and her colleagues in establishing a sustainable design and development firm. Nicole possessed the architectural skills, our partners had the engineering expertise, and I provided the financial knowledge. Nicole was a gifted designer, her work distinguished by its ability to minimize environmental impacts while also capturing a wonderful aesthetic. I conferred economic muscle through my contacts in the financial world that initially generated significant capital, which we invested in several large-scale developments.

Many factors contributed to our eventual demise. Our economic strategy was naive, based on the belief that a good concept along with a measure of idealism would inevitably surmount all obstacles. Our problem, however, was not just the uncertainty of innovation, in which something new almost always costs more and is, by definition, unfamiliar and risky. More basically, we had collaborated with some large-scale developers who possessed a very short-term horizon and looked for immediate profits, wanting to sell their developments soon after they were built. Long-term paybacks in energy and resource efficiency, or improved employee productivity that diminished the short-term bottom line, were viewed as "blue sky" abstractions, if not outright silliness. Also, most of the developers invested little of their own resources, relying on financing from large banks and foreign sources that were mainly motivated by the fastest return possible on their dollar. Contributions to the health of the natural environment or local communities were either ignored or regarded as irrelevant.

We also were hamstrung by government regulations; our plans violated conventional requirements for processing wastes, using permitted materials, or consuming energy. Originally intended to protect the public, these regulatory impediments had, over time, become rigid rules imposed by inflexible bureaucracies that preferred the dictates of standard operating procedures to dealing with something new and innovative.

In the end, our failure was largely self-inflicted, the product of overambition and a good deal of hubris. We struggled for more than five years before finally throwing in the towel. Nicole and I then parted, I heading back to the conventional world of finance while she went with an established architectural firm. My return to the world of ordinary finance, however, was in a much-reduced capacity. My abrupt departure from the large investment firm and subsequent business failure had left me with a tarnished reputation. Eventually, I landed a job as branch manager with a regional bank in a small coastal Massachusetts city. What I at first thought would be a short-term exile in time became a twenty-year career. But I did meet a wonderful woman who eventually became my wife and the mother of our two beautiful children.

I thus harbored few regrets. As a middle-aged man, I had found myself a solid member of a small city's economic elite, albeit a town a little long in the tooth, economically and socially a vestige of its former self. My work at the bank was often routine but still interesting. For the most part, I was appreciated by my colleagues and by the city's civic community as I tried to match resources with the potential both to do some good and to make a profit.

Much of the time, however, I operated on automatic pilot, cruising through my life more than creating it. My existence was safe, predictable, and largely secondhand. Even when I helped make good works happen, my satisfaction was mostly transient and focused on the accomplishments of others. Still, I was relatively content, finding joy in my family, friends, and the environment where we live. My wife was loving and caring, my two boys a constant source of pleasure. We lived in a restored house with a terrific view of the water, belonged to several clubs, and frequently explored the bay and its never-ending sources of beauty, wonder, and discovery. However, I still carried around inside me the nagging feeling of an unrealized self.

I continued to take special satisfaction in my lifelong passion for the natural world, quietly raging at the prevailing assumptions that equated progress with nature's disfigurement. Few among my friends and associates seemed to notice how much natural capital had already been lost, and how efforts at revitalizing the city continued to rely on the flawed logic that economic advancement requires environmental debasement. Despite my outrage at this insidious destruction, I remained largely silent—and sometimes even contributed to the prevailing paradigm through my various lending activities at the bank. I did almost nothing to stop the spreading pox, beyond an occasional feeble protest or superficial support for the local land trust. I sometimes proselytized to others, but this rarely resulted in any meaningful action.

My position at the bank had revealed to me how much of the region's environmental destruction had been spurred by external forces and financial interests. Most of the recent development of large shopping centers, corporate parks, and residential complexes, mainly in the suburbs, had been the work of multinational banks and corporations. The structures were almost always unattractive and flimsy, using excessive resources while generating enormous quantities of wastes and pollutants and destroying natural habitat. They also totally relied on vehicular transportation over mass transit or any pedestrian-friendly alternatives.

Meanwhile, like many others, I despaired over how little remained of the old downtown and waterfront, which consisted mainly of boarded-up stores, seedy bars, an old whaling museum, abandoned factories, ancient piers, and a legacy of industrial waste slowly leaching its chemical stew into the harbor. Despite the dereliction, the old city and waterfront still possessed considerable charm and enormous economic potential. The harbor continued to be a natural wonder of various historical and biological treasures. One could find in its shallow waters and along its estuarine flats and deeper channels a wealth of mollusks and crustaceans and a nursery for the bay's abundant fish populations. The marshes also attracted resident, migrating, and wintering waterfowl and, most miraculously, in recent winters the return of harbor and gray seals seemingly extirpated long ago. I often fantasized how some smart developer of particular boldness and imagination could make a fortune and do much good by restoring the commercial and environmental qualities of the old downtown harbor. This restoration could celebrate the commingling of human and natural history, allowing each to feed on the other, progressively enriching culture and nature until the two became more than they could ever be apart, a thing of wonder and beauty teeming with energy and connection.

Then, seemingly in answer to my fantasies, a rare opportunity presented itself, although I failed to recognize it at first. It started with a relatively modest proposal submitted to the bank by the whaling museum, which for years had struggled to attract enough visitors to cover its payroll and preserve its extraordinary collection of whaling artifacts. Plagued by obsolete exhibits, a decrepit building, the city's dubious image, and, ironically, contemporary sympathy for whales that identified whaling with the creature's demise, the museum had barely survived. It had recently hired a new executive director, who had concluded that only modernization and expansion could save the museum by appealing to a broader public interested in marine mammals and the sea. The museum proposed relocating to a renovated factory building beside the harbor and asked my bank to help finance the development. The museum board's strongest selling point was that it had already secured two-thirds of the $60 million needed from Silas Pease, patriarch of the city's once-great whaling family. But despite the pledge, the bank rejected the loan. I argued for its approval but was dismissed as biased and unrealistic.

Nonetheless, the fire of possibility had settled into my brain, and I could not stop thinking about the project. I speculated that, with some significant refocusing, it could be an enormous commercial, civic, and environmental success that would help restore the city and its harbor. One evening, in a moment of epiphany and perhaps hallucination, I decided that this was probably my last, best chance to accomplish something significant and fulfilling in my life. I proceeded to put thoughts to paper and over the next several days sketched a greatly revised plan. I decided that the original proposal had been fundamentally flawed by its limited focus on a single outcome, rendering the museum largely aloof from its deteriorated community. Investors would always remain skeptical about sinking resources into an unattractive, economically depressed neighborhood no matter how interesting the museum's new exhibits, restaurants, or stores might be. Paradoxically, the project had to be much bolder and more ambitious to succeed, broadening its vision from a single building and institution to the economic and ecological restoration of the entire downtown, embracing within it a spectrum of civic, commercial, and even residential uses. There would also need to be thematic coherence among these disparate elements, with the museum serving as the catalytic core for reconnecting people to the sea and its aquatic environment.

In my scheme, the museum as centerpiece would be the focus of education and entertainment, combining commerce, ecology, and culture. The museum's emphasis would be the marine world, but extended to include estuaries, wetlands, watersheds, rivers, and shores as well as the ocean. It would be a museum of science and technology and of natural history and environmental studies and would also include a theater, an art gallery, and anthropological displays, all bound together by the celebration of a single element vital to human life—water.

The museum would be the initial attraction, but the project would succeed or fail only by creating radiating circles of commercial, civic, and residential enterprise from that focal point. There would also need to be effective, easy vehicular access and parking, but cars and streets would be subordinated to the whole, with traffic held to the periphery rather than placed at the center of the project. A viable residential community would further border on and affirm the aquatic environment. Schools would also be organized around the relation of people to the sea, cutting across all traditional disciplines. Learning would occur in the classroom but be complemented by experience in the marine environment, theory joining with practice, the abstract with the personal and tangible.

The project would retrofit existing buildings but also construct new ones, all connecting the terrestrial with the aquatic and restoring ties to a healthy environment. Attractive waterfront views would be essential, structures evoking a positive connection between people and the sea. The architecture would blur lines separating the built from the natural environment, with exterior walls becoming a permeable skin to let the outside world in. People would be reminded of the aquatic environment not just through museum exhibits and decorative displays but also by the sight of an actual working harbor embedded into the flow of everyday life. Stores would face the waterfront; office, manufacturing, and residential space would be housed in retrofitted and new buildings lining the river and old canals. A linear park would parallel the waterways and be joined to pedestrian trails, outdoor recreational areas, and restored wetlands that eventually connected the city to its suburbs and, in time, the countryside.

All buildings would minimize energy and resource use as well as wastes and pollutants. Energy would be produced on site by exploiting sunlight, wind, and structural features that would lessen dependence on mechanical heating and cooling systems. The long-term goal would be to produce as much energy as consumed and to make waste an obsolete concept, with all discarded materials treated as valuable seed stock for future uses or returned safely to the natural environment. Buildings would be linked, with the waste heat of some becoming the heating and cooling sources for others. All materials and products would be recycled, and storm water collected and cleansed for flushing, cooling, and irrigating. Toxic chemicals would be prohibited in the paints, adhesives, glues, carpets, woods, and other furnishings, which would, whenever possible, be obtained from biodegradable and sustainably produced sources. Roadways would be designed to minimize erosion and runoff, with streets constructed of porous materials that would allow rainwater to percolate back into the ground. Landscaping would use native vegetation, enhancing the productivity of local ecosystems.

The days and evenings that followed were a fever of speculation and activity—a wild dream that in the cold light of day often seemed impossible, if not delusional. Any thought of bringing the concept before the bank would have been tantamount to professional suicide; the bank's conservative mindset would certainly have viewed these ideas as fantastic and troublesome. Still, possessed by my vision, I frantically continued to refine the plan. I remained emboldened by one important aspect of the original proposal I still counted on being possible: the $60 million commitment by the quixotic patriarch of the city's old whaling family. As a bank officer, I knew that he could afford the financing. However, I also knew he was furious about the bank's rejection of the museum proposal and about the bank officers' perceived lack of daring and imagination. He had even made threats about seeking other financing and moving his fortune to another bank. I assumed he was still interested in the project and might even be willing to extend his support to my much bolder, albeit more expensive, scheme if I could somehow bring the refashioned proposal to his attention.

In a fever in which the hot fantasy of imagination often clashed with the cold reality of what seemed possible, I continued to craft my case for a massive civic, commercial, and residential complex within a network of rehabilitated open space and restored harbor. I finally completed the document and, before I could think much about it or lose my courage, I boldly sent the proposal to the old patriarch. I heard nothing for more than a week, fearing more every day not only that had I offended him with my audacity but that he would inform the bank and I would be immediately dismissed. It was thus quite a shock when he called a week later. In more a monologue than a conversation, he informed me how much he liked the proposal and the prospect of partnering with me. He said that we needed to meet as soon as possible to discuss the next steps, and he promised one-fifth, or $100 million, of the estimated initial development cost—contingent on my raising the balance elsewhere. Finally, given the huge scale of the project, he said he expected me to resign immediately from the bank and completely devote myself to the project. Moreover, I had twelve months to raise the additional $400 million before his offer would expire.

I knew well how hopes of acquiring this amount of financial support could easily become the detritus of a failed dream. I discussed all this and more with my wife and a few close friends, but to my surprise and delight they all counseled me to take the chance. So the following week, I announced my resignation to the bank. Suddenly, I was frighteningly on my own, yet thrilled. I spent the first weeks hiring staff, refining the business plan, developing drawings, interviewing consultants, and beginning the gigantic task of raising a mountain of capital. Some wonderful architects, engineers, and businesspeople joined me, and together we developed what we viewed as a compelling and convincing proposal.

Over the new few months, we achieved many notable successes and encountered considerable skepticism. Then came a string of rejections, so many that I began to fantasize that the old patriarch had set me up for ruin. We cast an ever wider net and developed ever more supporting documentation. However, after nine months and despite having raised some $90 million, we were well short of our goal.

Finally, after we had contacted an extraordinary number of potential investors and gotten an equally remarkable number of rejections, we received a response indicating modest interest from Emerson Bates, the head of a venture capital fund managed as part of one of the country's largest educational endowments. Bates had once been in charge of the entire endowment, but after expanding it beyond anyone's wildest dreams, he had stepped away from general operations to concentrate on higher-risk investments that offered the potential for both significant financial return and major social benefit. Bates especially liked projects he described as bordering on the "is" of today and the "ought" of tomorrow.

Having concluded that our project fit this description, Bates requested that we meet with him and his colleagues. Two additional meetings followed, each in response to questions that forced us to revise our plans but that left the core concept intact. We then heard nothing for the next seven weeks. Our twelve-month deadline was approaching, our doubts growing. Finally, a letter arrived from Bates informing us that his group had decided to provide the balance of the financing needed. The next fifteen months brought a frenzy of finishing plans, formal submissions, political negotiations, regulatory approvals, and—most glorious of all—construction contracts.

When all was said and done, the project's greatest success turned out to be not the new museum or the commercial district but the establishment of a neighborhood of apartments, condominiums, town houses, and single-family homes. The public's imagination had been fired by the prospect of living in a place that included a restored historic harbor, a riverside park, outdoor recreational areas, pedestrian trails, and wildlife reserves. Families especially liked the idea of their children being able to play in open spaces near home, and everyone became addicted to the new fleet of water transport that had spontaneously emerged and turned the river, harbor, canals, and bay into an aquatic highway connecting the business and residential districts with new restaurants, recreational and entertainment attractions, and stores along the waterfront.

Pundits and politicians alike took credit for the project's mix of public and private uses within the restored harbor and historic area. Everyone praised the limited roadways and reduced motor traffic, the abundance of open space, and the combination of contemporary and traditional design. All extolled the new feeling of community and the surprising number of people from the suburbs who had purchased residences. These new urbanites said that they especially liked the greater opportunities for meeting neighbors, the reduced time spent driving, and the proximity of many cultural and environmental amenities along the waterfront. The initial surplus of vacant office space had been worrisome at first, but the problem eventually disappeared, as commerce followed the presence of a viable neighborhood and an attractive, healthy environment rather than the other way around.

My life continues to be consumed by the project, yet I am happy and at peace. I recognize that I have had the rarest of opportunities to engage life at its fullest by trying to accomplish something of lasting good. It reminds me of something I read by Dante:

"Upon your feet! This is no time to tire!"
my master cried. "The man who lies asleep
will never waken fame, and his desire

and all his life drift past him like a dream,
and the traces of his memory fade from time
like smoke in air, or ripples on a stream.

Now, therefore, rise. Control your breath, and call
upon the strength of soul that wins all battles
unless it sink in the gross body's fall.

There is a longer ladder yet to climb:
This much is not enough. If you understand me,
Show that you mean to profit from your time."[24]

11

ethics and everyday life

We have explored the many ways people's physical, mental, and spiritual well-being remains reliant on the quality of their connections to the natural world. This continuing dependence on nature stems from our species' having evolved in a natural, not artificial, world. Most of our physical, emotional, and intellectual tendencies developed in adaptive response to mainly natural stimuli and conditions. Yet like much of what makes us human, for these tendencies to become fully functional, they must be nurtured and developed through adequate learning and experience. People may possess an inherent inclination to affiliate with nature, but this is a birthright that must be earned if it is to serve our best interests and needs.

The beneficial experience of nature can be facilitated in many ways. In our modern, highly literate, and increasingly governed society, contact with the natural world is often fostered through school programs, government agencies and nongovernmental organizations, and new communication methods and technologies. Its accomplishment, however, must originate in the values and motivations of individual people and their sense of moral commitment and ethical responsibility for the natural world. If people lack sufficient knowledge, love, and faith in the value of nature, they will not be motivated to embrace their experiential dependence on the natural world.[1]

Unfortunately, modern society has lost sight of how much our health, productivity, and wholeness continue to rely on the quality of our connections to the natural world. We have separated ourselves from nature and degraded it in the dangerous delusion that we have become free from the constraints of the natural world and can aspire to transcend our biology and natural origins. The restoration of a healthy relationship with the natural world must originate not in our desire to "save" the planet but in a profound realization of our own self-interest. We will ultimately sustain only those things—whether species, buildings, or communities—that our values and ethics tell us contribute to our fitness and fulfillment.

Our consciousness reflects our values, which in turn drive our ethics. Our sense of responsibility for caring for the earth depends on recognizing how much we remain reliant on a multiplicity of connections to the natural world. An ethic that transforms our relationship to nature must embrace all our biophilic values—attraction, affection, aversion, reason, exploitation, dominion, spirituality, and symbolic communication. The core of this transformative ethic is the realization that we can achieve lives of meaning and satisfaction only by living in right relation to the world beyond ourselves.

A quartet of conditions will be necessary for this to occur, including:

- Engaging all our biophilic values, each revealed in balanced relation to the others, and each in adaptive and functional fashion.
- Having a strong emotional connection to nature that reflects both a passion for and a love of life and a universe of creation.
- Pursuing knowledge and understanding of the natural world, recognizing the limits of our intellect and the need to apply this understanding with humility and restraint.
- Recognizing that ultimately faith and reverent relation to the natural world will be necessary for us to flourish as individuals and as a species.

The great ecologist and ethicist Aldo Leopold recognized this reliance on values, love, intellect, and faith at the core of a transformative environmental ethic, when he suggested:

> There must be some force behind conservation more universal than profit, less awkward than government, less ephemeral than sport, something that reaches into all times and all places . . . something that brackets everything from rivers to raindrops, from whales to hummingbirds, from land-estates to window-boxes. . . . I can see only one such force: a respect for the land as an organism . . . out of love for and obligation to that great biota.[2]

Is a transformative environmental ethic a practical option or merely a rhetorical ideal and romantic vision? Is this goal realistic when we confront seemingly apocalyptic environmental challenges such as global pollution, massive biodiversity loss, extensive resource depletion, and the specter of atmospheric and climate change? Do we have the luxury of time to achieve what many view as the exceedingly difficult and long-term task of transforming our values and ethics toward the natural world? I believe there is no other option. Absent a basic reorientation of our values and ethics toward nature, humanity will never flourish or be fulfilled. Our regulatory and technical efforts to solve the great environmental challenges of our time inevitably will fall short, effecting temporary relief at best, and never a lasting cure.[3]

Moreover, a fundamental change in our ethical stance toward nature is far more pragmatic than often presumed. History reveals that at times a transformation in our basic values toward aspects of the natural world can occur quite quickly and exert lasting effects beyond those achieved by regulatory mandate or law. Two illustrations can be cited in this regard: the shift in values regarding an entire group of animals—the large cetaceans, or better known as "the great whales"; and the still unfolding ethical transformation involving an ecosystem, wetlands, which until recently was more pejoratively referred to as swamps.

THE GREAT WHALES

Perceptions of whales profoundly changed during the latter twentieth century, following a long history of hostile attitudes and excessive exploitation of these animals. This transformation in values eventually bestowed on whales a moral standing that drove major regulatory change. Moreover, this shift in values, behavior, and policy occurred in a relatively short period of time.[4]

Before the twentieth century, great whales were largely viewed as sources of oil, ivory, meat, and other material products, and as fishlike monsters of the sea. These creatures were relentlessly pursued and exploited. Moreover, most people regarded the whale harvest with pride, a demonstration that humans could dominate the largest creature the world had ever known in the most inhospitable of all environments, the open ocean. The whale was largely perceived as a distant and alien creature, more a monstrous fish, even if technically recognized as a mammal.

Reflecting the prevailing sentiments of the time, the *Mayflower* pilgrims, upon spying whales offshore shortly after arriving along the coast of New England, rushed for their guns to kill the animals. In an 1818 court case, *Maurice v. Judd*, the plaintiff protested a tax on whales as fish as erroneous, rightly pointing out these animals were "no more a fish than a man." More pragmatically, the jury concluded these animals for all intents and purposes were fish.[5] The perception of whales as strange and alien fishlike creatures continued well into the twentieth century, with whales classified as "fish catch." As recently as 1960, whale meat still accounted for a remarkable fifteen percent of the world's fish catch.[6]

By this time, the seeds of basic change in attitudes toward whales had been planted and were taking root. Once-dominant values based on exploitation, dominion, and aversion toward whales had been moderated through much of the developed world. Replacing these sentiments were far more appreciative and sympathetic values, including affection, attraction, intellectual interest, and even the spiritual celebration of this animal. This shift in consciousness toward whales became so pronounced that the animal emerged as an iconic symbol of contemporary conservation, prompting the president of the National Geographic Society in 1976, Gilbert Grosvenor, to remark: "The whale has become a symbol for a new way of thinking about our planet."[7]

Many factors contributed to this profound transformation in perception and relationship. A sense of urgency emerged from the realization that the great whales were in danger of extinction; many were disturbed by the prospect of this unique creature's being eliminated by the excesses of human ignorance and greed. The scientific community confirmed the animal's imperiled condition, the marine biologist Kenneth Norris noting: "No other group of large animals has had so many of its members driven to the brink of extinction."[8]

More sympathetic perceptions of whales were also prompted by significant advances in knowledge of this animal, much of it stemming from studies using new technology to observe whales in natural and captive settings. These studies revealed that whales possess exceptional intelligence, complex social lives, and extraordinary communication abilities, traits reminiscent of our own species. Enthusiasts began to extol the kindness of killer whales, the songs of the humpback whale, and the intellectual capacities of dolphins. In addition, millions flocked to view captive whales in aquariums, and an entirely new industry emerged, whale watching, which by 2010 generated an estimated two billion dollars in annual revenues, more than the economic value obtained from the harvest of whales for their meat and oil.[9] These changes reflected and encouraged a significant shift in attitudes toward whales. They also underlay the emergence of widespread opposition to whaling, particularly among the most economically advanced nations, except for Japan and Norway, which for cultural and historic reasons maintained their whaling industries.

These changes in values drove dramatic changes in policy and law. In the United States, the 1972 Marine Mammal Protection Act, thought to be the most ambitious wildlife law ever, was enacted. In the mid-1980s the International Whaling Commission mandated a moratorium on the commercial harvest of whales; until then, the IWC had been largely ineffectual in controlling the excessive exploitation of whales, and its historic focus had been the material utilization of these animals.[10]

These regulatory and policy changes were the consequence of fundamental changes in values and ethical assumptions about whales and the human relationship to them. Hostile perceptions that had prevailed for centuries and had encouraged the exploitation and domination of whales had greatly diminished, and in their place emerged a view of these animals as especially intelligent, attractive, ecologically important, and spiritually inspiring. Motivations of greed, ignorance, and hostility that had governed the relations of people and whales for millennia had been supplanted by the perception that these creatures were beautiful, wondrous, and admirable. The harvest of whales for their meat and oil became for many ethically repugnant and morally reprehensible.

Profound value shifts laid the foundation for the emergence of a transformative environmental ethic that motivated both public and political will to enact revolutionary changes in law and policy. Moreover, these changes in values and ethics occurred in a matter of decades. By contrast, government attempts at regulating the harvest of whales had been largely ineffectual for a much longer period of time. With stunning rapidity, whales had achieved a moral standing

31. The great whales have been intensively exploited as sources of oil, ivory, and meat, and most are now endangered. Profound changes in perceptions of these animals during the late twentieth century culminated in their being accorded a moral standing that encouraged their conservation and drove major changes in policy and law.

that motivated millions to defend their interests with passionate zeal and ethical intensity.

This dramatic shift in values and ethics was, of course, directed at a charismatic species whose perceived emotional and intellectual relationship to people fueled a moral transformation. Many identified and empathized with whales as if their plight and presumed suffering were akin to what people might experience under analogous circumstances. "Save the Whales" became for many a personal plea, not just a policy slogan.

WETLANDS

Could such a profound shift in values and ethics occur toward a more biologically remote species or even an inanimate feature of the natural world? Recent shifts in perceptions of an entire ecosystem suggest this is possible. The ecosystem in question comprises the marshy areas known as wetlands. Not only has a dramatic change in values and ethics toward this habitat happened, but as with the whales, this transformation has driven major shifts in regulatory policy and law, and this has occurred in a relatively short period of time, although this change remains a work in progress.

Wetlands are technically defined as areas subject to periodic and prolonged saturation at or near the soil surface. Both fresh- and saltwater wetlands are characterized by particular soils, plants, and animals that have adapted to the periodic presence of water and occasional and regular flooding. There are many kinds of wetlands, including tidal and freshwater marshes, wet meadows and prairies, prairie potholes, playas, vernal pools, bogs, fens, and forest, shrub, and mangrove swamps.[11]

For much of the public, wetlands were once collectively and pejoratively known as swamps. They were places to fear, avoid, and, wherever possible, exploit or convert to more useful and productive land. Their historic exploitation generally emphasized the harvest of grasses, trees, wildlife, and medicinal plants. Their material value was further measured in their potential for conversion, via draining, filling, or impounding, to presumably higher and better uses, such as agriculture, forestry, housing development, and transportation corridors.

In the prevailing scornful perception, swamps were dark, dismal, and fearsome, places of confusion and disorientation, quagmires easily stumbled into and hard to escape. They were perilous places, breeding grounds for disease and home to dangerous creatures—leeches, ticks, snakes, large predators and even evil spirits. The following depiction typifies this grim perspective:

Swamps are . . . godforsaken places that no man enters willingly. When they aren't infested with . . . horrors, they hide . . . hideous [creatures]. . . . They are the home of poisonous snakes and strange, incurable diseases. . . . Swamps are . . . dangerous and unsanitary. They . . . attract . . . insects, which . . . spread disease. . . . The sodden terrain makes traversing them on foot difficult; many swamps . . . are prone to heavy fog . . . making it easy to get lost. . . . Swamps are inhabited by dangerous animals. . . . Swamps are . . . cursed, haunted, full of monsters.[12]

Widespread antipathy toward swamps encouraged their avoidance and destruction. Wetlands were routinely filled, ditched, and drained, often to suppress disease, and were particularly viewed as breeding habitat for mosquitoes and other scorned insects. In the United States, wetlands destruction became nearly a civic duty, assisted by ever more powerful technologies. By the close of the twentieth century, the United States had eliminated more than half the 220 million acres of pre–European settlement wetlands. In the state of Iowa alone, more than ninety percent were destroyed and replaced by mainly agricultural land. By 2010 only Alaska had eliminated less than one percent of its original wetlands. As recently as the decade 1986–97, an average of fifty-eight thousand wetlands acres were lost in the United States each year, or more than half a million acres during that span; less conservative measures put the loss at one million acres.[13]

In the face of such grim statistics, a remarkable shift occurred during the latter part of the twentieth century in public attitudes toward wetlands in the United States and much of the developed world. Reflecting this change, a politically conservative and not especially environmentally oriented president, George W. Bush, declared in 2002 a national policy of "no net loss of wetlands."[14] This pronouncement reflected a broader transformation in the perceived value of wetlands. Rather than loathsome swamps viewed as dangerous and disease-ridden wastelands, wetlands began to be perceived as aesthetically attractive, materially beneficial, ecologically important, recreationally appealing, and even spiritually inspiring.[15]

A factor in this change was a rapidly expanding knowledge and understanding of the useful functions of wetlands. Scientific study documented such vital ecosystem services provided by wetlands as maintaining water supply and hydrologic regulation, flood and storm surge protection, fish nurseries and breeding habitat, waste decomposition and pollution control, and a variety of other ecological and material functions. Wetlands were described as one of the most biologically productive and diverse ecosystems on the planet. Wetlands

32. Wetlands are areas subject to periodic and prolonged water saturation at or near the soil surface. Once pejoratively known as swamps, wetlands were viewed as places to avoid, fear, exploit, and convert. A remarkable shift in attitude toward wetlands occurred during the second half of the twentieth century, and they are now widely perceived as ecologically important, aesthetically attractive, recreationally valuable, and even a source of spiritual inspiration.

were further celebrated for the boating, birding, fishing, hunting, and other recreational opportunities they provide. They were lauded as places of great beauty, aesthetic appeal, and even spiritual power.[16] Reflecting these newfound values, economic estimations credited wetlands in 2010 with contributing between $14 billion and $70 billion to the world's economy annually.[17]

A fundamental shift in the perceived value of wetlands had occurred. This change in consciousness and values was reflected in the emergence of a new ethic regarding this ecosystem that, as with whales, drove major changes in law and policy to conserve, protect and, ironically, restore wetlands that not long before had been deliberately destroyed. Moreover, this transformation in values and ethics had occurred in a relatively short period of time.

A TRANSFORMATIVE ENVIRONMENTAL ETHIC

The examples of whales and wetlands both suggest the potential practical significance of seeking a fundamental change in values and ethical relationships to the natural world. Yet many believe that this kind of transformation is unrealistic and irrelevant given the scale and urgency of our contemporary environmental crisis. Not only do these illustrations suggest otherwise, but I believe that absent such basic value and ethical change, our reliance on scientific, technical, economic, regulatory, and legal strategies to achieve environmental goals will be marginally effective and largely fail over time.

As noted, four conditions are necessary for a transformative environmental ethic to occur. First, all our biophilic inclinations to value nature must occur in functional and adaptive fashion. Moreover, these values must exist in balanced and mutually respectful relation to one another. This does not suggest that all our biophilic values will be equally important, or that they should be roughly equivalent across all individuals and groups. The human relationship to nature is richly diverse, dynamic, and creative, reflecting the shaping influence of experience, learning, and culture, and our evolutionary adaptation to different species and ecological circumstances. People will never feel the same way about a snake as they do about a swan, or toward a swamp and a savannah. Moreover, individuals and groups will differ in adaptive response to varying historic and cultural experience, religion, ethnicity, age, gender, and geographic location. We rightly celebrate this diversity, which reflects the creative genius of humanity and our remarkable capacity for progress and innovation.

Yet this variability does not suggest that one value of nature is intrinsically more important than another, or that some can be dispensed with in favor of others. Nor does it mean that all variations and differences are equally legitimate and worthy. All our biophilic values emerged as universal tendencies hammered into our genes because they reflected adaptive functions that advanced our health, fitness, and well-being over the course of human evolution and development. All our biophilic values must be functionally revealed if we are to be healthy and whole, even if the content and priority of these adaptations will vary among individuals and groups in functional response to varying conditions, cultures, experience, biology, and ecological circumstance. Each value renders a vital contribution to the human body, mind, and spirit, and each offers a suite of instrumental advantages. When all our biophilic values occur in functional, balanced, and complementary relation to one another, an essential foundation is laid for a transformative environmental ethic that motivates us to care for nature not out of some altruistic impulse but from a profound realization of our own self-interest.

Unfortunately, modern society has narrowly emphasized the benefits derived from treating nature mainly as a resource to be materially exploited and dominated. The result has been an ethic that views the natural world as primarily of source of material comfort and security. From this narrow perspective, the moral choice of action is a shallow cost-benefit analysis that largely ignores those biophilic values that do not lend themselves to economic estimation. By contrast, a transformative environmental ethic regards all our biophilic values as instrumental and beneficial, and needing to occur in balanced and respectful relation to one another. When this occurs, a web of relational dependency between people and nature takes place that yields a far more powerful ethic for caring for the earth. This more enlightened basis for our values and ethics toward nature is reflected in the views of the biologist René Dubos:

> Conservation of nature is based on human value systems that rather than being a luxury are a necessity for the preservation of mental health. Above and beyond the economic reasons for conservation there are aesthetic and moral ones, which are even more compelling. We are shaped by the earth. The characteristics of our environment in which we develop condition our biological and mental health and the quality of our life. Were it only for selfish reasons, we must maintain variety and harmony in nature.[18]

A transformative environmental ethic also depends on developing a deep emotional attachment to and love for nature. When this occurs, the degradation of the natural environment is perceived as not just a material deficit but as an act that fundamentally diminishes that which we cherish and adore. Lacking an emotional identification with and attachment to nature, it is impossible to morally defend its interest as if it were our own. As Aldo Leopold remarked: "We can be ethical only in relation to something we can see, feel, understand, love, or otherwise have faith in. . . . Conservation [emerges] out of love for and obligation to that great biota."[19]

A transformative environmental ethic also depends on the passion to know and comprehend the world beyond our selves, the world of nature and a universe of creation. This unyielding curiosity and sense of wonder about the natural world inevitably yield material and other practical advantages over time. More important than these narrow rewards, the passionate search for knowledge and discovery enriches not just our understanding and appreciation of nature but also our sense of self-worth and identity. This pursuit of the endless mysteries of the natural world further cautions us to be humble about how much we know, and to apply our understanding with restraint and respect.

Finally, a transformative environmental ethic necessitates a faith that only by living in right and moral relation to nature can we ever flourish and find fulfillment. We come to recognize that in nourishing our emotional attachment to the natural world, we deepen our capacity for love. We see in the beauty of the earth a magnificent accomplishment accessible to us each and every day. We find in even the tiniest of creatures and the smallest of elements an awesome power and strength. We realize that by building a tapestry of relational ties to the natural world, we can weave a cloak of enduring security that may be worn for all our days. We come to recognize that through our reverent respect for the earth we can participate in a community that will always embrace us with an ineffable feeling of connection to the vastness of the universe.

EVERYDAY LIFE

Can a transformative environmental ethic serve as a practical guide to everyday life? Or is this ethic of marginal relevance to the ordinary existence of people who must deal with the inevitable compromises of holding a job, raising a family, and coping with the limitations of normal life and the constraints of reality? There is no question that an ethic is an aspiration, an ideal of what should be, a line between what the world is and ought to be. But if it is meaningful and not merely rhetorical, an ethic must also serve as a guide to what is ultimately in our collective interest, a map that shows us how we can, as a society, pursue fitness and fulfillment.

The great challenge of today is to connect our understanding of nature's contribution to the human body, mind, and spirit to the demands of a world in which nature seems to be ever more in retreat. We must somehow find the means to move beyond experiencing nature as a marginal reality reflected in the occasional visit to a park or some faraway place to making it an integral and essential part of our everyday lives.

Without question, nature today has become an increasingly peripheral part of most people's lives. Yet we often fail to appreciate how much the natural world continues to be a vital aspect of our lives and can become even more so. Part of our blindness is a view of nature as something that occurs only outdoors and in places where the human presence is transient and other species and ecosystems prevail. This view prevents us from recognizing the many subtle and important ways the natural world continues to be part of our lives, from the food we eat, to the shelters we build, to the many images and symbols we use to facilitate communication, to how we design our structures and our art.

Still, we struggle with the reality of an increasingly fabricated and artificial world, and wonder whether nature can ever be more than a minor feature of our cities and suburbs, schools and hospitals, offices and manufacturing facilities, commercial centers and residential complexes. Despite these obstacles, the natural world can and must emerge as a practical and ethical necessity if we are to become physically, mentally, and spiritually whole. This will require conscious and deliberate action on our part motivated by the self-interested realization that to do otherwise invites a life of isolation and inadequacy.

How can we accomplish this daunting task? There are no simple or easy answers. What we offer here are suggestions and illustrations that conclude this chapter and this book. The first stems from a recent experience when I was professionally engaged to help resolve an environmental problem occurring at a large office tower in New York City. The second focuses on the imagined life of a young woman also living and working in New York.

Both illustrations occur in an urban location for good reason. Cities are where most of us live today and, barring catastrophe, where the world's population increasingly chooses to be. Unfortunately, the modern metropolis has historically pursued a paradigm of design and development that treats environmental degradation and separation from nature as an acceptable price to pay for advancing progress and civilization. The contemporary city is the site of our greatest impediments to achieving a world in which our values and ethics relating to the natural world can become benign and once again meaningfully nourish the human body, mind, and spirit. The outcome of this struggle could very well determine the future of our species.

AN URBAN OFFICE TOWER

Nowhere is the task of developing an ethically responsible relationship to nature more challenging than in the large office towers that make up the financial districts of most modern cities. Whether in Tokyo, Hong Kong, Mumbai, Dubai, Moscow, London, Rio de Janeiro, Mexico City, Atlanta, or New York, these icons of power appear very much alike, designed in an international style that typically affirms the normality of excess resource consumption, environmental degradation, separation from nature, and the irrelevancy of locality and place.

In 2011 I was engaged in a project at one of these buildings in the Wall Street area of lower Manhattan in New York City. The structure is the corporate headquarters of one of Wall Street's most renowned investment banking firms.

The building is a relatively new office tower, completed in 2009, with more than two million square feet of floor space, rising more than eight hundred feet high. The building was designed to minimize its environmental impact, and had received the United States Green Building Council's third highest Gold LEED rating.

I became involved in the building's possible retrofit because of the suspicion that it was causing many bird deaths due to collisions with its glass façade. The problem of birds dying from building collisions has significantly increased with the expanded use of glass as a building material during the modern era. This extensive use of glazing, especially on the exterior envelope of buildings, has resulted from major technological advances in the structural strength, durability, clarity, and insulating properties of glass as a building material.[20]

While the data is still insufficient to draw definitive conclusions, in North America alone, an estimated one to two billion annual bird deaths have been linked to collisions with building glass. The multiple hazards include highly transparent glass, which the birds fail to recognize as an impenetrable barrier; reflective glass that confuses the birds, particularly when nearby vegetation is mirrored in the glass; and brightly lit buildings that attract birds, especially during the late evening hours. The problem of bird collisions has been most acute during the fall and spring migratory seasons, times when large numbers of birds travel long distances, pausing for rest and feeding or due to overcast or inclement weather conditions.

I was hired to assess the extent of the problem at this office tower, and, if I found evidence of extensive mortality, to recommend design solutions that might mitigate the problem. I was also encouraged to recommend ways that rather than just seeking to solve this specific problem might offer a more affirmative biophilic outcome: ideally, such a strategy might enhance the food and habitat needs of birds, while at the same time improving employees' comfort and productivity by providing a positive experience of nature.

Evidence of a problem was suggested by several dead birds having been found near the building during the autumn preceding our project. A number of characteristics of the building's design and location suggested a high potential for bird mortality, including its highly transparent glass façade, its site at the narrow tip of Manhattan Island, where a variety of terrestrial and aquatic habitats converge, the limited open space of the highly developed area, and the building's proximity to a number of other high-rise glass buildings, some of which had experienced high bird mortality.

To obtain a more precise estimate of bird deaths at the building, New York City Audubon was engaged to conduct a four-month study during the 2011 spring migration season. The research omitted the more hazardous fall migratory period due to time and budgetary constraints. A significant problem of bird deaths was nonetheless identified during the four-month study. Based on actual dead birds found during this period, and extrapolations to the fall migration and other seasons, an estimated one hundred bird deaths were thought to occur annually at this building due to collisions with its glass, or roughly one thousand mortalities over a decade. If accurate, this collision rate is among the highest in New York City, exceeded only by what has been found at the Jacob Javits Convention Center, the Metropolitan Museum of Art, and the World Financial Center.

Considering the impacts of other glass buildings across New York City, it has been estimated that eighty thousand annual bird mortalities occur as a consequence of this single factor alone. [21] Extrapolated to all of the world's burgeoning cities and high-rise building construction, the possibility exists that billions of birds die each year as a result of colliding with glass buildings.

We proposed a number of ways to mitigate the problem at this building, including changes to the glazing in especially vulnerable locations, alterations in the glass design, changes in the building's lighting operations, and various landscape and building-design features. In addition, a number of biophilic design solutions were recommended that, while meant to protect birds, were also intended to address their need for food and cover, and to enrich the employees' comfort and productivity through more satisfying contact with the natural environment. These biophilic design possibilities included:

- The introduction of vegetation into designated areas, where birds could rest and feed, and employees could relax and enjoy an aesthetically attractive outdoor setting while conducting business. These areas would be designed to avoid increased risks to birds being attracted to the sites. The location of these areas included an already constructed but not yet utilized "green roof," as well as interior and exterior ground floor spaces.
- The design of an interior "park system" in a variety of locations throughout the building, particularly in the large thirteenth-floor lobby and dining area. Vegetation and information about bird conservation would be introduced into these areas, where employees could rest and meet. Some live displays of birds would also be added.
- The production of entertaining and informative written and video material to educate employees about the values and benefits of birds, and to demonstrate that people and nature can coexist and enhance each other even in the most populated urban areas.

The central consideration here is not the specifics of either the low-environmental-impact or biophilic design recommendations but rather the question whether birds and people can coexist in mutually reinforcing and respectful relation to one another in a modern city. Beyond technology, this outcome fundamentally hinges on our values and ethics. It demands that people knowingly and deliberately choose to share their world with the likes of warblers, woodpeckers, and woodcocks, among the birds that needlessly died by colliding with this structure. A few thousand or even a few billion bird deaths due to building collisions may seem a trivial consideration, a small price to pay for the extraordinary technological attributes of a modern office tower. From an arguably more enlightened perspective, these deaths seem meaningless and cruel, the technological and engineering triumph an insufficient reason for extinguishing the lives of creatures possessing a will to live no less urgent than our own, and adding so much to the human experience.

Can the well-paid and, some would argue, overrewarded employees of one of the richest companies in the richest country in the world move beyond ignorance of and indifference to this problem to a more celebratory affirmation of the value of birds and their contribution to the human condition? I believe this is possible, and indeed necessary for the flourishing of birds and people alike. A city and an office tower are masterworks of human creation and technological accomplishment. But to be successful habitats for people and nonhuman animals alike, they must affirm life and our connection to nature. By combating the needless destruction of innocent others, and welcoming the opportunity to enhance the lives of these creatures, people can enrich and affirm themselves.

During the course of our data collection, we encountered dead blackburnian, chestnut-sided, parula, and black and white warblers. Just the other day, while working at my desk on the third floor of my house, perched high among the branches of tall oaks, I was thrilled by the sight of the orange, dark black, and bright white feathers of a blackburnian warbler moving quickly through a nearby tree. The warbler is an actual and symbolic wonder. It possesses a host of aesthetic, emotional, intellectual, material, ecological, and spiritual rewards. My work at the office building caused me to imagine a world without warblers: a barren place where the spectacle of purposeful life would become diminished and replaced by a more pervasive deadness. Warblers constitute one thread among many that transform inanimate water, rock, and soil into a fountain of living energy. They represent an irreplaceable bridge that links nature with humanity. Our species stands at the pinnacle of creation, aspiring to be its leading edge. We can achieve this lofty perch only by serving as a nurturing source for life rather than as the cause of its debasement or degradation.

33. The blackburnian warbler has beautiful orange feathers against a background of dark black and bright white. It offers a host of ecological, emotional, intellectual, material, and spiritual rewards. A world lacking warblers would be a more barren place where the spectacle of purposeful life was diminished.

A YOUNG ADULT LIVING IN THE MODERN CITY

I conclude the book by imagining the life of a twenty-five-year-old woman. She is a recent college graduate, working at a marketing firm in New York. Her office, on the seventeenth floor of a forty-six-story building, is a windowless cubicle lit by bright overhead lights; in it are a desk, a chair, a computer and monitor, a printer, and some file cabinets, all made from largely artificial materials. She lives in a small downtown apartment, about all she can afford at this stage of her career. Her apartment is on the seventh floor of a twelve-story building surrounded by similarly tall buildings. It has one window each in the living room, bedroom, and bathroom, the views partially blocked by adjacent buildings. There is a small park not far from her building, which she occasionally visits.

When not working, she mostly sees friends or relatives, shops, watches television, cooks, reads, surfs the Net, answers her email, and talks on the phone, and she sometimes goes with others to a movie, concert, restaurant, or bar. For the most part, she likes her life, including her job, which is interesting and pays well for a person her age, with good prospects for advancement in the future. She has a number of good friends, a nice boyfriend, and a loving family she wishes she saw more. Yet she is somewhat frustrated by the lack of variety in her life and wishes it offered more interesting activities and deeper meaning.

She doesn't think much about nature, and when she does she mostly regards it as something occasionally seen from afar—on visits to the nearby park or a rare camping trip, sometimes in a television show or a book or magazine article about some wild animal or place, even some pictures on her wall or her favorite panda bear screen saver. She is therefore surprised and at first doubtful when she sees a magazine article that makes the amazing claim that contact with nature can add satisfaction, beauty, and purpose to one's life, even significantly contribute to physical and mental health and happiness. The author of the article further contends that these benefits can occur far more easily than generally assumed and even in our largest cities, like New York. Curious, she reads the entire article, finding its thesis convincing and exciting.

The article begins with the suggestion that the satisfying experience of nature means more than just being outside, although the author stresses that there is no better way to enjoy and benefit from the natural world. Still, the author asserts, in today's world, where people spend most of their time indoors and in front of one screen or another, the experience of nature can be cultivated and enriched even in these settings. Whether indoors or outdoors, at home or at work, at school or at play, the author insists, a person benefits from increased contact with nature. The article includes practical suggestions of what people can do to expand their satisfying experience of nature, whether indoors, outside but relatively close to home and work, or in more distant and remote locations. The author stresses that all kinds of contact with nature exert a beneficial effect: pictures, stories, television shows, houseplants, pets, visits to local parks, and traveling to more distant lands and places. Our young New York woman eventually adopts many of the article's suggestions, and indeed these steps profoundly change her life for the better.

She was a little surprised by the article's emphasis on the indoors, as she always had thought of nature as something that occurs outside. Still, after reading the article and reflecting further, she realized how much her indoor life was already connected to the natural world—and could be even better linked through pictures, reading, video, views, decoration, and design.

She read about the benefits of natural materials, including wood, cotton, wool, leather, and stone. The author stressed that these natural materials have textures, patterns, and colors that are inherently appealing to people, because while each looks alike—an oak panel similar to another piece of oak—they all vary in some slight way, as well as change over time. She decided to make some modest changes to her carpets, chairs, curtains, couch, and other furnishings by replacing artificial with natural materials, and she was delighted to find that these adjustments to her apartment made it more attractive and satisfying than the plastic and polyester that was replaced. She was so pleased that she enlisted her boyfriend to help her construct new countertops and floor coverings of stone and clay in the kitchen and bathroom; these also added patterns, colors, and an occasional depiction of plants, butterflies, and shells.

The author further encouraged putting pictures on the walls of attractive landscapes, trees, birds, and other wildlife. She used prints and photos, even bought a painting or two, which added beauty to her apartment, as well as gave it a more lively feel; and, she never tired of looking at and discovering new features she hadn't noticed before in these pictures. She also purchased several oversized books that contained amazing depictions of coral reefs, tropical forests, mountain chains, savannahs, oceans, deserts, and rivers. She not only loved the books but was surprised by the many friends who were riveted by them, and the spirited discussions they provoked about people, places, and critters.

Another recommendation in the article was to emphasize natural lighting, natural ventilation, and views to the outside in one's home and workplace. Her apartment had only three windows, but she discovered that small changes in the placement of the furniture and curtains allowed more natural light into the apartment, while improving her views to the outside. She was pleased to realize that she could now see some distant trees, and before long she was observing the birds and squirrels that braved the noise, traffic, and people to live there. The trees also added interest and color, but the animals became company and entertainment, even though they remained unaware of her.

A further recommendation involved bringing into the home live plants and, if practical, even animals. She started with flowers and houseplants. Not only did they add color and life to her apartment, but she found that she enjoyed tending to the plants and getting to know more about them. Then she took the most daring step yet: she purchased a small fish tank and stocked it with some fascinating creatures. She learned a great deal about her fish and grew fond of caring for them and maintaining their habitat. She was surprised to discover that looking at the fish was calming and restorative, especially after a long day's work. Then, even more boldly, she got a cat, which took a good deal of her time, but was even more rewarding: this animal became one of her best friends, whom she loved dearly and came to see as part of her family.

The article's author also proposed making changes at work, especially for those who, like our young woman, worked in a windowless office. As with the apartment, the author recommended introducing plants and pictures of nature. She did, and many of her colleagues commented on how much more interesting, attractive, and stimulating her cubicle had become. A few also followed her lead.

She was surprised and a little apprehensive when her supervisor came to talk to her about these changes. But rather than chastise her, the supervisor complimented her on her example, and said that the alterations had significantly improved employee comfort and morale. Indeed, the supervisor asked her for a copy of the article, then passed it along to her own superiors, with the proposal that the recommendations espoused there be more widely adopted.

Much to everyone's delight, major design alterations occurred some months later, including increased exposure to natural lighting, the introduction of plants, and the establishment of common areas where employees could sit, relax, and have small meetings with views to the river and distant hills beyond. An outdoor sitting area with plants and flowers was also constructed on a flat roof, which previously had been a surface of asphalt and tar. The flowers, shrubs, and small trees attracted birds, butterflies, and other insects. The new green roof became one of the most popular places in the building for breaks, informal lunches, small meetings; people also went there to work creatively by themselves or with others.

She and her boss became good friends. She learned that her boss had always viewed herself as a "nature-lover," having grown up with a passion for the outdoors. Because of the article and the significant improvements at work, her boss decided that she and her family needed to do more about bringing nature into their overscheduled suburban lives. Consequently, she, her husband, and their children decided to spend more time outdoors together, and they redesigned their house and yard to include a greater diversity of vegetation, natural materials, and shapes and forms inspired by nature. They also installed a butterfly garden, a bird feeder, and a wildlife food plot, then purchased a spotting scope and web camera, which practically brought the critters inside.

One premise of the article was that no matter how clever and creative one might be at bringing nature into the home or workplace, these experiences can never sufficiently substitute for actual contact with nature in the outdoors.

The author divided the outdoors into places relatively close to where one lived and more distant, remote, and wild places. Even the largest cities, she learned, had more parks and open space than most people realized. In New York, for example, more than one-quarter of the city remained undeveloped, with nearly twenty percent of its area in parks.

There were two small parks in her neighborhood, and she began to spend more time there. After repeated visits, she found they contained a surprising number and variety of trees, flowers, shrubs, birds, squirrels, butterflies, bees, and other insects. One had a small pond where she encountered frogs, turtles, and fish, and on two occasions she saw small snakes, which made her a little nervous. These parks were also filled with children playing and adults walking their dogs; it was, she discovered, a good place to meet new and interesting people, despite the occasional character she had to avoid.

She also learned that not far away by bus or subway were much larger parks, a few far wilder than she had imagined. Some of these large parks had programs with outings that exposed her to the plants, animals, geological features, and natural and human history of the city. She attended a number of programs and learned a great deal about the forests, marshes, creeks, ponds, and wildlife of New York. One time her group collected wild berries and mushrooms; they even caught some fish, which she brought back to her apartment and made into a delicious meal, impressing the heck out of the friends she invited over to share the feast. She also visited the city's amazing zoos, botanical gardens, and natural history museums, which contained incredible numbers and varieties of plants and animals from across the world, and also offered many interesting programs and trips.

She became especially fascinated by birds, which she learned lived just about everywhere in the city. She started to learn how to identify them, and liked the variation of species depending on whether she was in a forest, field, or wetland, next to a river or lake, or on a beach by the ocean. At the same time, she began to be depressed by the realization of the harm people did birds, even if unintentionally, by pollution and development. This new awareness motivated her to join the local Audubon Society, which taught her about birds and their conservation, as well as offering great trips in and around the city to see and experience birds and other wildlife.

The article concluded with praise for the splendors and benefits of more remote and wilder places beyond the city. The author stressed that these areas offered enjoyment, satisfaction, and engagement with nature that no city park or human-controlled area could ever provide, and were more deeply satisfying than even the best pictures, television shows, or Imax films about nature.

Until then, her most distant trips had been to resorts in Florida and the Caribbean, which were fun, but she often found the experience shallow, artificial, expensive, and exploitative. The article's author also encouraged her to visit places like Florida and the Caribbean, but more for their extraordinary coral reefs, beaches, and astonishing assortment of plants and animals, some quite rare and unique. She eventually went on a number of these trips and found them fascinating, enjoyable, and informative, as well as an occasion to meet new people. Still, these trips were difficult to organize and costly.

She could, however, implement another suggestion from the article on a more regular basis by traveling to wild places not far from home. There were a number of opportunities to do so relatively near New York, and some of these trips turned out to be amazing experiences and adventures. Some were quite challenging, and a few times she had some pretty close calls and was almost injured, but she found that she always rose to the occasion. Especially fond memories included fording a wild river, climbing a steep canyon, happening upon a nervous mother bear with her cubs, and scrambling to find shelter in a scary thunder and lightning storm. She never forgot these experiences, and they made for good stories for years to come.

These trips also taught her new skills, like reading maps, using a compass and GPS, cooking outdoors, hiking and climbing, camping, identifying plants, animals, and stars, collecting wild foods, fly fishing, even a little hunting. Although these skills were hardly relevant to her life in the city, she found them satisfying and somehow they made her feel surer about herself and more independent.

Certain trips left her contented and at peace with herself and the world in a way that she had never known before. On one occasion she felt such a strong and enduring sense of connection that she returned home with a deeper feeling for the meaning of her life. This experience occurred in a state forest about forty miles north of the city. She had gone there with friends for a weekend camping trip. It was early spring, and they arrived midmorning to begin a ten-mile hike into the backcountry to the camping site they had reserved for the weekend. There were six friends altogether, and they divided into three groups of two hikers each, setting out separately for the trek to the campsite.

The hike was strenuous but incredibly enjoyable. They saw many birds starting to pair up and nest, some white-tailed deer, a variety of animal tracks, and the scat of owls, bears, and coyotes. At around noon, she and her companion stopped for lunch near a small spring-fed marsh, with cattails and tall grass at both ends and open shallow water in between. Before lunch, they split up to explore the area. She climbed up a rocky hill above the wetlands and stumbled upon purple trillium, and just downslope was an entire hillside of bright yellow coltsfoot. It was like a beautiful wild garden, especially after the long winter drabness, and she sat there enjoying the color before returning to the grassy meadow above the wetlands.

She lay down and closed her eyes, taking in the raspy sound of red-winged blackbirds and the shriller cries of blue jays. She opened her eyes and, looking up, noticed the new green leaves starting to leaf out on the trees. A flicker of movement caught her eye in the upper branches, and she heard the distinctive insectlike calls of migrating warblers. She grabbed her binoculars and was rewarded by the sight of the tan stripe and yellow head patch of a chestnut-sided warbler, then the zebralike stripes of a black and white warbler, and finally the red, white, and black feathers of a redstart. She spied another movement in the lower branches and was thrilled to see what looked like a piece of the sky with wings, a bluebird, and then, in the shrubs nearby, the brilliant pink and white of a rose-breasted grosbeak.

It was all quite magical, but also real. A smile crept across her face, and she felt deep contentment. She lay back on the grass, and looking up she saw the ever-changing shapes of clouds marching across the bright blue sky. She didn't fall asleep exactly, but drifted into a kind of semiconsciousness. She floated, selfless, rising, carried along with the clouds. She was eventually brought back to earth by the resonant rumblings of bullfrogs, and then an orchestra of spring peepers added their accompaniment, followed by a chorus of wind rustling through the leaves. On high, she could barely hear the hypnotic whistling of snipes' wings flapping overhead.

She felt at that moment that little separated her from these sounds, sights, and creatures. She experienced an ineffable feeling of connection to all the creation that surrounded her—the wind, the trees, the critters, the water, the clouds, even the distant universe beyond. Her distinctness lost meaning, and she felt an intermingling, a merging with the vast community of others traveling together through space and time. She felt nurtured and at peace in a way she never had known before.

After that moment beside the marsh, she held fast to a conviction that no matter what she faced in life, she would never lose her feeling of belonging to something beyond that also embraced her, something that gave her life meaning and significance. She tried to explain to her friend what she had experienced, but it was impossible to fully convey. Rather than adding his explanation, he shared with her a book he had brought with him that included something John Muir had written about a somewhat similar experience. She thought it perfectly captured what she had felt. Muir wrote:

> Climb the mountains and get their good tidings. Nature's peace will flow into you as sunshine flows into trees. The winds will blow their own freshness into you . . . while cares will drop away from you like leaves of Autumn. . . . Everybody needs beauty as well as bread, places to play in and pray in, where nature may heal and give strength to body and soul.[22]

NOTES

INTRODUCTION

1. E. O. Wilson, *On Human Nature* (Cambridge: Harvard University Press, 1979); D. Palmer, *Human Evolution Revealed* (London: Mitchell Beazley, 2010).

2. R. Carson, *The Sense of Wonder* (New York: HarperCollins, 1998), 100.

3. H. Beston, *The Outermost House* (New York: Ballantine, 1971).

4. E. O. Wilson, *Biophilia: The Human Bond with Other Species* (Cambridge: Harvard University Press, 1984); S. Kellert and E. O. Wilson, eds., *The Biophilia Hypothesis* (Washington, DC: Island, 1993).

5. E. Fromm, *The Anatomy of Human Destructiveness* (New York: Holt, Rinehart and Winston, 1973).

6. Wilson, *Biophilia*; S. Kellert, *Kinship to Mastery: Biophilia in Human Evolution and Development* (Washington, DC: Island, 1997).

7. R. Carson, *Silent Spring* (Boston: Houghton Mifflin, 1962).

1. ATTRACTION

1. E. O. Wilson, *The Diversity of Life* (Cambridge: Harvard University Press, 1992); en.wikipedia.org/wiki/beetle.

2. A. Evans and C. Bellamy, *An Inordinate Fondness for Beetles* (New York: Henry Holt Reference, 1996), 14; "Might Be Most Beautiful Insect in the Universe," www .designswan.com/archives/might-be-most-beautiful-insect-in-the-universe.html.

3. N. Myers, *The Sinking Ark* (New York: Pergamon), 46.

4. C. Saxon, cartoon, *New Yorker*, 1983, www.condenaststore.com/-sp/It-s-good-to-know-about-trees-Just-remember-nobody-ever-made-any-big-mo-New-Yorker-Cartoon-Prints_i8562934_.htm, forestry.about.com/od/forestrycareers/f/money_career.htm (Charles Saxon papers, Columbia University Libraries, Archival Collection).

5. E. O. Wilson, personal communication; cf. video, *Biophilic Design: The Architecture of Life*, www.bullfrogfilms.com.

6. A. Leopold, *The Sand County Almanac, with Other Essays on Conservation from Round River* (New York: Oxford University Press, 1996), 240.

7. Ibid., 137.

8. E. O. Wilson, *Biophilia: The Human Bond with Other Species* (Cambridge: Harvard University Press, 1984).

9. W. Rauschenbusch, Personal Prayers, www.emailmeditations.com/Archives/01–23-08.pdf.

10. G. Hildebrand, *The Origins of Architectural Pleasure* (Berkeley: University of California Press, 1999); J. Appleton, *The Experience of Landscape* (London: Wiley, 1975).

11. Leopold, *Sand County Almanac*, 137.

12. B. Mandelbrot, *The Fractal Geometry of Nature* (San Francisco: W. H. Freeman, 1983); en.wikipedia.org/wiki/Fractal.

13. S. Gould, "A Biological Homage to Mickey Mouse," www.monmsci.net/~kbaldwin/mickey.pdf; en.wikipedia.org/wiki/Neotony.

14. R. Ulrich, "Biophilia, Biophobia, and Natural Landscapes," in *The Biophilia Hypothesis*, ed. S. Kellert and E. O. Wilson (Washington, DC: Island, 1993), 91; R. Ulrich, "Human Responses to Vegetation and Landscapes," *Landscape and Urban Planning* 12 (1986).

15. Quoted in R. Dubos, *The Wooing of the Earth* (London: Althone, 1980), 119.

16. A. Thornhill, "Darwinian Aesthetics," in *Evolutionary Psychology*, ed. D. Buss (London: Allyn and Bacon, 1999), 549.

17. See, for example, references cited in S. Kellert, J. Heerwagen, and M. Mador, eds., *Biophilic Design: The Theory, Science, and Practice of Bringing Buildings to Life* (New York: Wiley, 2008), and S. Kellert, *Building for Life: Understanding and Designing the Human-Nature Connection* (Washington, DC: Island, 2005). Some illustrations: J. Heerwagen and B. Hase, "Building Biophilia: Connecting People to Nature," *Environmental Design + Construction*, March–April 2001; J. Heerwagen, "Green Buildings, Organizational Success, and Occupant Productivity," *Building Research and Information* 28 (2000); J. Heerwagen et al., "Environmental Design, Work, and Well Being," *American Association of Occupational Health Nurses Journal* 43 (1995); J. Heerwagen and G. Orians, "Adaptations to Windowlessness: A Study of the Use of Visual Décor in Windowed and Windowless Offices," *Environment and Behavior* 18 (1986); J. Heerwagen, J. Wise, D. Lantrip, and M. Ivanovich, "A Tale of Two Buildings: Biophilia and the Benefits of Green Design," US Green Buildings Council Conference, November 1996; J. Heerwagen, "Do Green Buildings Enhance the Well Being of Workers? Yes," *Environmental Design + Construction*, July 2000; R. Kaplan, "The Role of Nature in the Context of the Workplace," *Landscape and Urban Planning* 26 (1993); C. Tennesen and B. Cimprich, "Views to Nature: Effects on Attention," *Journal of Environmental Psychology* 15 (1995).

18. See, for example, references cited in Kellert, Heerwagen, and Mador, *Biophilic Design*, and Kellert, *Building for Life*. Some illustrations: E. Friedmann et al., "Animal Companions and One-Year Survival of Patients Discharged from a Coronary Care Unit," *Public Health Reports* 95 (1980); E. Friedmann, "Animal-Human Bond: Health and Wellness," in *New Perspectives on Our Lives with Companion Animals*, ed. A. Katcher and A. Beck (Philadelphia: University of Pennsylvania Press, 1983); H. Frumkin, "Beyond Toxicity: Human Health and the Natural Environment," *American Journal of Preventive Medicine* 20 (2001); C. Cooper-Marcus and

M. Barnes, eds., *Healing Gardens: Therapeutic Landscapes in Healthcare Facilities* (New York: Wiley, 1999); A. Katcher and G. Wilkins, "Dialogue with Animals: Its Nature and Culture," in Kellert and Wilson, *Biophilia Hypothesis*; A. Katcher et al., "Looking, Talking, and Blood Pressure: The Physiological Consequences of Interaction with the Living Environment," in Katcher and Beck, *New Perspectives*; H. Searles, *The Nonhuman Environment: In Normal Development and in Schizophrenia* (New York: International Universities Press, 1960); A. Taylor et al., "Coping with ADD: The Surprising Connection to Green Places," *Environment and Behavior* 33 (2001).

19. See, for example, references cited in Kellert, Heerwagen, and Mador, *Biophilic Design*, and Kellert, *Building for Life*. Some illustrations: Heerwagen and Hase, "Building Biophilia"; Heerwagen, "Green Buildings, Organizational Success, and Occupant Productivity"; J. Heerwagen et al., "Environmental Design, Work, and Well Being," *American Association of Occupational Health Nurses Journal* 43 (1995).

20. D. Dutton, *The Art Instinct: Beauty, Pleasure, and Human Evolution* (New York: Bloomsbury, 2009).

21. Ibid., 52.

22. Ibid., 58.

23. F. Church, *The Heart of the Andes*, 1859 (New York Metropolitan Museum of Art, www.metmuseum.org/toah/works-of-art/09.95); A. Bierstadt, *The Rocky Mountains, Lander's Peak*, 1863 (New York Metropolitan Museum of Art, www.metmuseum.org/toah/works-of-art/07.123).

24. William Wordsworth, *The Prelude*, www.everypoet.com/archive/poetry//William_Wordsworth/william_wordsworth _298.htm; L. Chawla, "Spots of Time: Manifold Ways of Being in Nature in Childhood," in *Children and Nature: Psychological, Sociocultural, and Evolutionary Investigations*, ed. P. Kahn Jr. and S. Kellert (Cambridge: MIT Press, 2002).

25. Quoted in A. de Botton, *The Art of Travel* (New York: Vintage, 2002), 150.

26. Ibid., 151.

27. Leopold, *Sand County Almanac*, 96.

2. REASON

1. "Descartes' Epistemology," Stanford Encyclopedia of Philosophy, plato.stanford.edu/entries/descartes-epistemology/.

2. Ibid.

3. A. Leopold, *The Sand County Almanac, with Other Essays on Conservation from Round River* (New York: Oxford University Press, 1996).

4. C. Lévi-Strauss, *The Savage Mind* (Chicago: University of Chicago Press, 1966); H. Shunk, "In What Respects Are Animals 'Good to Think With'? An Evaluation of Claude Levi-Strauss Animal Comparative Theory in Totemism," goldsmiths.academia.edu/HenrikSchunk/Papers/103325/In_what_res_alution_of_Claude_Levi-Strauss_animal_comperative_theory_in_totemism.

5. E. Lawrence, "The Sacred Bee, the Filthy Pig, and the Bat out of Hell: Animal Symbolism as Cognitive Biophilia," in *The Biophilia Hypothesis*, ed. S. Kellert and E. O. Wilson (Washington, DC: Island, 1993).

6. E. O. Wilson, *The Diversity of Life* (Cambridge: Harvard University Press, 1992).

7. K. von Frisch, *Bees: Their Vision, Chemical Senses, and Language* (London: Cape Editions, 1968), 13; E. O. Wilson, "Biophilia and the Conservation Ethic," in Kellert and Wilson, *The Biophilia Hypothesis.*

8. R. Sebba, "The Landscapes of Childhood: The Reflections of Childhood's Environment in Adult Memories and in Children's Attitudes," *Environment and Behavior* 23 (1991).

9. M. Bloom et al., *Taxonomy of Educational Objectives: The Classification of Educational Goals; Handbook 1, Cognitive Domain* (New York: Longman, 1956).

10. P. Shepard, *The Others: How Animals Made Us Human* (Washington, DC: Island, 1996).

11. J. Diamond, "New Guineans and Their Natural World," in Kellert and Wilson, *The Biophilia Hypothesis, 258.*

12. Ibid., 261.

13. R. Nelson, "Searching for the Lost Arrow: Physical and Spiritual Ecology in the Hunter's World," in Kellert and Wilson, eds., *The Biophilia Hypothesis.*

14. R. Nelson, "Understanding Eskimo Science," *Audubon Magazine*, September–October 1993, 102–9.

15. Nelson, "Searching for the Lost Arrow," 207–9.

16. W. Morris, ed., *The American Heritage Dictionary of the English Language* (Boston: Houghton Mifflin, 1976).

17. Nelson, "Understanding Eskimo Science."

18. S. McVay, Prologue to Kellert and Wilson, *The Biophilia Hypothesis.*

3. AVERSION

1. B. Lopez, *Of Wolves and Men* (New York: Scribner's, 1978).

2. Quoted ibid., 137.

3. L. D. Mech, *The Wolf* (New York: Doubleday, 1981).

4. See, for example: F. Harrington and P. Pacquet, *Wolves of the World* (New York: Simon and Schuster, 1982); en.wikipedia.org/wiki/Gray_wolf.

5. M. Jawer and M. Micozzi, *The Spiritual Anatomy of Emotion* (Rochester, VT: Park Street, 2009), 17.

6. Ibid., 26.

7. Ibid.

8. Ibid., 27.

9. Ibid.

10. Ibid.

11. See C. Jung, ed., *Man and His Symbols* (Garden City, NY: Doubleday, 1964); J. Campbell, *The Hero with a Thousand Faces* (Princeton: Princeton University Press, 1972); James Frazer, *The Golden Bough* (Oxford: Oxford University Press, 1994).

12. A. Öhman, "Face the Beast and Fear the Face: Animal and Social Fears as Prototypes for Evolutionary Analyses of Emotion," *Psychophysiology* 23 (1986); R. Ulrich, "Biophilia, Biophobia, and Natural Landscapes," in *The Biophilia Hypothesis*, ed. S. Kellert and E. O. Wilson (Washington, DC: Island, 1993).

13. S. Minerka et al., "Observational Conditioning of Snake Fear in Rhesus Monkeys," *Journal of Abnormal Psychology* 93 (1984).

14. S. Kellert, "Values and Perceptions of Invertebrates," *Conservation Biology* 7 (1993).

15. J. Hillman, "Going Bugs," *Spring: A Journal of Archetype and Culture* (1988), 59.

16. Ibid.

17. Kellert, "Values and Perceptions of Invertebrates."

18. Lopez, *Of Wolves and Men.*

19. Ibid., 180–81.

20. P. Matthiessen, *Wildlife in America* (New York: Viking, 1989); S. Kellert, *The Value of Life: Biological Diversity and Human Society* (Washington, DC: Island, 1996).

21. Quoted in K. Dunlap, *Saving America's Wildlife* (Princeton University Press, 1988), 26.

22. Quoted in Lopez, *Of Wolves and Men*, 137.

23. Ibid., 163.

24. Kellert, *The Value of Life*; S. Kellert et al., "Perceptions of Wolves, Mountain Lions, and Grizzly Bears in North America," *Conservation Biology* 10 (1996).

25. S. Flader, *Thinking Like a Mountain: Aldo Leopold and the Evolution of an Ecological Attitude toward Deer, Wolves, and Forests* (Madison: University of Wisconsin Press, 1994).

26. A. Leopold, *The Sand County Almanac, with Other Essays on Conservation from Round River* (New York: Oxford University Press, 1996), 129–30.

27. Kellert, *The Value of Life*, 108–10.

28. Ibid., 107.

29. S. Kellert, "Public Views of Wolf Restoration in Michigan," *Trans North American Wildlife and Natural Resources Conference* 56 (1991); Kellert et al., "Perceptions of Wolves."

30. R. Nelson, "Searching for the Lost Arrow: Physical and Spiritual Ecology in the Hunter's World," in Kellert and Wilson, *The Biophilia Hypothesis.*

31. W. Morris, ed., *The American Heritage Dictionary of the English Language* (Boston: Houghton Mifflin, 1976).

32. en.wikipedia.org/wiki/Light_pollution; www.forspaciousskies.com; C. Rich and T. Longcore, *Ecological Consequences of Artificial Night Lighting* (Washington, DC: Island, 2006).

4. EXPLOITATION

1. J. Boyd and S. Banzhaf, "What Are Ecosystem Services?" *RFF DP* 06–02, January 2006, www.rff.org/rff/documents/rff-dp-06–02.pdf; G. Daily, *Nature's Services* (Washington, DC: Island, 1997).

2. birds.audubon.org/species/amewoo.

3. A. Leopold, *The Sand County Almanac, with Other Essays on Conservation from Round River* (New York: Oxford University Press, 1996).

4. en.wikipedia.org/wiki/Demographics_of_the_United_States.

5. B. Groombridge, ed., *Global Biodiversity* (London: Chapman and Hall, 1992).

6. D. Pimentel, "Economics and Environmental Benefits of Biodiversity," *BioScience* 47 (1997).

7. Groombridge, *Global Biodiversity*, 365.

8. FAO, The State of the World's Fisheries, www.fao.org/docrep/013/i1820e/i1820e00.htm.

9. S. Kellert, "Values and Perceptions of Invertebrates," *Conservation Biology* 7 (1993).

10. Pimentel, "Economics and Environmental Benefits."

11. Kellert, "Values and Perceptions of Invertebrates."

12. R. Costanza et al., "The Value of the World's Ecosystem Services and Natural Capital," *Ecological Economics* 25 (1998).

13. E. O. Wilson, *The Diversity of Life* (Cambridge: Harvard University Press, 1992).

14. See, e.g., S. Kellert, *The Value of Life: Biological Diversity and Human Society* (Washington, DC: Island, 1996); M. Duda et al., *The Sportsman's Voice: Hunting and Fishing in America* (State College, PA: Venture, 2010).

15. J. Ortega y Gasset, *Meditations on Hunting*, trans. Howard B. Wescott (New York: Scribner's, 1986), 110–11.

16. P. Matthiessen, *Wildlife in America* (New York: Viking, 1989); V. Ziswiller, *Extinct and Vanishing Animals* (London: English University Press, 1967).

17. Quoted in Matthiessen, *Wildlife in America*, 192.

18. Leopold, *Sand County Almanac*, 108–9.

19. Kellert, *The Value of Life*.

20. Keystone species, The Free Dictionary, www.thefreedictionary.com/keystone+species.

21. L. White Jr., "The Historical Roots of Our Ecological Crisis," *Science* 155 (1967).

5. AFFECTION

1. W. Morris, ed., *The American Heritage Dictionary of the English Language* (Boston: Houghton Mifflin, 1976).

2. www.publicradio.org/applications/formbuilder/projects/joke_machine/joke_page.php?car_id=453770&joke_cat=Animal; lasvegasbadger.blogspot.com/2010/03/dogwife-joke-funny-but-very-true.html.

3. E. Fromm, *The Anatomy of Human Destructiveness* (New York: Holt, Rinehart and Winston, 1973), 366.

4. See, e.g., R. Kall, *Children and Their Development* (New York: Prentice Hall, 2006); B. Hopkins, ed., *The Cambridge Encyclopedia of Child Development* (Cambridge: Cambridge University Press, 2005).

5. See, e.g., A. Beck and A. Katcher, *Between Pets and People: The Importance of Animal Companionship* (West Lafayette, IN: Purdue University Press, 1996); E. Friedmann et al., "Animal Companions and One-Year Survival of Patients Discharged from a Coronary Care Unit," *Public Health Reports* 95 (1980); E. Friedmann, "Animal-Human Bond: Health and Wellness," in *New Perspectives on Our Lives with Companion Animals*, ed. A. Katcher and A. Beck (Philadelphia: University of

Pennsylvania Press, 1983); H. Frumkin, "Beyond Toxicity: Human Health and the Natural Environment," *American Journal of Preventive Medicine* 20 (2001); C. Cooper-Marcus and M. Barnes, eds., *Healing Gardens: Therapeutic Landscapes in Healthcare Facilities* (New York: Wiley, 1999); A. Katcher and G. Wilkins, "Dialogue with Animals: Its Nature and Culture," in *The Biophilia Hypothesis*, ed. S. Kellert and E. O. Wilson (Washington, DC: Island, 1993); A. Katcher et al., "Looking, Talking, and Blood Pressure: The Physiological Consequences of Interaction with the Living Environment," in Katcher and Beck, *New Perspectives*; H. Searles, *The Nonhuman Environment: In Normal Development and in Schizophrenia* (New York: International Universities Press, 1960); B. Levinson, *Pets and Human Development* (Springfield, IL: Thomas 1972); J. Serpell, *In the Company of Animals* (Oxford: Basil Blackwell, 1986).

6. K. Thomas, *Man and the Natural World* (New York: Pantheon, 1983).

7. Idea borrowed from Jonathan Swift, "A Modest Proposal," www.pagebypage books.com/Jonathan_Swift/A_Modest_Proposal/).

8. Humane Society of the United States, U.S. Pet Ownership Statistics, www .humanesociety.org/issues/pet_overpopulation/facts/pet_ownership_statistics.html.

9. See the sources in note 5.

10. Friedmann, "Animal-Human Bond."

11. Friedmann et al., "Animal Companions and One-Year Survival."

12. Ibid.

13. S. T. Coleridge, "The Rime of the Ancient Mariner," www.online-literature .com/coleridge/646/.

14. Friedmann, "Animal-Human Bond."

15. Katcher et al., "Looking, Talking, and Blood Pressure."

16. Katcher and Wilkins, "Dialogue with Animals."

17. Serpell, *In the Company of Animals*, 114–15.

18. P. Shepard, "On Animal Friends," in Kellert and Wilson, *The Biophilia Hypothesis*.

19. A. Leopold, *The Sand County Almanac, with Other Essays on Conservation from Round River* (New York: Oxford University Press, 1996), 230, 239.

20. S. Kellert, J. Heerwagen, M. Mador, eds. *Biophilic Design: The Theory, Science, and Practice of Bringing Buildings to Life* (New York: Wiley, 2008). For a fuller description of low environmental impact and biophilic design see chapter 10.

21. Leopold, *Sand County Almanac*.

22. See, for example: en.wikipedia.org/wiki/Bambi_effect; M. Cartmill, *A View of Death in the Morning* (Cambridge: Harvard University Press, 1993); S. Kellert, *The Value of Life* (Washington, DC: Island, 1996); W. Morris, ed., *The American Heritage Dictionary* (Boston: Houghton Mifflin, 1976).

23. R. Nelson, "Searching for the Lost Arrow: Physical and Spiritual Ecology in the Hunter's World," in Kellert and Wilson, *The Biophilia Hypothesis*.

6. DOMINION

1. L. White Jr., "The Historical Roots of Our Ecological Crisis," *Science* 155 (1967); K. Thomas, *Man and the Natural World* (New York: Pantheon, 1983);

P. Coates, *Nature: Western Attitudes since Ancient Times* (Berkeley: University of California Press, 1998).

2. Thomas, *Man and the Natural World*, 25, 29.

3. White, "Historical Roots."

4. J. Passmore, *Man's Responsibility for Nature: Ecological Problems and Western Traditions* (New York: Scribner's, 1974).

5. niv.scripturetext.com/genesis/1.htm; notesontheholybible.blogspot.com/2008/03/notes-on-genesis-5-mans-dominion-over.html.

6. en.wikipedia.org/wiki/world_population.

7. P. Vitousek et al., "Human Appropriation of the Products of Photosynthesis," *BioScience* 36 (1991).

8. Ibid.; E. O. Wilson, *The Diversity of Life* (Cambridge: Harvard University Press, 1992).

9. en.wikipedia.org/wiki/Demographics_of_the_United_States.

10. White, "Historical Roots."

11. Keystone species, The Free Dictionary, www.thefreedictionary.com/keystone+species.

12. See, for example M. Gauvain and M. Cole, eds., *Readings on the Development of Children* (New York: Worth, 2005).

13. Quoted by Rick Brame, personal communication (National Outdoor Leadership School, Lander, WY).

14. Quoted in S. Kellert and V. Derr, *National Study of Outdoor Wilderness Experience* (New Haven: Yale University School of Forestry and Environmental Studies, 1998), 88–89, 175.

15. A. Ewert, *Outdoor Adventure Pursuits: Foundations, Models, and Theories* (Scottsdale, AZ: Publishing Horizons, 1989); see also B. Driver, P. Brown, and G. Peterson, eds., *Benefits of Leisure* (State College, PA: Venture, 1991); B. Driver et al., eds., *Nature and the Human Spirit* (State College, PA: Venture, 1999).

16. Kellert and Derr, *National Study of Outdoor Wilderness Experience.*

17. R. Schreyer, *The Role of Wilderness in Human Development*, General Technical Report SE-51 (Fort Collins, CO: USDA Forest Service, 1988).

18. See, e.g., www.childrenandnature.org/research/volumes.

19. R. Dubos, *The Wooing of Earth* (London: Althone, 1980), 68.

20. Ibid.; G. Piel, ed., *The World of René Dubos: A Collection of His Writings* (New York: Henry Holt, 1990).

21. R. Dubos, "Symbiosis of the Earth and Humankind." Science 193 (1976), 459–62. As quoted in Dubos, *The Wooing of Earth*, 281, 286.

22. S. Kellert, J. Heerwagen, and M. Mador, eds. *Biophilic Design: The Theory, Science, and Practice of Bringing Buildings to Life* (New York: John Wiley, 2008).

23. Dubos, *The Wooing of Earth*, 182.

24. Ibid., 109–10.

25. W. Berry, "The Regional Motive," in *A Continuous Harmony: Essays Cultural and Agricultural* (New York: Harcourt, 1972), 68–69.

26. Quoted in C. Beverdige and P. Rocheleau, *Frederick Law Olmsted: Designing the American Landscape* (New York: Universe, 1998).

27. R. Candido et al., "The Naturally Occurring Historical and Extant Flora of Central Park, New York City, New York, 1857–2007," *Journal of the Torrey Botanical Society* 134 (2007); R. Candido et al., "A First Approximation of the Historical and Extant Vascular Flora of New York City: Implications for Native Plant Species Conservation," *Journal of the Torrey Botanical Society* 13 (2004).

28. www.ive.cuny.edu/nynn/nature/life/birds.htm; cbc.amnh.org/center/programs/birds-ny.html; B. Carleton, "The Birds of Central and Prospect Parks," *Proceedings of the Linnaean Society of New York*, 66–70 (1958).

29. C. Vornberger, *Birds of Central Park* (New York: Harry N. Abrams, 2008).

30. White, "Historical Roots."

31. Ronald Reagan, as paraphrased widely, including ibid. The remark Reagan actually made—before he was governor, when he was campaigning for the office in 1966—was less poetic and marginally less inflammatory: "I think, too, that we've got to recognize that where the preservation of a natural resource like the redwoods is concerned, that there is a common sense limit. I mean, if you've looked at a hundred thousand acres or so of trees—you know, a tree is a tree, how many more do you need to look at?" See Snopes.com, www.snopes.com/quotes/reagan/redwoods.asp, citing Lou Cannon, *Governor Reagan: His Rise to Power* (New York: Public Affairs, 2003), 177 and note.

32. www.imdb.com/title/tt0499549/quotes.

33. R. Perschel, "Work, Worship, and the Natural World: A Challenge for the Land Use Professions," in *The Good in Nature and Humanity: Connecting Science, Religion, and Spirituality with the Natural World*, ed. S. Kellert and T. Farnham (Washington, DC: Island, 2002).

7. SPIRITUALITY

1. H. Rolston, *Philosophy Gone Wild* (Buffalo, NY: Prometheus, 1986), 88.

2. A. Schweitzer, "The Ethics of Reverence for Life," *Albert Schweitzer: An Anthology*, ed. C. R. Joy (New York: Harper, 1947), also available at www1.chapman.edu/schweitzer/sch.reading4.html; A. Schweitzer, *The Philosophy of Civilization* (New York: Prometheus, 1987), also available at www1.chapman.edu/schweitzer/sch.reading1.html; A. Schweitzer, *Out of My Life and Thought* (Baltimore: Johns Hopkins University Press, 1998); en.wikipedia.org/wiki/Albert_Schweitzer.

3. Schweitzer, "The Ethics of Reverence for Life"; Schweitzer, "The Philosophy of Civilization."

4. "The Discovery and Meaning of Reverence for Life," Albert Schweitzer, Life and Thought, www.albertschweitzer.info/discovery.html, quoting A. Schweitzer, *Out of My Life and Thought* (Baltimore: Johns Hopkins University Press, 1998).

5. Schweitzer, "The Philosophy of Civilization"; "Reverence for Life," www.en.wikipedia.org/wiki/Reverence_for_Life.

6. Schweitzer, *Out of My Life and Thought*, 156.

7. Ibid., 236.

8. Schweitzer, "The Ethics of Reverence for Life," 262.

9. J. Steinbeck, *Log from the Sea of Cortez* (Mamaroneck, NY: Appel, 1941), 93.

10. E. O. Wilson, "Biophilia and the Conservation Ethic," in *The Biophilia Hypothesis*, ed. S. Kellert and E. O. Wilson (Washington, DC: Island, 1993).

11. W. Whitman, "Song of Myself," *Leaves of Grass* (London: Putnam, 1997).

12. A. Huxley, *The Perennial Philosophy* (New York: Harper and Row, 1990).

13. M. E. Tucker, "Religion and Ecology: The Interaction of Cosmology and Cultivation," in *The Good in Nature and Humanity: Connecting Science, Religion, and Spirituality with the Natural World*, ed. S. Kellert and T. Farnham (Washington, DC: Island, 2002).

14. R. Nash, *The Rights of Nature: A History of Environmental Ethics* (Madison: University of Wisconsin Press, 1989), 113.

15. L. White Jr., "The Historical Roots of Our Ecological Crisis," *Science* 155 (1967); K. Thomas, *Man and the Natural World* (New York: Pantheon, 1983); P. Coates, *Nature: Western Attitudes since Ancient Times* (Berkeley: University of California Press, 1998).

16. Tucker, "Religion and Ecology," 81.

17. J. Passmore, *Man's Responsibility for Nature: Ecological Problems and Western Traditions* (New York: Scribner's, 1974).

18. C. Lévi-Strauss, *The Savage Mind* (Chicago: University of Chicago Press, 1966); R. Nelson, "Searching for the Lost Arrow: Physical and Spiritual Ecology in the Hunter's World," in *The Biophilia Hypothesis*, ed. S. Kellert and E. O. Wilson (Washington, DC: Island, 1993); R. Nelson, "Understanding Eskimo Science," *Audubon*, September–October 1993.

19. Nelson, "Searching for the Lost Arrow."

20. Ibid., 205, 217.

21. Ibid., 223–24; R. Redfield, *The Primitive World and Its Transformations* (Ithaca, NY: Cornell University Press, 1953).

22. B. Taylor, *Dark Green Religion: Nature, Spirituality, and the Planetary Future* (Berkeley: University of California Press, 2009).

23. L. M. Wolfe, ed., *John of the Mountains: The Unpublished Journals of John Muir* (New York: Knopf, 1945); www.sierraclub.org/john_muir_exhibit/writings/mountain_thoughts.aspex; P. Browning, ed., *John Muir in His Own Words: A Book of Quotations* (Lafayette, CA: Great West, 1988); www.sierraclub.org/john_muir_exhibit/writings/favorite_quotations.aspx.

24. E. Howell, J. Harrington, and S. Glass, *Introduction to Restoration Ecology* (Washington, DC: Island, 2011); W. Jordan, G. Lubick, *Making Nature Whole* (Washington, DC: Island, 2009).

25. G. Van Wieren, "Restored Earth, Restored to Earth: Christianity, Environmental Ethics, and Ecological Restoration," Ph.D. diss., Yale University, 2011.

26. Ibid., 15.

27. Ibid., 76.

28. F. House, *Totem Salmon: Life Lessons from Another Species* (Boston: Beacon, 1999).

29. Ibid., 13.

8. SYMBOLISM

1. E. O. Wilson, *Biophilia: The Human Bond with Other Species* (Cambridge: Harvard University Press, 1984), 101.

2. S. Booth, ed., *Shakespeare's Sonnets* (New Haven: Yale University Press, 1977), sonnet 18.

3. R. Mabey, *Nature Cure* (London: Pimlico, 2006), 19–20.

4. Elephant Symbol, www.animal-symbols.com/elephant-symbol.html; I. Douglas-Hamilton and O. Douglas-Hamilton, *Battle for the Elephants* (New York: Viking, 1992); C. Moss, *Elephant Memories* (New York: Morrow, 1988).

5. en.wikipedia.org/wiki/butterfly; Boggs et al., *Butterflies: Evolution and Ecology Taking Flight* (Chicago: University of Chicago Press, 2003); R. Pyle, *Handbook for Butterfly Watchers* (Boston: Houghton Mifflin, 1984).

6. R. Gagliardi, "The Butterfly and Moth as Symbols in Western Art," *Cultural Entomology Digest* 4 (1997).

7. en.wikipedia.org/wiki/Serpent_(symbolism); J. Campbell, *The Masks of God*, vol. 3, *Occidental Mythology* (New York: Viking, 1965).

8. Wilson, *Biophilia*, 84.

9. E. Lawrence, "The Sacred Bee, the Filthy Pig, and the Bat Out of Hell: Animal Symbolism as Cognitive Biophilia," in *The Biophilia Hypothesis*, ed. S. Kellert and E. O. Wilson (Washington, DC: Island, 1993).

10. See, e.g., B. Bettelheim, *The Uses of Enchantment* (New York: Vintage, 1977); C. Jung, ed., *Man and His Symbols* (Garden City: Doubleday, 1964); P. Shepard, *Thinking Animals: Animals and the Development of Human Intelligence* (New York: Viking, 1978); P. Shepard, *The Others: How Animals Made Us Human* (Washington, DC: Island, 1996).

11. E. B. White, *The Trumpet of the Swan* (New York: HarperCollins, 2000).

12. en.wikipedia.org/wiki/Anatidae; en.wikipedia.org/wiki/Trumpeter_Swan.

13. J. Updike, Review of *The Trumpet of the Swan*, *New York Times*, June 28, 1970.

14. Lawrence, "The Sacred Bee."

15. www.childrenandnature.org; Kaiser Foundation, "Generation M2: Media in the Lives of 8- to 18-Year-Olds," Kaiser Family Foundation Study, January 2010.

16. I. Opie and P. Opie, *The Oxford Dictionary of Nursery Rhymes* (Oxford: Oxford University Press, 1997); en.wikipedia.org/wiki/Sing_a_Song_of_Sixpence.

17. For other examples go to amazon.com and browse "children's books," then "animals."

18. E. Leach, "Anthropological Aspects of Language: Animal Categories and Verbal Abuse," in *New Directions in the Study of Language*, ed. E. H. Lenneberg, (Cambridge: MIT Press, 1975).

19. www.vanityfair.com/magazine, 2011 editions, particularly June 2011.

20. www.economist.com/printedition/2009–12-12.

21. S. Elliot, "Super Bowl Was Animal Lovers Paradise," *New York Times*, February 13, 1996.

22. William Wordsworth, "Lines Written in Early Spring," Poetry Foundation, www.poetryfoundation.org/poem/181415.

23. Daniel Webster, *The Writings and Speeches of Daniel Webster*, national ed. (Boston: Little, Brown, 1903); highered.mcgraw-hill.com/sites/dl/free/0072879130/40803/chap09elem1.htm.

24. www.william-shakespeare.info/act1-script-text-julius-caesar.htm.

25. www.brainyquote.com/quotes/authors/w/winston_churchill.html, pages 3, 4, 6.

26. Lawrence, "The Sacred Bee"; Bettelheim, *The Uses of Enchantment*; Jung, *Man and His Symbols*; Shepard, *Thinking Animals*; Shepard, *The Others*.

27. The Best Online Classic Children's Books, www.mainlesson.com/display booksbytitle.php.

28. H. Searles, *The Nonhuman Environment: In Normal Development and in Schizophrenia* (New York: International Universities Press, 1960), 3.

29. Shepard, *Thinking Animals*.

30. Ibid., 249.

31. D. Thomas, *Quite Early One Morning* (New York: New Directions, 1965), 4, 6.

32. J. Campbell, *The Hero with a Thousand Faces* (Princeton: Princeton University Press, 1972); J. Frazer, *The Golden Bough* (Oxford: Oxford University Press, 1994); Jung, *Man and His Symbols*; C. Lévi-Strauss, *The Savage Mind* (Chicago: University of Chicago Press, 1966); R. Redfield, *The Primitive World and Its Transformations* (Ithaca, NY: Cornell University Press, 1953); R. Nelson, *Make Prayers to the Raven* (Chicago: University of Chicago Press, 1983).

33. Lawrence, "The Sacred Bee."

34. S. Kellert, J. Heerwagen, and M. Mador, eds., *Biophilic Design* (New York: John Wiley, 2008); S. Kellert, *Building for Life* (Washington, DC: Island, 2005).

35. O. Jones, *The Grammar of Ornament* (London: Studio Editions, 1986).

36. Ibid., 2.

37. Lawrence, "The Sacred Bee."

38. W. Whitman, "Song of Myself," *Leaves of Grass* (London: Putnam, 1897).

39. en.wikipedia.org/wiki/Peregrine_Falcon.

40. R. Carson, *Silent Spring* (Boston: Houghton Mifflin, 1962).

9. CHILDHOOD

1. en.wikipedia.org/wiki/Spring_Peeper.

2. R. Pyle, "Eden in a Vacant Lot: Special Places, Species, and Kids in the Neighborhood of Life," in *Children and Nature: Psychological, Sociocultural, and Evolutionary Investigations*, ed. P. Kahn and S. Kellert (Cambridge: MIT Press, 2002).

3. H. L. Burdette and R. C. Whitaker, "Resurrecting Free Play in Young Children: Looking beyond Fitness and Fatness to Attention, Affiliation, and Affect," *Archives of Pediatric and Adolescent Medicine* 159 (2005), www.archpediatrics.com.

4. H. Searles, *The Nonhuman Environment: In Normal Development and in Schizophrenia* (New York: International Universities Press, 1960).

5. B. Hopkins, ed., *The Cambridge Encyclopedia of Child Development* (Cambridge: Cambridge University Press, 2005).

6. www.childrenandnature.org/research/volumes.

7. R. Dyson-Hudson and E. Alden, "Human Territoriality: An Ecological Assessment," *American Anthropologist* 80 (1978); R. Ardrey, *The Territorial Imperative* (New York: Atheneum, 1966).

8. R. Louv, *Last Child in the Woods: Saving Our Children from Nature-Deficit Disorder* (Chapel Hill, NC: Algonquin, 2005), 34.

9. R. Pyle, *The Thunder Tree: Lessons from an Urban Wildland* (Boston: Houghton Mifflin, 1993), 145–47.

10. See, for example: www.childrenandnature.org/research/volumes; S. Kellert, *Building for Life* (Washington, DC: Island, 2005); J. Dunlap and S. Kellert, eds., *Companions in Nature* (Cambridge: MIT Press, 2012); Louv, *Last Child in the Woods*.

11. www.childrenandnature.org/research/volumes; Kellert, *Building for Life*; Dunlap and Kellert, *Companions in Nature*; Louv, *Last Child in the Woods*.

12. www.childrenandnature.org; en.wikipedia.org/wiki/No_Child_Left_Inside_ (movement).

10. DESIGN

1. S. Kellert, *Building for Life* (Washington, DC: Island, 2005); S. Kellert, J. Heerwagen, and M. Mador, eds., *Biophilic Design* (New York: John Wiley, 2008); T. Beatley, *Green Urbanism* (Washington, DC: Island, 2000); T. Beatley, *Biophilic Cities* (Washington, DC: Island, 2010).

2. Kellert, *Building for Life*; "Buildings and Their Impact on the Environment: A Statistical Summary," www.epa.gov/greenbuilding/pubs/gbstats.pdf.

3. D. Orr, "Architecture as Pedagogy," in *Reshaping the Built Environment*, ed. C. Kibert (Washington, DC: Island, 1999).

4. United States Green Building Council LEED rating systems, www.usgbc.org/LEED.

5. J. Wines, *The Art of Architecture in the Age of Ecology* (New York: Taschen, 2000).

6. J. Heerwagen and B. Hase, "Building Biophilia: Connecting People to Nature," *Environmental Design and Construction*, March–April 2001.

7. M. Miller, *Chartres Cathedral* (New York: Riverside, 1997); G. Hildebrand, *The Origins of Architectural Pleasure* (Berkeley: University of California Press, 1999).

8. G. Hildebrand, *The Wright Space: Pattern and Meaning in Frank Lloyd Wright's Houses* (Seattle: University of Washington Press, 1991).

9. D. Pearson, *New Organic Architecture: The Breaking Wave* (Berkeley: University of California Press, 2001).

10. S. Kellert, "Dimensions, Elements, and Attributes of Biophilic Design," in Kellert, Heerwagen, and Mador, *Biophilic Design*; Kellert, *Biophilic Design: The Architecture of Life*, www.bullfrogfilms.com. For other useful related perspectives, see J. Benyus, *Biomimicry* (New York: William Morrow, 1997); K. Bloomer, *The Nature of Ornament* (New York: Norton, 2000); G. Hersey, *The Monumental Impulse* (Cambridge: MIT Press, 1999).

11. Kellert, Heerwagen, and Mador, *Biophilic Design*.

12. E. Relph, *Place and Placelessness* (London: Pion, 1976), 6.

13. See, for example, references cited in Kellert, Heerwagen, and Mador, *Biophilic Design*, and Kellert, *Building for Life*. For further illustrations see Heerwagen and Hase, "Building Biophilia"; J. Heerwagen, "Green Buildings, Organizational Success, and Occupant Productivity," *Building Research and Information* 28 (2000); J. Heerwagen et al., "Environmental Design, Work, and Well Being," *American Association of Occupational Health Nurses Journal* 43 (1995); J. Heerwagen and G. Orians, "Adaptations to Windowlessness: A Study of the Use of Visual Décor in Windowed and Windowless Offices," *Environment and Behavior* 18, (1986); J. Heerwagen, J. Wise, D. Lantrip, and M. Ivanovich, "A Tale of Two Buildings: Biophilia and the Benefits of Green Design," *US Green Buildings Council Conference*, November 1996; J. Heerwagen, "Do Green Buildings Enhance the Well Being of Workers? Yes," *Environmental Design + Construction*, July 2000; R. Kaplan, "The Role of Nature in the Context of the Workplace," *Landscape and Urban Planning* 26 (1993); C. Tennesen, and B. Cimprich, "Views to Nature: Effects on Attention," *Journal of Environmental Psychology* 15 (1995); T. Hartig et al., "Restorative Effects of the Natural Environment," *Environment and Behavior* 23 (1991).

14. Heerwagen, "Do Green Buildings Enhance the Well Being of Workers?"; Heerwagen and Hase, "Building Biophilia."

15. See, for example, references cited in www.childrenandnature.org/research/volumes; G. Kats, *Greening America's Schools: Costs and Benefits* (Washington, DC: Capital E, 2006).

16. See, for example, references cited in Kellert, Heerwagen, and Mador, *Biophilic Design*, and Kellert, *Building for Life*. Representative studies include E. Friedmann et al., "Animal Companions and One-Year Survival of Patients Discharged from a Coronary Care Unit," *Public Health Reports* 95 (1980); E. Friedmann, "Animal-Human Bond: Health and Wellness," in *New Perspectives on Our Lives with Companion Animals*, ed. A. Katcher and A. Beck, eds. (Philadelphia: University of Pennsylvania Press, 1983); R. Ulrich, "Biophilia, Biophobia, and Natural Landscapes," in *The Biophilia Hypothesis*, ed. S. Kellert and E. O. Wilson (Washington, DC: Island, 1993); R. Ulrich, "How Design Impacts Wellness," *Healthcare Forum Journal* 20 (1992); H. Frumkin, "Beyond Toxicity: Human Health and the Natural Environment," *American Journal of Preventive Medicine* 20 (2001); C. Cooper-Marcus and M. Barnes, eds., *Healing Gardens: Therapeutic Landscapes in Healthcare Facilities* (New York: Wiley, 1999); A. Katcher and G. Wilkins, "Dialogue with Animals: Its Nature and Culture," in Kellert and Wilson, *The Biophilia Hypothesis*; A. Katcher et al., "Looking, Talking and Blood Pressure: The Physiological Consequences of Interaction with the Living Environment," in Katcher and Beck, *New Perspectives on Our Lives with Companion Animals*; H. Searles, *The Nonhuman Environment: In Normal Development and in Schizophrenia* (New York: International Universities Press, 1960); A. Taylor et al., "Coping with ADD: The Surprising Connection to Green Places," *Environment and Behavior* 33 (2001).

17. R. Ulrich, "Biophilic Theory and Research for Healthcare Design," in Kellert, Heerwagen, and Mador, *Biophilic Design*; personal communication, Center for Health Systems and Design, College of Architecture, Texas A&M University.

18. Kellert, *Building for Life*.

19. F. Kuo, "Coping with Poverty: Impacts of Environment and Attention in the Inner City," *Environment and Behavior* 33 (2001); F. Kuo et al., "Transforming Inner-City Landscapes: Trees, Sense of Safety, and Preference," *Environment and Behavior* 30 (1998); W. Sullivan and F. Kuo, "Do Trees Strengthen Urban Communities, Reduce Domestic Violence?" Forestry Report R8-FR 56, USDA Forest Service, Atlanta: Southern Regions, USDA Forest Service.

20. Kuo, "Coping with Poverty."

21. J. Corbett and M. Corbett, *Designing Sustainable Communities: Learning from Village Homes* (Washington, DC: Island, 2000), 31.

22. M. Francis, "Village Homes: A Case Study in Community Design," *Landscape Journal* 21 (2002); R. Moore and C. C. Marcus, "Healthy Planet, Healthy Children: Designing Nature into the Daily Spaces of Childhood," in Kellert, Heerwagen, and Mador, *Biophilic Design*.

23. Quoted in Corbett and Corbett, *Designing Sustainable Communities*, 21.

24. Dante, *Inferno*, trans. J. Ciardi (New York: New American Library, 1954), canto 24, lines 46–57.

11. ETHICS AND EVERYDAY LIFE

1. S. Kellert and G. Speth, eds., *The Coming Transformation: Values to Sustain Human and Natural Communities* (New Haven: Yale University School of Forestry and Environmental Studies Publication Series, 2009).

2. A. Leopold, "The Meaning of Conservation," handwritten notes, 1946, quoted in *The Essential Aldo Leopold: Quotations and Commentaries*, ed. C. Meine and R. L. Knight (Madison: University of Wisconsin Press, 1999), 309.

3. S. Kellert, "A Biocultural Basis for an Environmental Ethic," in Kellert and Speth, *The Coming Transformation*; S. Kellert, "For the Love and Beauty of Nature," in *Moral Ground*, ed. K. D. Moore and M. P. Nelson (San Antonio: Trinity University Press, 2010).

4. D. Lavigne, S. Kellert, and V. Scheffer, "The Changing Place of Marine Mammals in American Thought," in *Marine Mammals*, ed. J. Twiss and R. Reeves (Washington, DC: Smithsonian Press); S. Kellert, *The Value of Life* (Washington, DC: Island, 1996).

5. E. Dolin, *Leviathan: The History of Whaling in America* (New York: Norton, 2009).

6. Lavigne, Kellert, Scheffer, "The Changing Place of Marine Mammals."

7. Ibid.

8. K. Norris, "Marine Mammals and Man," in *Wildlife and America*, ed. H. P. Brokaw (Washington, DC: Council on Environmental Quality, 1978).

9. Whale Watching Worldwide—Report Released, www.ecolarge.com/2009/06/whale-watching-worldwide-report-released.

10. M. Bean, *The Evolution of National Wildlife Law* (New York: Praeger, 1982).

11. water.epa.gov/lawsregs/guidance/wetlands/definitions.cfm.

12. tvtropes.org/pmwiki/pmwiki.php/Main/SwampsAreEvil.

13. T. E. Diehl, "Status and Trends of Wetlands in Conterminous United States, 1986 to 1997," www.citeulike.org/group/342/article/4030617.

14. www.law.ufl.edu/conservation/waterways/waterfronts/pdf/no_net_loss.pdf; en.wikipedia.org/wiki/No_net_loss_wetlands_policy.

15. T. Dahl and G. Allord, "History of Wetlands in the Conterminous United States," water.usgs.gov/nwsum/WSP2425/history.html.

16. The Ramsar Mission, www.ramsar.org/cda/en/ramsar-home/main/ramsar/1%5e7715_4000_0_.

17. E. Barbier, M. Acreman, and D. Knowler, *Economic Valuation of Wetlands* (Gland, Switzerland: Ramsar Convention Bureau, 1997).

18. R. Dubos, *The Wooing of Earth* (London: Althone, 1980), 126.

19. Leopold, *Sand County Almanac*, 230, 239.

20. S. Kellert, *Building for Life* (Washington, DC: Island, 2005); D. Klem. "Bird-Window Collisions," *Wilson Bulletin* 101 (1989); D. Klem, "Bird Injuries, Cause of Death, and Recuperation from Collisions with Windows," *Journal of Field Ornithology* 61 (1990); D. Klem, "Glass: A Deadly Conservation Issue for Birds," *Bird Observer* 34 (2006); D. Klem et al., "Architectural and Landscape Risk Factors Associated with Bird-Glass Collisions in an Urban Environment," *Wilson Journal of Ornithology* 12 (2009); C. Seewagen, "Bird Collisions with Windows: An Annotated Bibliography," *American Bird Conservancy*, 2010; Dr. Christine Sheppard, personal communication, csheppard@abcbirds.org.

21. New York City Audubon, *Bird-Safe Building Guidelines* (New York: Audubon, 2008).

22. en.wikiquote.org/wiki/John_Muir.

ACKNOWLEDGMENTS

The writing and publication of this book owe a great debt of thanks to many who have been particularly helpful and inspiring. First, I want to thank my editor at Yale University Press, Jean Thomson Black, whose support, incredibly good advice, and time devoted to the project were exceptional and very much appreciated. I also want to give special thanks to my agent, Gillian MacKenzie, whose constructive suggestions helped shape the book's focus, structure, and organization. Readers of manuscript drafts provided much needed editorial advice and support, most particularly Dan Witter, Cheryl Charles, Tom Lovejoy, and Gretel Van Wieren. The copyediting of Dan Heaton was invaluable and certainty contributed to a more readable and accurate manuscript.

I also want to thank two Yale School of Forestry and Environmental Studies students. First, a doctoral student, Adrian Cerezo, who provided much assistance and encouragement at an early stage of the book, and second, a master's degree student, Matthew Arnold, who helped with many aspects of the illustrations and formatting of the book. Sara Hoover of Yale University Press also provided much-needed technical support and advice. Finally, Margaret Riley assisted in assembling the book's references, and Laurie Bozzuto, my friend and faculty support person at Yale, gave me invaluable assistance with many details of the manuscript.

A book that encompasses so much of my career inevitably owes a debt of gratitude to many people who have contributed to the development of these ideas, understandings, and perspectives. It is impossible to acknowledge all who have played this crucial role, and I apologize for the inevitable oversights and omissions. In recent years, I particularly want to thank the contributions of Judith Heerwagen, Elizabeth Lawrence, Richard Louv, Louise Chawla, and Gus Speth. Over the longer term, there have been a few individuals who have especially influenced my thinking, most particularly Edward O. Wilson, Aldo Leopold, and René Dubos.

Various students of mine played important roles, particularly Nicole Ardoin, Adrian Cerezo, Tori Derr, Julie Dunlap, Syma Ebbin, Tim Farnham, Iona Hawken, Marty Mador, Bob Powell, Sorrayut Ratanapojnard, Rich Reading, Ali Senauer, Ben Shepard, Shannon Spencer, Terry Terhaar, Critter Thompson, and Rich Wallace.

My wife, Cilla, as always, provided immeasurable support, encouragement, and, patience at an especially challenging time in our lives. Both my daughters, Emily and Libby, offered critical suggestions, support, and advice. Partially overlapping the time when I wrote this book, I faced some significant personal challenges. Family and friends offered extraordinary support during this period, and among friends, I owe a special thanks to John and Amy, Tim and Susie, and Ham and Ceci.

ILLUSTRATION CREDITS

Figure 1, from left: Ian Grove-Stephensen; Abigail Batchelder; Michael L. "Mike" Baird, flickr.bairdphotos.com; Chea Phal; Catherine Scott, Cazpix Photography; Quinn Dombrowski; ND Strupler, Creative Commons

Figure 2, John Good, National Park Service

Figures 3, 9, 22, Matthew Browning

Figures 4, 12, 14, 15, 23, author

Figure 5, Jeffrey Pavlin, Creative Commons

Figure 6, Lisa Charles Watson

Figure 7, U.S. Fish and Wildlife Service

Figure 8, "Lobocba_15," www.arteyfotografia.com.ar, Creative Commons

Figure 10, Hilary Chambers, Creative Commons

Figure 11, U.S. Department of Energy

Figure 13, Louis Agassiz Fuertes, 1874–1927, *Birds of New York* (Albany: University of the State of New York, 1910)

Figure 16, Kevin Hamilton, Student Conservation Association

Figure 17, Lorena Woodrow Burke, Denison University Library Archives

Figure 18, Library of Congress

Figure 19, Tad Arensmeier, Creative Commons

Figure 20, Warshaw Collection of Business Americana, Archives Center, National Museum of American History, Smithsonian Institution

Figure 21, Owen Jones, 1809–74, *The Grammar of Ornament,* 1868

Figure 24, www.shutterstock.com

Figure 25, Dimitry B., Creative Commons

Figure 26, Franklin Heijnen, Creative Commons

Figure 27, Jimmy Harris, Creative Commons

Figure 28, Seth Werkheiser, Creative Commons

Figure 29, top, Gordon Carlisle; bottom, Roger Ulrich

Figure 30, Eric Fredericks, Creative Commons

Figure 31, Richard Giddens, Creative Commons

Figure 32, George Gentry, U.S. Fish and Wildlife Service

Figure 33, Bill Majoros, Creative Commons

INDEX